The Garden of Eating

A COMPLETE
KOSHER COOKBOOK

Yeshiva Degel HaTorah was guided from its inception by one of the
great role models of Torah teachers, HaRav Mordechai Schwab צז"ל.
His profound sensitivity and understanding of children built the
foundation of a Torah school that demonstrates the significance of
Jewish study and the importance of Jewish behavior. Every aspect of
the Yeshiva's operation is carefully orchestrated by his son,
the *menahel*, Rabbi Moshe Schwab שליט"א. The radiant, smiling faces
of Yeshiva Degel HaTorah's students reflect the devotion and warmth
of their *rebbeim* and teachers. It is with *hakaras ha-tov* that the
parents of Yeshiva Degel HaTorah present this cookbook.

A Project of Women's League of
Yeshiva Degel Hatorah Maamar Mordechai

The Garden of Eating

A COMPLETE KOSHER COOKBOOK

JERUSALEM FELDHEIM PUBLISHERS NEW YORK

First published 1998
Hardcover edition: ISBN 0-87306-867-x

Copyright © 1998 by
Feldheim Publishers

FELDHEIM PUBLISHERS
POB 35002 / Jerusalem, Israel

200 Airport Executive Park
Nanuet, NY 10954

Printed in Israel

10 9 8 7 6 5 4 3 2 1

Editor: Ann Chapler
Project Coordinator: Chana Leah Oppenheim
Nutritional analysis provided by:
Chanie Raice, M.S., R.D., C.D.E., Medical Nutrition Therapist

Special thanks to:
Rivkie Ebstein, Tammy Eckstein, Hadassah Lang, Rochelle Moskowitz,
Toby Raice, Rochel Leah Rotbard

Cookbook Committee:

Rivki Aderet	Faigi Fisch	Rochelle Moskowitz
Shani Bree	Esti Flegman	Rochel Leah Rotbard
Rochel Cherns	Malke Glovinsky	Tamara Schwed
Tammy Eckstein	Malke Kleinman	Elisheva Spaner
Shoshi Feldheim	Fradi Lampert	Helen Yurowitz

Cover illustration: Helen Yurowitz

Recipe contributors:

Yehudis Abramson	Malka Gehler	Toby Raice
Rivki Aderet	Malke Gestetner	Tzipora Reitman
Dvora Adler	Malke Glovinsky	Devorah Rokowsky
Chany Amsel	Sherie Gross	Baila Rosenbaum
Chani Ausband	Menucha Kahan	Laura Rosenberg
Mrs. Babayov	Rena Kaplan	Rochel Leah Rotbard
Mrs. Ben Arbon	Suri Katz	Chani Schonfeld
Rochel Braun	Chavie Katzman	Tamara Schwed
Shani Bree	Rivky Kaufman	Barbara Shafran
Ann Chapler	Malke Kleinman	Wendi Shafran
Rochel Chapler	Gitty Kramer	Bashie Sommerfeld
Rochel Cherns	Sharone F. Kramer	Elisheva Spaner
Aviva Davidson	Fradi Lampert	Leah Spilman
Lina Drillman	Chaya Landerer	Helen Spitz
Deanna Ebstein	Dina Lang	Judy Steinberger
Rivkie Ebstein	Chavie Lang	Cilka Steinmetz
Tammy Eckstein	Shaindy Lazarus	Malka Steinmetz
Shaindy Ehrman	Chavi Leiner	Kreindy Stern
Shoshi Feldheim	Mashi Levine	Rivka Tillim
Tzvia Feldman	Rena Levine	Rivki Vann
Faigy Fisch	Beatrice Levy	Bruchy Weiser
T. Fischer	Roz Levy	Peri Weisz
Estie Flegman	Chana Mark	Helen Yurowitz
Gila Forchheimer	Brocha Minzer	Yentie Zafir
Naomi Franklin	Chana Leah Oppenheim	Shira Zolty
	Rochel Racht	

Whether in our Kitchens or in our Hearts...

MRS. YEHUDIS ABRAMCZYK
in honor of
MRS. ESTHER HIRSCH

MRS. CHANY AMSEL
in honor of
MRS. PHYLLIS LEVY
MRS. LILLY AMSEL

MRS. SORA BURNBAUM
in honor of
MRS. PEARL PEARSON

MRS. ANN CHAPLER
in honor of
MRS. BEATRICE LEVY
MRS. ROCHEL CHAPLER
MRS. GERTRUDE MINTZ
MRS. LOLA SHAFRAN a"h

MRS. ROCHEL CHERNS
in honor of
MRS. J. SALB
MRS. M. CHERNS

MRS. TZIPORA EHRMAN
in honor of
MRS. BUBBY HERMAN

MRS. SHAINDY EHRMAN
in honor of
MRS. TOVA HERZOG
MRS. GITTY EHRMAN

MRS. MALKY GEHLER
in honor of
MRS. FREDA MILLER a"h
MRS. FANNY ROTENBERG a"h

MRS. CHAVA KASTEN
in honor of
MRS. S. TILLIM

MRS. MALKY KONSTAM
in honor of
MRS. RIVKA WEINSTEIN

MRS. SHARONE KRAMER
in honor of
MRS. MARY WHITE
MRS. ELAINE WHITE
MRS. ZYRA KRAMER

MRS. LIBA KRAMER
in honor of
MRS. RUTH RENNERT a"h

MRS. MASHI LEVINE
in honor of
MRS. BEATRICE LEVINE

MRS. CHANIE LIPSCHUTZ
in honor of
REBBETZIN ITTA BRACHA
LIPSCHUTZ a"h

MRS. ROCHELLE MOSKOWITZ
in honor of
MRS. EVA LICHTIG
MRS. SURI MOSKOWITZ

MRS. ESTHER NEWHOUSE
in honor of
REBBETZIN S. YUDASIN
REBBETZIN R. NEWHOUSE

MRS. CHANA LEAH OPPENHEIM
in honor of
MRS. SOPHIE SATANOVSKY
MRS. JULIA OPPENHEIM
MRS. DEBBIE BEYMAN

MRS. MINA PILCHICK
in honor of
THE CHILDREN AT YESHIVA
DEGEL HaTORAH

We Honor Those Who Inspire Us...

MRS. CHANIE POSEN
in honor of
RABBI MOSHE SCHWAB
MRS. ROZ MYEROWITZ
MRS. LIZ COHEN

MRS. CHANA RAICE
in honor of
MRS. MARGARET ROSSKAMM

MRS. TOBY RAICE
in honor of
MRS. ANNA FOGEL a"h
MRS. SHAINDEL RAICE a"h
MRS. BETTY NAGEL

MRS. TZIPORA REITMAN
in honor of
MRS. SHIRLEY JAFFE

MRS. DEBORAH ROKOWSKY
in honor of
MRS. RUTH KATZ
MRS. MARIKA ROKOWSKY

MRS. SUSIE ROSENBERG
in honor of
MRS. NELLA MERMELSTEIN
MRS. EVA ROSENBERG

MRS. MIRIAM SALVAY
in honor of
GRANDMA SARAH SALVAY

MRS. SORA SCHWAB
in honor of
REBBETZIN R. WIESNER
REBBETZIN Y. SCHWAB

MRS. CHANA SEPTIMUS
in honor of
MRS. R. NEZRI
MRS. CHARLENE RUBENSTEIN
JUDITH ROSE

MRS. HELEN SPITZ
in honor of
MRS. ESTHER GUNZ
MRS. SURI SPITZ
MRS. MIREL KIZELNIK

MRS. MALKA ROCHEL STEINMETZ
in honor of
MRS. GITTIE RUDINSKY
MRS. HELEN STEINMETZ

MRS. CILKA STEINMETZ
in honor of
MRS. FRIEDA SCHMOOKLER

MRS. MIRIAM TRESS
in honor of
MRS. D. ZOBERMAN

MRS. SHERRY WEINSTEIN
in honor of
MRS. SALLY DIAMOND

MRS. YENTIE ZAFIR
in honor of
MRS. TZIPORA MIRIAM STAHL
MRS. HINDY ZAFIR

MRS. MICHELLE ZAKON
in honor of
MRS. BERNICE SCHNEIDER
CRAVATTS a"h
MRS. GLORIA ZAKON

FOR A REFUAH SHLEMA FOR
CHAYA LEAH BAS CHAVA

In Appreciation:

Special thanks to the following restaurants and caterers who have contributed recipes and ideas for this cookbook:

CYRK *Fine Foods, Inc.*
162 Rt. 59
Monsey, N.Y.
914-356-3006

The Natural Place
6 Maple Leaf Rd.
Monsey, N.Y.
914-352-6859

Monsey Glatt
Monsey Glatt Plaza
190 Rt. 59
Monsey, N.Y.
914-425-MEAT

Jerusalem Plaza
Monsey Glatt Plaza
190 Rt. 59
Monsey, N.Y.
914-426-1500

Sabel's Catering
3-D Route 59
Monsey, N.Y.
914-356-0000

Supreme Health Food Center
25 Main Street
Monsey, N.Y.
914-426-6004

The nutritional values contained in this cookbook are based on the ingredients provided in each recipe. Individual products may vary somewhat in their specific ingredients, i.e., added nutrients, etc. So you are urged to check the information provided on each food package you use.

The nutritional value information was included for general reference purposes and is not meant to guide people with special medical or dietary needs. Those people should consult their dietician or physician.

Nutritional information was not provided for what we considered to be the rich fruit and other desserts.

CONTENTS

Before Beginning

Useful Information

Standard Measurements

pinch = ⅛ teaspoon (tsp.) or less
3 teaspoons = 1 tablespoon
2 tablespoons = 1 fluid ounce
2 tablespoons = ⅛ cup
4 tablespoons = ¼ cup
5⅓ tablespoons = ⅓ cup
8 tablespoons = ½ cup

12 tablespoons (Tbsp.) = ¾ cup
16 tablespoons = 1 cup
1 pound (lb.) = 16 ounces (oz.)
1 cup = ½ pint = 8 ounces
2 cups = 1 pint = 16 ounces
4 cups = 2 pints = 1 quart
4 quarts = 1 gallon

Equivalents

1 stick margarine = 4 oz.
1 square chocolate = 1 oz.
1 cup uncooked rice = 3 to 4 cups cooked rice
1 lemon, squeezed = 3 Tbs. lemon juice
1 orange, squeezed = 6 Tbs. or ⅓ cup orange juice
8-10 egg whites = 1 cup egg whites
12-14 egg yolks = 1 cup egg yolks

Substitutions

INGREDIENT	SUBSTITUTE
1 cup self-rising flour	1 cup all-purpose flour, ½ tsp. salt, plus 1 tsp. baking powder
1 cup cake flour	1 cup minus 2 Tbs. all-purpose flour plus 2 Tbs. cornstarch
1 cup all-purpose flour	1½ cups bread crumbs or 1 cup rolled oats
1 cup wheat flour	¾ cup cornmeal or 1½ cups rolled oats
1 tsp. baking powder	¼ tsp. baking soda plus ½ tsp. cream of tartar
1 cup sugar	1⅓ cups brown sugar or 1½ cups powdered sugar
1 cup powdered sugar	1 cup granulated sugar plus 1 tsp. cornstarch
½ cup brown sugar	2 Tbs. molasses in ½ cup granulated sugar
1 cup honey	1¼ cups sugar plus ¼ cup liquid

1 pkg. vanilla sugar	1 tsp. vanilla extract
2 sticks margarine	1 cup shortening
1 cup butter	1 cup vegetable shortening plus ½ tsp. salt
1 square unsweetened chocolate	3 Tbs. cocoa plus 1 Tbs. margarine
6-oz. pkg. semi-sweet chocolate pieces, melted	2 squares unsweetened chocolate plus 2 Tbs. oil and ½ cup sugar
1 cup milk	½ cup non-dairy creamer plus ½ cup water
1 cup buttermilk	1 Tbs. vinegar or lemon juice plus milk to make 1 cup (let stand for 5 min.), or 1 cup yogurt
1 Tbs. cornstarch (for thickening)	2 Tbs. flour
1 Tbs. flour (for thickening)	½-⅔ Tbs. cornstarch
1 fresh garlic clove	⅛ tsp. garlic powder or 1 tsp. garlic salt
2 Tbs. minced onion	1 tsp. onion powder
1 Tbs. fresh herbs	1 tsp. dried herbs
1 cup ketchup	1 cup tomato sauce, ½ cup sugar, plus 2 Tbs. vinegar
1 cup tomato juice	½ cup tomato sauce plus ½ cup water
2 cups tomato sauce	¾ cup tomato paste plus 1 cup water
white wine	an equal amount of apple cider or apple juice

Cooking Terms

Baste — To moisten foods during cooking with gravy or liquid.

Blanch — To immerse in rapidly boiling water and allow to cook slightly.

Blend — To mix until smooth by hand or in a blender.

Coat — To cover entire surface of food with flour, bread crumbs, etc.

Cream — To soften margarine or butter by beating it at room temperature. Margarine or butter is often creamed together with sugar to make a smooth, soft paste.

Cube — To cut into square pieces.

Degrease — To remove fat from the surface of stews or soup. Usually cooled in the refrigerator so that fat hardens and is easy to remove.

Dice — To cut into small, square pieces.

Dredge — To coat lightly with flour, sugar, or meal.

Fold — To add ingredients such as whipped cream or beaten egg whites gently, without loss of air.

Garnish	To add decorative or appetizing touches to food.
Glaze	To coat with syrup, icing, or jelly.
Julienne	To cut vegetables into thin strips.
Marinate	To allow food to stand in a liquid to add flavor and tenderize.
Mince	To chop or cut food into very small pieces.
Parboil	To boil in liquid until partially cooked.
Pare	To remove the outermost skin of a fruit or vegetable.
Poach	To cook gently in simmering liquid.
Purée	To mash foods until perfectly smooth.
Sauté	To cook or brown food in a small quantity of hot fat.
Scald	To heat to just below boiling point.
Score	To make shallow gashes or slits with a sharp utensil.
Sear	To brown surface of meat quickly in a skillet by intense heat.
Sift	To put dry ingredients through a sieve or sifter.
Simmer	To cook in liquid just below boiling point.
Steep	To soak in boiling water to extract or to enhance flavor.
Stir-fry	To cook small pieces of food very quickly in hot oil, moving the food around as it cooks.
Toss	To combine ingredients with a lifting motion.
Whip	To beat rapidly to incorporate air and increase volume.

Herbs and Spices

Allspice	Use in baked goods and desserts. Especially good with fruits, sweet potatoes, squash, and turnips.
Anise seed	Use in baked goods; especially good in apple pie. Use also in sauces and marinades for poultry.
Basil	Use in any tomato-based dish to soften the tomato taste. Can be added to salad dressing.
Bay leaf	Use to season stews and soups (remove before serving).
Caraway seed	Use in cabbage dishes.
Cardamom seed	Use in baked goods such as cookies or fruit pies.
Celery seed	Use in salads and dressings.
Chervil	Use in salads and dressings.
Cinnamon	Use in sweet baked goods. Use also with squash, sweet potatoes, applesauce, and baked apples.
Cloves	Use in baked desserts. Good on sweet potatoes, squash,

	and beets. Whole cloves can be used for marinades.
Coriander	Use in spicy baked goods and poultry stuffing.
Cumin	Good in soups, stews (adds a Mexican flavor), and in devilled and scrambled eggs.
Dill	Can be added to any salad or vegetable. Good with fish.
Fennel	Use in sauces for poultry.
Ginger	Use in baked goods. Try a pinch in beef stew.
Mace	Use in pound cakes or fruit cakes. Add to chicken or tuna.
Marjoram	Use in meat stews or marinades for meat. Good in salads and dressings, and on green vegetables.
Mint	Tasty on fruit desserts, especially pineapple. Good with peas, carrots, and beets.
Mustard	Ground mustard sharpens flavor of any sauce.
Nutmeg	Use in baked goods, custard puddings, and lemon-based desserts. Good in creamed dishes.
Oregano	Use in any tomato-based dish.
Rosemary	Use with poultry or lamb. A little bit adds flavor to salads.
Saffron	Use in many rice-based dishes.
Sage	Use in stuffing for poultry.
Savory	Use in salads and dressings. Sprinkle on cauliflower, broccoli, cabbage, and green beans.
Sesame seeds	Use in desserts and breads. Can also be added to salads and dressings.
Tarragon	Use in sauces and marinades for meat and poultry. Add to salads and dressings.
Thyme	Use in many ways with poultry (stuffing, dressing). Good in salads and dressings.
Turmeric	Can be added to cooking rice (will turn it light yellow).

*And Now
We Begin . . .*

Challahs, Breads, and Muffins

Traditional Challah
Always Delicious Challah
Water Challah
Pumpernickel Bread
Whole-Wheat Challah
Spelt Challah
Whole-Wheat Bread
Garlic Bread
Banana Chip Muffins

Golden Muffins
"LITE" Whole-Wheat Bread
Banana Bread
Zucchini Muffins
"LITE" Whole-Wheat Cinnamon Buns
Blueberry Muffins
Low-Fat Bran Muffins
Corn Muffins
Oat Muffins

Challahs, Breads, and Muffins

Traditional Challah

1 2-oz. cube fresh yeast
½ cup + ½ cup warm water
½ cup sugar
1 Tbs. salt

½ cup oil
2 eggs
4 cups + 1–1½ cups flour
egg yolk for brushing

Dissolve yeast in ½ cup warm water and let stand for 5 minutes. Put 4 cups of flour in a large bowl. Make a well and add yeast mixture, sugar, salt, oil, eggs, and ½ cup warm water. Mix well with either a wooden spoon or mixer, using dough hook on low speed. Add another 1-1½ cups flour until kneadable. Knead until smooth and elastic (approximately 10-15 minutes). Form into a round shape, oil top and cover with cloth. Let rise until double in bulk (approximately 2 hours). Punch down and knead lightly. Shape loaves (either 1 large, 2 medium, or 3 small) and brush with egg yolk. Let rise in pan or on cookie sheet for approximately ½ hour. Bake at 350° for 45 minutes for large or medium challahs, or 35 minutes for small challahs. Loaves should sound hollow when tapped with a spoon on the bottom.

NUTRITIONAL INFORMATION PER SERVING:			Serving Size: 1¼ oz. Total Servings: 30	
Calories	135	Cholesterol	14 mg	Protein 3 g
Calories from fat	38	Sodium	218 mg	**PERCENT OF DAILY VALUE**
Fat	4 g	Carbohydrates	21 g	Iron 7 %
Saturated Fat	1 g	Fiber	1 g	

Always Delicious Challah

1 stick margarine
1 cup boiling water
2 oz. cube fresh yeast
1 Tbs. + ¾ cup sugar
1⅓ cups lukewarm water
3 eggs

1 Tbs. salt
3 cups + 3 cups + 3 cups
  flour
1 egg yolk
2 tsp. sugar

In a large bowl dissolve margarine in the boiling water. In a smaller bowl put yeast, 1 Tbs. sugar, and lukewarm water. To the margarine mixture, add eggs, salt, ¾ cup sugar, and 3 cups flour. Mix well. Add yeast mixture and mix. Add 3 more cups of flour and mix well. Then add the remaining 3 cups of flour and knead. Put in a greased bowl and cover. Let rise 2 hours at room temperature or overnight in the refrigerator. Shape loaves and let rise another ½ hour. Brush loaves with egg yolk and top with 2 tsp. sugar. Bake at 400° for 10 minutes and then at 350° for 30 minutes.

NUTRITIONAL INFORMATION PER SERVING:		Serving Size: 1½ oz. Total Servings: 40		
Calories	145	Sodium	192 mg	**PERCENT OF DAILY VALUE**
Calories from fat	27	Carbohydrates	26 g	Vitamin A	4 %
Fat	3 g	Fiber	1 g	Calcium	1 %
Saturated Fat	1 g	Protein	4 g	Iron	8 %
Cholesterol	16 mg			

Water Challah

2 oz. cube fresh yeast
1 Tbs. + ¾ cup sugar
½ cup + 2½ cups warm
  water

9 cups flour
½ cup oil
½ Tbs. salt

Dissolve yeast and 1 Tbs. sugar in ½ cup warm water. Place flour in a large bowl and make a well in the middle. Add 2½ cups water, oil, ¾ cup sugar, salt and yeast mixture. Mix until blended. Knead dough. Place in a greased bowl, cover with a towel and let rise until doubled in size. Punch down and knead again. Braid into loaves and let rise again for ½ hour. Bake at 350° for 45 minutes.

NUTRITIONAL INFORMATION PER SERVING:		Serving Size: 1¼ oz. Total Servings: 40			
Calories	138	Cholesterol	0 mg	Protein	3 g
Calories from fat	27	Sodium	107 mg		
Fat	3 g	Carbohydrates	24 g	**PERCENT OF DAILY VALUE**	
Saturated Fat	0 g	Fiber	1 g	Iron	7 %

Pumpernickel Bread

2 pkgs. dry yeast
1 Tbs. sugar
1 Tbs. salt
1 Tbs. oil
1½ cups warm water

2 cups rye flour
2 cups whole-wheat flour
2½ cups unbleached white flour

In a large bowl, mix together yeast, sugar, salt, oil, and water. Combine flours and add to the yeast mixture. Mix until well blended (if mixture is sticky, add a little flour), and knead until smooth (about 10 minutes). Oil a large bowl and place the dough in it. Cover with a towel and put in a warm place to rise for 1 hour. Punch dough down, place on a lightly floured board, cover with a towel and leave for 10 minutes. Cut dough in half and shape into loaves. Put dough into greased loaf pans, and cover again to rise until well rounded (about 30 minutes). Bake at 375° for 1 hour. Tap loaf — if it sounds hollow, it's done.

NUTRITIONAL INFORMATION PER SERVING:		Serving Size: 1½ oz. Total Servings: 20			
Calories	144	Sodium	321 mg	**PERCENT OF DAILY VALUE**	
Calories from fat	11	Carbohydrates	29 g	Calcium	1 %
Fat	1 g	Fiber	4 g	Iron	9 %
Saturated Fat	0 g	Protein	5 g		
Cholesterol	0 mg				

Whole-Wheat Challah

2 oz. cube fresh yeast
2 cups warm water
¼ cup oil
1 Tbs. salt

1 cup brown sugar
4 cups + 4 cups whole-
    wheat flour
1 egg

Place yeast into water and let stand for 5 minutes. Add oil, salt, sugar, and 4 cups of flour to yeast mixture. Knead dough. Add remaining flour and knead again. Cover and let rise for 1½ hours. Braid and let rise again for 30 minutes. Brush challahs with beaten egg. Bake at 350° for ½ hour.

NUTRITIONAL INFORMATION PER SERVING:			Serving Size: $1^1/_5$ oz. Total Servings: 40		
Calories	117	Sodium	165 mg	**PERCENT OF DAILY VALUE**	
Calories from fat	17	Carbohydrates	23 g	Calcium	1 %
Fat	2 g	Fiber	3 g	Iron	8 %
Saturated Fat	0 g	Protein	4 g		
Cholesterol	5 mg				

Spelt Challah

2 Tbs. dry yeast
2 cups warm water
2 lb. spelt flour

⅓ cup oil
⅓ cup honey
1 tsp. salt

Dissolve yeast in the warm water. Add flour and remaining ingredients. Knead at least 5 minutes — dough will be slightly sticky. Cover and let rise in a warm place for 1 hour. Shape into round challahs or rolls (this dough cannot be shaped into braids easily). Let rise for ½ hour. Bake at 375° for about 20 to 30 minutes, or until lightly browned on top and hollow-sounding when tapped on bottom. Delicious!

NUTRITIONAL INFORMATION PER SERVING:			Serving Size: $1^4/_5$ oz. Total Servings: 30		
Calories	148	Saturated Fat	0 g	Carbohydrates	18 g
Calories from fat	26	Cholesterol	0 mg	Fiber	4 g
Fat	2 g	Sodium	72 mg	Protein	12 g

Whole-Wheat Bread

2 pkgs. dry yeast
5 cups warm water
⅔ cup honey
1 cup oil

4 eggs (optional)
5 lbs. whole-wheat pastry
    flour
2 Tbs. salt

Mix yeast in warm water and honey until it dissolves. Add oil, and eggs if using, and mix. Add flour and salt, and knead. Let rise 1½ hours, punch down and form loaves or rolls. Let rise again for 45 minutes. Bake at 350° until golden brown and sides pull away from edges of pan.

NUTRITIONAL INFORMATION PER SERVING:[*]		Serving Size: 2½ oz. Total Servings: 100			
Calories	105	Sodium	132 mg	**PERCENT OF DAILY VALUE**	
Calories from fat	25	Carbohydrates	18 g	Calcium	1 %
Fat	3 g	Fiber	3 g	Iron	6 %
Saturated Fat	0 g	Protein	3 g		
Cholesterol	9 mg				

* Analysis includes eggs

Garlic Bread

1 loaf French or Italian
    bread
¼ cup margarine

1 large or 2 small cloves
    garlic, crushed

Slice loaf of bread to about ½ inch from the bottom so that the loaf remains intact at the bottom. Melt margarine and add crushed garlic. Let stand for 15 minutes. Spread the cut surface of each slice with garlic sauce. Heat in oven at 375° for 10 to 12 minutes.

NUTRITIONAL INFORMATION PER SERVING:		Serving Size: 2 oz. Total Servings: 9			
Calories	172	Sodium	312 mg	**PERCENT OF DAILY VALUE**	
Calories from fat	65	Carbohydrates	23 g	Vitamin A	7 %
Fat	7 g	Fiber	2 g	Iron	10 %
Saturated Fat	1 g	Protein	4 g		
Cholesterol	0 mg				

Banana Chip Muffins

1½ cups whole-wheat pastry
   flour
½ tsp. baking soda
1 tsp. baking powder
⅓ cup melted butter or
   margarine

2 eggs, beaten
3 bananas
½ cup honey
½ cup chopped walnuts
6 oz. carob chips
½ cup shredded coconut

Preheat oven to 375°. Grease a muffin tin. Mix flour with baking soda
and baking powder. Add melted butter (or margarine) and beaten
eggs. Purée bananas with honey and add to mixture. Mix well. Add
walnuts, carob chips, and coconut. Blend well. Spoon into muffin tins.
Bake for 30 minutes.

NUTRITIONAL INFORMATION PER SERVING:		Serving Size: $3^3/5$ oz. Total Servings: 12			
Calories	340	Sodium	144 mg	PERCENT OF DAILY VALUE	
Calories from fat	165	Carbohydrates	41 g	Vitamin A	10 %
Fat	18 g	Fiber	4 g	Vitamin C	4 %
Saturated Fat	5 g	Protein	7 g	Calcium	10 %
Cholesterol	36 mg			Iron	8 %

Golden Muffins

¼ cup margarine, softened
¼ cup firmly packed brown
   sugar
2 eggs
1 Tbs. lemon juice
1 Tbs. water
1 cup finely shredded
   carrots, lightly packed

1 cup all-purpose flour
2 tsp. baking powder
½ tsp. salt
¼ tsp. ground ginger
½–¾ cup chopped almonds,
   pecans, or walnuts

Beat together margarine and sugar until creamy. Add eggs and beat
until light and fluffy. Stir in lemon juice, water, and shredded carrots.
Stir until well blended. In a separate bowl, combine flour with baking
powder, salt, and ginger. Sift into carrot mixture. Add chopped nuts.

Stir just enough to moisten all dry ingredients. Spoon into greased, 2½-inch muffin cups, ⅔-full. Bake at 400° for 20 minutes or until muffins spring back when lightly touched.

NUTRITIONAL INFORMATION PER SERVING:			Serving Size: 1³/₅ oz. Total Servings: 12	
Calories	148	Sodium	152 mg	**PERCENT OF DAILY VALUE**
Calories from fat	78	Carbohydrates	15 g	Vitamin A 40 %
Fat	9 g	Fiber	1 g	Vitamin C 2 %
Saturated Fat	1 g	Protein	4 g	Calcium 3 %
Cholesterol	36 mg			Iron 6 %

"LITE" Whole-Wheat Bread
Compliments of The Natural Place, Monsey, NY

¼ cup dry yeast
1 cup + 5½ cups warm
    water
5 lb. 100% LITE Whole-Wheat
    Flour*

¼ cup LIMA Sea Salt
¼ cup raw white honey
¼ cup safflower oil
1 egg

Dissolve yeast in 1 cup of warm water and set aside until it bubbles. Combine flour and salt. Add honey, oil, yeast mixture, and remaining water. Knead well (approximately 10 to 12 minutes in a mixer). Place dough in a floured bowl, cover and let rise in a warm place for 1 hour. Divide into 6 equal parts and form them into balls. Shape each ball into a loaf and place into greased loaf pans. Cover and let rise for ½ hour. Brush with beaten egg. Bake at 375° for 50 minutes.

*available only at The Natural Place

NUTRITIONAL INFORMATION PER SERVING:			Serving Size: 1¹/₃ oz. Total Servings: 120	
Calories	72	Sodium	162 mg	**PERCENT OF DAILY VALUE**
Calories from fat	8	Carbohydrates	14 g	Calcium 1 %
Fat	1 g	Fiber	3 g	Iron 5 %
Saturated Fat	0 g	Protein	3 g	
Cholesterol	2 mg			

Banana Bread

2 eggs
½ cup oil
¼ cup sugar
1 tsp. vanilla
¼ cup orange juice

2–3 small bananas, mashed
2 cups flour
½ tsp. baking powder
¾ tsp. baking soda

Mix first 5 ingredients. Add remaining ingredients and mix well. Pour into 2 small greased loaf pans (7½ x 4 inches). Bake at 350° for approximately 45 minutes.

NUTRITIONAL INFORMATION PER SERVING:		Serving Size: 2¼ oz. Total Servings: 20			
Calories	121	Sodium	123 mg	PERCENT OF DAILY VALUE	
Calories from fat	58	Carbohydrates	15 g	Vitamin A	1%
Fat	6 g	Fiber	2 g	Vitamin C	6 %
Saturated Fat	1 g	Protein	2 g	Calcium	2 %
Cholesterol	23 mg			Iron	3 %

Zucchini Muffins

3 cups flour
1½ cups sugar
1 tsp. cinnamon
1 tsp. salt
1 tsp. baking powder

¾ tsp. baking soda
2 medium zucchini
3 eggs
1 cup oil
1 cup (6 oz.) chocolate chips

Mix first 6 dry ingredients. Peel and grate zucchini to measure 2 cups and add to flour mixture. Blend eggs and oil. Add to flour mixture. Stir well until moistened. Add chocolate chips to batter and pour into paper-lined muffin tins. Bake at 350° for 25 minutes.

NUTRITIONAL INFORMATION PER SERVING:		Serving Size: 2½ oz. Total Servings: 24			
Calories	231	Sodium	124 mg	PERCENT OF DAILY VALUE	
Calories from fat	107	Carbohydrates	30 g	Vitamin A	2 %
Fat	12 g	Fiber	1 g	Vitamin C	3 %
Saturated Fat	1 g	Protein	3 g	Calcium	1 %
Cholesterol	27 mg			Iron	6 %

"LITE" Whole-Wheat Cinnamon Buns

Compliments of The Natural Place, Monsey, NY

Dough:
¼ cup dry yeast
1 cup + 2¾ cups warm fruit
    juice
5 lb. 100% LITE Whole-Wheat
    Flour*
3½ tsp. cinnamon
2½ tsp. LIMA Sea Salt
8 organic eggs
1½ cups raw white honey

2½ cups safflower oil

*Filling, per roll (each roll
    makes 8 buns):*
safflower oil (approx. 1 Tbs.)
2 tsp. cinnamon
¾ cup SUCANAT (evaporated
    sugar cane juice)
Yellow raisins

Dissolve yeast in 1 cup warm fruit juice. Set aside until it bubbles. Meanwhile, combine flour, cinnamon, and salt. Add eggs, honey, oil, yeast mixture, and remaining fruit juice. Knead well (approximately 10 to 12 minutes in a mixer). Place dough in a floured bowl, cover and set aside to rise for 1 hour. Punch down and let rise another ½ hour. Divide dough into 6 equal parts and form them into balls. Roll out one ball to ¼-inch thick. Brush with a thin layer of oil. Sprinkle entire surface lightly with cinnamon. Coat with a nice layer of SUCANAT. Sprinkle with raisins. Roll up dough. Cut into ¾-inch thick slices and place them flat an on oiled baking sheet. Cover and let rise for ½ hour. Repeat with remaining balls. Bake in 325° oven for 20 to 25 minutes or until golden brown.

*available only at The Natural Place

NUTRITIONAL INFORMATION PER SERVING:				Serving Size: 4 oz. Total Servings: 48	
Calories	400	Sodium	15 mg	**PERCENT OF DAILY VALUE**	
Calories from fat	161	Carbohydrates	56 g	Vitamin A	2 %
Fat	18 g	Fiber	6 g	Vitamin C	1 %
Saturated Fat	2 g	Protein	8 g	Calcium	7 %
Cholesterol	36 mg			Iron	22 %

Blueberry Muffins

2 cups whole-wheat flour	2 eggs
½ tsp. cinnamon	1 cup applesauce
½ tsp. baking soda	¼ cup oil
½ tsp. salt	1 cup blueberries

In a large bowl, mix flour, cinnamon, baking soda, and salt. In a small bowl, beat eggs and add applesauce and oil. Pour into flour mixture and mix well. Stir in blueberries. Pour mixture into greased muffin cups until ⅔-full. Bake at 425° for ½ hour or until brown.

NUTRITIONAL INFORMATION PER SERVING:			Serving Size: 2¼ oz. Total Servings: 15		
Calories	153	Sodium	109 mg	**PERCENT OF DAILY VALUE**	
Calories from fat	44	Carbohydrates	23 g	Vitamin A	1%
Fat	5 g	Fiber	1 g	Vitamin C	2 %
Saturated Fat	1 g	Protein	4 g	Calcium	2 %
Cholesterol	28 mg			Iron	11 %

Low-Fat Bran Muffins

1 cup wheat bran	2 eggs
1 cup whole-wheat flour	1 cup apple juice
1 tsp. baking soda	½ cup honey
½ cup raisins	

Mix bran, flour, baking soda, and raisins. Beat together eggs and juice, then add honey. Mix all ingredients well. Spoon into 12 muffin cups lined with paper. Bake at 400° for 10 to 12 minutes.

NUTRITIONAL INFORMATION PER SERVING:			Serving Size: 2¼ oz. Total Servings: 12		
Calories	127	Sodium	82 mg	**PERCENT OF DAILY VALUE**	
Calories from fat	12	Carbohydrates	29 g	Vitamin A	1 %
Fat	1 g	Fiber	2 g	Calcium	2 %
Saturated Fat	0 g	Protein	3 g	Iron	8 %
Cholesterol	36 mg				

Corn Muffins

1 cup yellow cornmeal
1 cup flour
¼ cup sugar
pinch of salt
3 tsp. baking powder

1 egg
1 cup milk
¼ cup oil
½ tsp. vanilla extract

Preheat oven to 400°. In a large bowl, combine all dry ingredients. Add remaining ingredients and blend thoroughly. Line muffin pan with cupcake papers (or use non-stick pan). Fill ¾-full with batter. Bake 15 to 20 minutes until golden brown.
Variation: Chocolate chips or blueberries may be added to the batter.

NUTRITIONAL INFORMATION PER SERVING:		Serving Size: 2 oz. Total Servings: 12		
Calories	152	Sodium	112 mg	**PERCENT OF DAILY VALUE**
Calories from fat	55	Carbohydrates	21 g	Vitamin A 2 %
Fat	6 g	Fiber	2 g	Calcium 4 %
Saturated Fat	1 g	Protein	3 g	Iron 5 %
Cholesterol	21 mg			

Oat Muffins

½ cup whole-wheat pastry
    flour
½ cup all-purpose flour
1½ cups rolled oats
2 tsp. baking powder
½ tsp. baking soda

1 tsp. cinnamon
1 egg
1 cup soy milk
1 Tbs. canola oil
3 Tbs. barley malt or maple
    syrup

Preheat oven to 375°. In a bowl, combine all dry ingredients. In a second bowl, combine egg, soy milk, oil, and either barley malt or maple syrup, and mix. Pour into flour mixture and mix well. Spoon into muffin tray and bake at 375° for 18 minutes.

NUTRITIONAL INFORMATION PER SERVING:		Serving Size: 1⁴/₅ oz. Total Servings: 12		
Calories	111	Sodium	95 mg	**PERCENT OF DAILY VALUE**
Calories from fat	24	Carbohydrates	18 g	Vitamin A 1 %
Fat	3 g	Fiber	2 g	Vitamin C 0 %
Saturated Fat	0 g	Protein	4 g	Calcium 7 %
Cholesterol	18 mg			Iron 7 %

Soups and Accompaniments

Soups and Accompaniments

Hearty Vegetable Soup

Compliments of Sabel's Catering, Monsey, NY

⅓ cup green split peas
⅓ cup yellow split peas
⅓ cup pearl barley
½ cup lima beans
8 qts. water
½ yellow squash, sliced
½ green squash, sliced
1 stalk celery, sliced
1 carrot, sliced
1 onion, diced
1 white potato, cubed

1 sweet potato, cubed
½ cup fresh peas
½ cup fresh green beans, cut in chunks
3 bay leaves
3 tsp. vegetable soup base (optional)
salt, pepper, onion powder, garlic powder (or any other spice you like), to taste

Put split peas, beans, and barley in a bowl and set aside. Boil water in a large pot and add bean mixture. Cook for ½ hour. Then add vegetables, bay leaves, soup base, and spices. Bring to a boil, then lower flame and cook for 1½ to 2 hours, stirring occasionally. Remember to remove bay leaves before serving.

NUTRITIONAL INFORMATION PER SERVING:				Serving Size: 8½ oz. Total Servings: 20	
Calories	76	Sodium	334 mg	**PERCENT OF DAILY VALUE**	
Calories from fat	2	Carbohydrates	15 g	Vitamin A	13 %
Fat	0 g	Fiber	1 g	Vitamin C	11 %
Saturated Fat	0 g	Protein	4 g	Calcium	3 %
Cholesterol	0 mg			Iron	7 %

Tomato Soup (Dairy)

1 onion, chopped
1 stalk celery, chopped
4 Tbs. oil
2–3 Tbs. flour
1 cup water

1 cup milk
1 tsp. salt
pepper, to taste
1 15-oz. can tomato sauce
1–2 Tbs. sugar

Sauté onion and celery in oil. Stir in flour. Add water, milk, salt, and pepper. Bring to a boil and let it thicken. Then add tomato sauce and sugar, and warm through for 5 to 10 minutes.

NUTRITIONAL INFORMATION PER SERVING:				Serving Size: 7 oz. Total Servings: 6	
Calories	172	Sodium	847 mg	**PERCENT OF DAILY VALUE**	
Calories from fat	96	Carbohydrates	17 g	Vitamin A	11 %
Fat	11 g	Fiber	2 g	Vitamin C	12 %
Saturated Fat	2 g	Protein	3 g	Calcium	9 %
Cholesterol	6 mg			Iron	5 %

Squash Soup

4 large zucchini squash
2 potatoes

1 pkg. onion soup mix
1½ qts. water

Peel and slice squash and potatoes. Place in a pressure cooker (or regular pot). Add onion soup mix and water to cover. Cook in pressure cooker for 20 minutes (or in a regular pot until vegetables are tender). Then blend in a blender to produce a nice, creamy soup. When doubling the recipe, only 1½ pkgs. of onion soup mix are needed — not 2.

NUTRITIONAL INFORMATION PER SERVING:				Serving Size: 8 oz. Total Servings: 10	
Calories	69	Sodium	1023 mg	**PERCENT OF DAILY VALUE**	
Calories from fat	8	Carbohydrates	14 g	Vitamin A	5 %
Fat	1 g	Fiber	3 g	Vitamin C	27 %
Saturated Fat	0 g	Protein	3 g	Calcium	5 %
Cholesterol	1 mg			Iron	6 %

2 Tbs. flour
6 cups water
½ cup barley
2 tsp. salt
½ tsp. pepper
½ tsp. paprika

3–4 carrots, sliced
3 stalks celery, sliced

In a soup pot, lightly sauté onion in a small amount of oil. Add mushrooms, carrots, and celery. Continue to stir and sauté until tender. Add flour and mix well. Add water, barley, and seasonings. Simmer for 2 hours.

NUTRITIONAL INFORMATION PER SERVING:				Serving Size: 8 oz. Total Servings: 10	
Calories	67	Sodium	455 mg	**PERCENT OF DAILY VALUE**	
Calories from fat	7	Carbohydrates	14 g	Vitamin A	102 %
Fat	1 g	Fiber	3 g	Vitamin C	8 %
Saturated Fat	0 g	Protein	3 g	Calcium	3 %
Cholesterol	0 mg			Iron	10 %

Oatmeal Soup (Meat)

5 medium potatoes, diced
2 carrots, diced
any type of meat, cut into
   cubes (approx. 1 lb.)

6–8 cups water
salt, to taste
2 Tbs. instant oatmeal

Place potatoes and carrots in a 4-quart pot. Add meat, and water to cover. Add a pinch of salt, then add oatmeal. Cook on low flame for 1 hour. Watch that soup doesn't boil over.

NUTRITIONAL INFORMATION PER SERVING:				Serving Size: 8 oz. Total Servings: 12	
Calories	132	Sodium	394 mg	**PERCENT OF DAILY VALUE**	
Calories from fat	37	Carbohydrates	15 g	Vitamin A	42 %
Fat	4 g	Fiber	1 g	Vitamin C	24 %
Saturated Fat	2 g	Protein	9 g	Calcium	1 %
Cholesterol	20 mg			Iron	9 %

Cabbage Soup (Meat)

1 large onion, chopped
oil (approx. 6 Tbs.)
1 cabbage, shredded
2–3 carrots, shredded
1 8-oz. can tomato sauce
1 46-oz. can tomato juice or purée
1 15-oz. can or 1½ cups sauerkraut

1 lb. flanken or any soup meat
meat bones
salt, garlic powder, pepper, paprika, to taste
3 qts. water (approx.)

Sauté onion in oil until soft. Add cabbage and carrots, and sauté. Pour in tomato sauce, tomato juice, and sauerkraut. Add meat, bones, seasonings, and water as needed. Bring to a boil and simmer for 2½ to 3 hours.

NUTRITIONAL INFORMATION PER SERVING:				Serving Size: 8 oz. Total Servings: 16	
Calories	202	Sodium	600 mg	**PERCENT OF DAILY VALUE**	
Calories from fat	141	Carbohydrates	10 g	Vitamin A	63 %
Fat	16 g	Fiber	3 g	Vitamin C	84 %
Saturated Fat	5 g	Protein	6 g	Calcium	6 %
Cholesterol	22 mg			Iron	11 %

Chicken Soup

10–12 cups water
1 chicken (3–4 lbs.)
3 carrots
2 stalks celery
2 turnips
1 onion
1 parsnip

1 squash and/or 2 cloves of garlic, optional
1 Tbs. salt
pepper, to taste
spray of parsley
dill

Fill pot with water and add chicken. Add all ingredients except parsley and dill. Bring to a boil and skim foam off top. Add parsley and dill. Cover pot. Simmer 1½ to 2 hours. Strain soup and pour into containers. Chill. Before reheating, remove layer of fat from top of soup.

NUTRITIONAL INFORMATION PER SERVING:		Serving Size: 10 oz. Total Servings: 18			
Calories	169	Sodium	505 mg	**PERCENT OF DAILY VALUE**	
Calories from fat	55	Carbohydrates	6 g	Vitamin A	45 %
Fat	6 g	Fiber	1 g	Vitamin C	15 %
Saturated Fat	4 g	Protein	22 g	Calcium	16 %
Cholesterol	82 mg			Iron	19 %

Lentil Soup

4 qts. water
1 16-oz. pkg. lentils
2 large onions, diced
oil for sautéing
3–4 large tomatoes (you
    may substitute canned
    tomatoes)

2 tsp. oregano
2 tsp. basil
2 tsp. salt
pepper, to taste
2 carrots
2 stalks celery

Boil up a large pot of water (can use an 8-quart pot) and add lentils. In a second pan, sauté onions in oil. Add to lentils. Add chopped tomatoes, oregano, basil, salt, and pepper. Grate in carrot and celery. Cook 1 to 2 hours.

NUTRITIONAL INFORMATION PER SERVING:		Serving Size: 7 oz. Total Servings: 20			
Calories	45	Sodium	232 mg	**PERCENT OF DAILY VALUE**	
Calories from fat	2	Carbohydrates	9 g	Vitamin A	31 %
Fat	0 g	Fiber	3 g	Vitamin C	25 %
Saturated Fat	0 g	Protein	3 g	Calcium	2 %
Cholesterol	0 mg			Iron	7 %

Corn Soup (Dairy)

1 cup chopped carrot
¼ cup chopped red pepper
¼ cup chopped onion
2 heaping Tbs. OSEM Adif
    Soup Mix (chicken flavor,
    parve)
2 cups water

2 cups milk
¼ cup flour
1 tsp. salt, or to taste
¼ tsp. pepper, or to taste
1 8-oz. can of corn
1½ cups shredded cheese

In a soup pot, combine carrots, red pepper, and onion. Dissolve soup mix in water and add to pot. Bring to a boil, then reduce heat, cover and simmer for 15 minutes. In a separate bowl, combine milk, flour, salt, and pepper. Stir into soup. Cook until bubbly, stirring to prevent lumps; then cook 1 minute more. Remove from heat and add corn and cheese. Cover pot until cheese is melted.

NUTRITIONAL INFORMATION PER SERVING:		Serving Size: 4½ oz. Total Servings: 12		
Calories	130	Sodium	829 mg	**PERCENT OF DAILY VALUE**
Calories from fat	69	Carbohydrates	9 g	Vitamin A 53 %
Fat	8 g	Fiber	1 g	Vitamin C 12 %
Saturated Fat	5 g	Protein	7 g	Calcium 21 %
Cholesterol	24 mg			Iron 4 %

French Onion Soup (Dairy)

8 cups water
8 medium onions
3 Tbs. onion soup powder or
    1 pkg. onion soup mix
4 slices white American
    cheese, shredded
½ cup milk
2 tsp. flour
1 tsp. salt

½ tsp. pepper
2 tsp. garlic powder
1 carrot (optional)
1 8-oz. can mushrooms
    (optional)
bread (1 slice per serving)
mozzarella cheese, ½ oz.
    slice, shredded, per
    serving

Bring water to a boil in a large pot. Cut onions into quarters and add to water. Add remaining ingredients, except bread and mozzarella, and cook, covered, on low flame for 1 hour. Before serving, top each bowl of soup with a slice of bread and shredded mozzarella cheese.

NUTRITIONAL INFORMATION PER SERVING:				Serving Size: 9 oz. Total Servings: 12	
Calories	109	Sodium	642 mg	**PERCENT OF DAILY VALUE**	
Calories from fat	35	Carbohydrates	12 g	Vitamin A	23 %
Fat	4 g	Fiber	2 g	Vitamin C	11 %
Saturated Fat	1 g	Protein	7 g	Calcium	10 %
Cholesterol	11 mg			Iron	3 %

Vegetable Soup (Meat)

3 Tbs. oil
2 onions, diced
6 large potatoes, diced
1 large squash, diced
2 carrots, shredded
2 stalks celery, diced
1 large clove of garlic, minced

dried dill, parsley, celery salt, and pepper — a pinch of each or to taste
3 chicken frames
½ cup barley

In a large 8-quart soup pot, heat oil. Add ingredients in order — all except barley. Fill pot with 3 quarts of water, to 2 inches from the top. Cook 1 hour. Add barley. Cook 1½ to 2 hours more.

NUTRITIONAL INFORMATION PER SERVING:				Serving Size: 8 oz. Total Servings: 20	
Calories	97	Sodium	124 mg	**PERCENT OF DAILY VALUE**	
Calories from fat	28	Carbohydrates	14 g	Vitamin A	26 %
Fat	3 g	Fiber	2 g	Vitamin C	20 %
Saturated Fat	0 g	Protein	4 g	Calcium	2 %
Cholesterol	3 mg			Iron	5 %

Minestrone Soup

¼ cup olive oil
1 small onion, chopped
4 cloves of garlic, crushed
1 cup small lima beans or
   navy beans
10 cups water
2 stalks celery, diced
3 carrots, sliced

2 potatoes, diced
1 tsp. oregano
1 tsp. basil
½ tsp. salt
¼ tsp. pepper
2 cups canned tomatoes
½ cup any type of pasta

In a soup pot, heat oil and sauté onion and garlic. Add beans and water. Simmer for 1½ hours. Add celery, carrots, and potatoes, and enough water to cover. Add seasonings and bring to a boil. Reduce heat and simmer, covered, for 1 hour. Add tomatoes, cook for 20 minutes, then stir in pasta and cook 10 minutes more.

NUTRITIONAL INFORMATION PER SERVING:				Serving Size: 7 oz. Total Servings: 15	
Calories	120	Sodium	140 mg	**PERCENT OF DAILY VALUE**	
Calories from fat	36	Carbohydrates	17 g	Vitamin A	53 %
Fat	4 g	Fiber	3 g	Vitamin C	13 %
Saturated Fat	1 g	Protein	5 g	Calcium	4 %
Cholesterol	0 mg			Iron	10 %

Tomato Soup

1 46-oz. can tomato juice
4 cups water
1 tsp. salt, or to taste

2 Tbs. sugar, or to taste
⅛ tsp. pepper
½ cup brown rice

Combine all ingredients. Bring to a boil. Reduce heat and simmer for 1½ hours.

NUTRITIONAL INFORMATION PER SERVING:				Serving Size: 8 oz. Total Servings: 8	
Calories	82	Sodium	857 mg	**PERCENT OF DAILY VALUE**	
Calories from fat	4	Carbohydrates	19 g	Vitamin A	11 %
Fat	0 g	Fiber	2 g	Vitamin C	49 %
Saturated Fat	0 g	Protein	2 g	Calcium	2 %
Cholesterol	0 mg			Iron	7 %

Tasty Vegetable Soup

2 onions, chopped
3–4 garlic cloves, minced
1 Tbs. vegetable or corn oil
1 4-oz. can tomato sauce
3 10-oz. pkgs. frozen
    vegetables (any kind)*

1 28-oz. can crushed
    tomatoes
3½ cups water
2 bouillon cubes
1 tsp. salt
¼ tsp. pepper

Sauté onion and garlic in oil. Add tomato sauce and stir. Add remaining ingredients. Bring to a boil. Reduce heat and simmer 1½ to 2 hours.

NUTRITIONAL INFORMATION PER SERVING:*		Serving Size: 8 oz. Total Servings: 12		
Calories	55	Sodium	545 mg	**PERCENT OF DAILY VALUE**
Calories from fat	6	Carbohydrates	11 g	Vitamin A 16 %
Fat	1 g	Fiber	2 g	Vitamin C 34 %
Saturated Fat	0 g	Protein	2 g	Calcium 7 %
Cholesterol	0 mg			Iron 9 %

* Nutritional information is based on French-style green beans.

Fruit Soup

1 30-oz. can fruit cocktail
1 pkg. red jello
1 pkg. vanilla pudding (non-
    instant)

dash of cinnamon
1 tsp. lemon juice
⅛–¼ cup sugar

In a 4-quart pot, mix all ingredients. Add enough water to almost fill pot. Bring to a boil, lower flame, and cook over low heat for 15 minutes. **Do not** cover pot (or it'll boil over).

NUTRITIONAL INFORMATION PER SERVING:		Serving Size: 6 oz. Total Servings: 12		
Calories	109	Sodium	79 mg	**PERCENT OF DAILY VALUE**
Calories from fat	0	Carbohydrates	27 g	Vitamin A 2 %
Fat	0 g	Fiber	0 g	Vitamin C 3 %
Saturated Fat	0 g	Protein	1 g	Calcium 1 %
Cholesterol	0 mg			Iron 1 %

Onion Soup

6 large onions, diced
4 Tbs. oil
3 qts. water
2 bouillon cubes

1 tsp. salt, or to taste
¼ tsp. pepper
6 Tbs. (approx.) flour
5 Tbs. water

Sauté onions in oil until soft (not brown). Pour in water with bouillon cubes, salt, and pepper. Make a paste with flour and water. Mix into soup and cook slowly about 45 minutes.

NUTRITIONAL INFORMATION PER SERVING:			Serving Size: 8 oz. Total Servings: 12		
Calories	92	Sodium	508 mg	**PERCENT OF DAILY VALUE**	
Calories from fat	42	Carbohydrates	11 g	Vitamin C	10 %
Fat	5 g	Fiber	2 g	Calcium	3 %
Saturated Fat	1 g	Protein	2 g	Iron	2 %
Cholesterol	0 mg				

Fluffy Kneidels

4 eggs, separated
½ cup water
⅓ cup oil
1 tsp. + 1 Tbs. salt

dash of pepper
1 cup matzah meal
1½ qts. water

Beat egg whites until stiff. Add yolks. Combine eggs with water, oil, 1 tsp. salt, and pepper. Mix well, add matzah meal, and stir thoroughly. (Mixture should not be too loose. If necessary, add a little more matzah meal.) Let stand in refrigerator for 20 minutes. Boil water and add 1 Tbs. of salt. Form mixture into balls and drop into boiling water. Cook 20 minutes.

NUTRITIONAL INFORMATION PER SERVING:			Serving Size: 1 kneidel Total Servings: 12		
Calories	121	Sodium	199 mg	**PERCENT OF DAILY VALUE**	
Calories from fat	70	Carbohydrates	9 g	Vitamin A	4 %
Fat	8 g	Fiber	0 g	Calcium	1 %
Saturated Fat	2 g	Protein	3 g	Iron	3 %
Cholesterol	71 mg				

Kreplach

Filling:
¾ lb. ground meat
1 egg
pepper, onion powder, garlic
    powder, to taste

Dough:
1¾ cups flour
2 eggs
½ tsp. salt
3 Tbs. oil

Combine filling ingredients and refrigerate. Combine dough ingredients. Roll out on lightly floured wax paper. Cut out circles with a glass. Place a small amount of filling mixture onto each circle of dough. Fold over and pull dough into a triangle shape. Pinch closed with wet fingers. Reroll scraps of dough and repeat. Drop into a 3-quart pot of boiling water and cook for 30 to 45 minutes. (At this point, the kreplach can be cooled and frozen.) Reheat in a pot of boiling soup.

NUTRITIONAL INFORMATION PER SERVING:		Serving Size: 1 krepel Total Servings: 10		
Calories	244	Sodium	149 mg	**PERCENT OF DAILY VALUE**
Calories from fat	133	Carbohydrates	17 g	Vitamin A 3 %
Fat	15 g	Fiber	1 g	Calcium 1 %
Saturated Fat	5 g	Protein	10 g	Iron 11 %
Cholesterol	93 mg			

Egg Drops for Soup

1 egg, beaten
dash of salt

3 Tbs. flour
¼ cup cold water

Stir together all ingredients until smooth. Drop slowly from end of spoon into boiling soup. Cover soup and cook 5 minutes.

NUTRITIONAL INFORMATION PER SERVING:		Serving Size: ¾ oz. Total Servings: 6		
Calories	27	Sodium	100 mg	**PERCENT OF DAILY VALUE**
Calories from fat	8	Carbohydrates	3 g	Vitamin A 1 %
Fat	1 g	Fiber	0 g	Iron 1 %
Saturated Fat	0 g	Protein	1 g	
Cholesterol	36 mg			

Salads, Dressings, Dips, Relishes, and Sauces

Boston Leaf Mandarin Salad
Bean Salad
Corn Salad
Israeli Couscous Salad
Coleslaw
"No Check" Salad
Waldorf Salad
Zucchini and Squash Salad
Marinated Salad
Tabouli Salad
Cucumber Salad
Georgian Salad
Health Salad
Festive Cucumber Salad
Russian Salad
Beet Salad
Broccoli Salad
Three-Bean Salad
Deviled Eggs
Potato Salad
Vegetable Trifle
Almond Mandarin Salad
Tal's Potato Salad
Purple Cabbage Salad
String Bean Salad
Helen's Pink Salad

Cabbage Salad
Marinated Vegetable Salad
Georgi's Salad
Jennifer's Broccoli Salad
French Dressing
Garlic Dressing
Italian Dressing
Lemon Vinaigrette Dressing
Savory Salad Dressing
Russian Dressing
Yogurt-Nut Dip
Tangy Avocado Dip
Creamy Avocado Dip
Tofu Dip
Creamy Dip
Spinach Salad Dip
Fresh Cranberry Relish
Sweet and Sour Sauce
Dill Sauce
Pepper Relish
Fish Sauce
Cranberry with Character
Cranberry Fruit Sauce
Fruit Sauce
Tomato Relish

Salads, Dressings, Dips, Relishes, and Sauces

Boston Leaf Mandarin Salad

2 heads of Boston leaf
   lettuce
1 16-oz. box mushrooms
½ cup sliced almonds
1 8-oz. can mandarin
   orange segments,
   drained

Dressing:
¼ cup freshly squeezed
   lemon juice
¼ cup olive oil
¾ cup mayonnaise
¼ cup sugar
⅛ cup vinegar
garlic powder and black
   pepper, to taste

Prepare lettuce for salad. Slice mushrooms. Toast almonds at 250° for 10 minutes until golden. Combine orange segments with lettuce, mushrooms, and almonds. Mix dressing ingredients together and pour over vegetables.

NUTRITIONAL INFORMATION PER SERVING:				Serving Size: 4 oz. Total Servings: 20	
Calories	134	Sodium	84 mg	**PERCENT OF DAILY VALUE**	
Calories from fat	109	Carbohydrates	6 g	Vitamin A	3 %
Fat	12 g	Fiber	1 g	Vitamin C	8 %
Saturated Fat	2 g	Protein	2 g	Calcium	2 %
Cholesterol	5 mg			Iron	4 %

Bean Salad

1 16-oz. can green beans
1 16-oz. can wax beans
1 16-oz. can kidney beans
1 16-oz. can chickpeas
   (garbanzo beans)
1 15-oz. can corn

1 red onion
¾ cup sugar
⅓ cup oil
½ cup vinegar
1 tsp. salt
½ tsp. pepper

Drain canned beans and corn and mix together. Slice onion and mix
with beans and corn. Combine sugar, oil, vinegar, salt, and pepper,
and pour over beans and corn. Marinate for one day.

NUTRITIONAL INFORMATION PER SERVING:				Serving Size: 5½ oz. Total Servings: 15	
Calories	196	Sodium	548 mg	**PERCENT OF DAILY VALUE**	
Calories from fat	68	Carbohydrates	29 g	Vitamin A	2 %
Fat	8 g	Fiber	5 g	Vitamin C	10 %
Saturated Fat	1 g	Protein	5 g	Calcium	4 %
Cholesterol	0 mg			Iron	13 %

Corn Salad

2 11-oz. cans corn niblets
1 medium red pepper
1 medium green pepper
½ cup chopped scallions
¼ cup fresh parsley
1 cup oil

½ cup vinegar
½ cup lemon juice
1 tsp. sugar
2 tsp. salt
¼ tsp. basil

Drain corn and put in bowl. Chop peppers, scallions, and parsley into
small pieces and add to corn. Mix in remaining ingredients.

NUTRITIONAL INFORMATION PER SERVING:				Serving Size: 5½ oz. Total Servings: 8	
Calories	313	Sodium	767 mg	**PERCENT OF DAILY VALUE**	
Calories from fat	253	Carbohydrates	17 g	Vitamin A	5 %
Fat	28 g	Fiber	2 g	Vitamin C	62 %
Saturated Fat	4 g	Protein	2 g	Calcium	2 %
Cholesterol	0 mg			Iron	6 %

Israeli Couscous Salad

1 12-oz. pkg. Israeli
    couscous
8 oz. canned or frozen
    (thawed) white corn
    niblets
1 green pepper, diced
1 red pepper, diced
¼ cup pimentos, diced

Dressing:
½ cup oil
½ cup lemon juice (from
    fresh lemons)
1 tsp. salt
¼ cup chopped dill
½ tsp. garlic powder

Cook couscous according to directions on package. Combine couscous with vegetables. Mix together ingredients for dressing. Pour over couscous and mix well. Adjust salt and garlic powder to taste.

NUTRITIONAL INFORMATION PER SERVING:				Serving Size: 3½ oz. Total Servings: 10	
Calories	250	Sodium	275 mg	**PERCENT OF DAILY VALUE**	
Calories from fat	103	Carbohydrates	32 g	Vitamin A	2 %
Fat	11 g	Fiber	6 g	Vitamin C	41 %
Saturated Fat	1 g	Protein	5 g	Calcium	4 %
Cholesterol	0 mg			Iron	8 %

Coleslaw

1 cabbage
3 carrots
1 green pepper
4 Tbs. lemon juice

½ cup sugar
½ Tbs. salt
10 Tbs. mayonnaise

Shred cabbage, carrots, and green pepper. Combine vegetables with lemon juice, sugar, and salt. Add mayonnaise and mix well.

NUTRITIONAL INFORMATION PER SERVING:				Serving Size: 5 oz. Total Servings: 12	
Calories	143	Sodium	357 mg	**PERCENT OF DAILY VALUE**	
Calories from fat	85	Carbohydrates	15 g	Vitamin A	66 %
Fat	9 g	Fiber	3 g	Vitamin C	97 %
Saturated Fat	1 g	Protein	2 g	Calcium	6 %
Cholesterol	7 mg			Iron	3 %

"No Check" Salad

1 12-oz. bag BODEK
   coleslaw
1 12-oz. bag BODEK purple
   cabbage
2 bunches scallions, sliced
½ cup sliced almonds
¾ cup oil

¼ cup sugar
½ tsp. pepper
4 Tbs. sesame seeds
2 tsp. salt
2 tsp. wine vinegar
¼ cup hot water

Mix first 3 ingredients and add almonds. In a separate bowl, combine the remaining ingredients and mix well. Pour over vegetables and marinate. Fast and kosher — no checking!

NUTRITIONAL INFORMATION PER SERVING:		Serving Size: 4 oz. Total Servings: 12			
Calories	229	Sodium	11 mg	**PERCENT OF DAILY VALUE**	
Calories from fat	183	Carbohydrates	11 g	Vitamin A	23 %
Fat	20 g	Fiber	3 g	Vitamin C	53 %
Saturated Fat	2 g	Protein	4 g	Calcium	13 %
Cholesterol	0 mg			Iron	10 %

Waldorf Salad

3 apples
1 cup diced celery
½ cup mayonnaise

2 tsp. lemon juice
1 cup chopped walnuts

Peel and cube apples. Add celery and mayonnaise. Mix. Add lemon juice. Mix well, then add walnuts and mix.

NUTRITIONAL INFORMATION PER SERVING:		Serving Size: 6 oz. Total Servings: 4			
Calories	446	Sodium	175 mg	**PERCENT OF DAILY VALUE**	
Calories from fat	360	Carbohydrates	20 g	Vitamin A	4 %
Fat	40 g	Fiber	4 g	Vitamin C	11 %
Saturated Fat	4 g	Protein	8 g	Calcium	4 %
Cholesterol	16 mg			Iron	8 %

Zucchini and Squash Salad

3 zucchini
3 yellow squash
1 tsp. + ¾ tsp. salt

½ cup white wine vinegar
2 Tbs. sugar
¼ tsp. pepper

Cut zucchini and yellow squash into 4-inch-long thin strips and place into a large bowl. Toss with 1 tsp. salt. Cover and let stand ½ hour. Uncover and squeeze out as much liquid as possible. Stir in vinegar, sugar, pepper, and ¾ tsp. salt. Cover and refrigerate at least 1 hour.

NUTRITIONAL INFORMATION PER SERVING:		Serving Size: 5½ oz. Total Servings: 6			
Calories	33	Sodium	626 mg	PERCENT OF DAILY VALUE	
Calories from fat	2	Carbohydrates	9 g	Vitamin A	5 %
Fat	0 g	Fiber	2 g	Vitamin C	19 %
Saturated Fat	0 g	Protein	2 g	Calcium	3 %
Cholesterol	0 mg			Iron	4 %

Marinated Salad

3 carrots
2 green squash
1 red onion
1 red pepper
1 green pepper
1 yellow pepper
1 15-oz. can baby corn
1 12-oz. can mushrooms

1 12-oz. bag frozen string
    beans, defrosted
2–3 cloves garlic
¾ cup vinegar
½ cup oil
½ cup sugar
2 tsp. salt

Slice carrots, squash, and onion. Slice peppers into strips. Cut each baby corn into thirds. Mix all vegetables together and set aside. Cook together the garlic cloves, vinegar, oil, sugar, and salt, and pour over vegetables while hot. Marinate overnight. Makes about 4 quarts.

NUTRITIONAL INFORMATION PER SERVING:		Serving Size: 5½ oz. Total Servings: 15			
Calories	145	Sodium	379 mg	PERCENT OF DAILY VALUE	
Calories from fat	71	Carbohydrates	18 g	Vitamin A	55 %
Fat	8 g	Fiber	2 g	Vitamin C	52 %
Saturated Fat	1 g	Protein	2 g	Calcium	3 %
Cholesterol	0 mg			Iron	9 %

Tabouli Salad

1 cup dry bulgur wheat
1½ tsp. salt
1½ cups boiling water
¼ cup lemon juice
1 tsp. crushed fresh garlic
½ cup chopped scallions

¼ cup olive oil
2 medium tomatoes, diced
1 cup chopped parsley
  (packed)
1 cucumber, diced

Mix bulgur and salt. Pour boiling water over bulgur and allow it to sit, covered, for 15 minutes. Add remaining ingredients and chill.

NUTRITIONAL INFORMATION PER SERVING:				Serving Size: 7½ oz. Total Servings: 4	
Calories	271	Sodium	826 mg	**PERCENT OF DAILY VALUE**	
Calories from fat	129	Carbohydrates	33 g	Vitamin A	23 %
Fat	14 g	Fiber	9 g	Vitamin C	63 %
Saturated Fat	2 g	Protein	6 g	Calcium	7 %
Cholesterol	0 mg			Iron	17 %

Cucumber Salad

3 medium cucumbers
2 medium onions
1 cup water
1 cup white vinegar

1 Tbs. sugar
1 Tbs. salt
⅛ tsp. pepper

Score cucumbers by running a fork down each of their sides. Cut into thin slices. Thinly slice onions. In a large bowl, combine water, vinegar, sugar, salt, and pepper. Stir in cucumbers and onions. Cover and marinate salad in refrigerator for at least 5 hours before serving.

NUTRITIONAL INFORMATION PER SERVING:				Serving Size: 6 oz. Total Servings: 8	
Calories	34	Sodium	807 mg	**PERCENT OF DAILY VALUE**	
Calories from fat	1	Carbohydrates	8 g	Vitamin A	3 %
Fat	0 g	Fiber	1 g	Vitamin C	14 %
Saturated Fat	0 g	Protein	1 g	Calcium	4 %
Cholesterol	0 mg			Iron	11 %

Georgian Salad

2 eggplants, peeled
2 zucchini
2 red peppers
2 green peppers
2 medium red onions

5 cloves of garlic
½ cup oil
5 Tbs. apple cider vinegar
1 tsp. salt, or to taste

Cut eggplants and zucchini into small cubes and steam until very soft. While they cool, cut peppers into long thin strips, cut onions into thin rings, and crush garlic. In a large salad bowl, combine all the vegetables. Add oil, vinegar, and salt. Mix well. Chill overnight.

NUTRITIONAL INFORMATION PER SERVING:			Serving Size: 5½ oz. Total Servings: 10	
Calories	144	Sodium	222 mg	**PERCENT OF DAILY VALUE**
Calories from fat	100	Carbohydrates	10 g	Vitamin A 5 %
Fat	11 g	Fiber	2 g	Vitamin C 89 %
Saturated Fat	1 g	Protein	2 g	Calcium 3 %
Cholesterol	0 mg			Iron 11 %

Health Salad

1 bunch celery
1 lb. carrots
1 green pepper
1 red pepper
1 red onion

1 small onion
¼ cup sugar
¼ cup oil
¼ cup vinegar

Thinly slice all vegetables in food processor. Then add sugar, oil, and vinegar. Mix. The longer it marinates, the better it tastes.

NUTRITIONAL INFORMATION PER SERVING:			Serving Size: 5½ oz. Total Servings: 8	
Calories	132	Sodium	54 mg	**PERCENT OF DAILY VALUE**
Calories from fat	63	Carbohydrates	17 g	Vitamin A 202 %
Fat	7 g	Fiber	3 g	Vitamin C 58 %
Saturated Fat	1 g	Protein	1 g	Calcium 5 %
Cholesterol	0 mg			Iron 10 %

Festive Cucumber Salad

10–12 small cucumbers	1 red pepper
2 carrots	¾ cup lemon juice
1 red onion	½ cup oil
1 white onion	¾ cup sugar
1 green pepper	3 tsp. salt

Thinly slice all vegetables. Mix together remaining ingredients and pour over vegetables. Chill. Amount of dressing can be proportionately increased or decreased to taste.

NUTRITIONAL INFORMATION PER SERVING:			Serving Size: 6 oz. Total Servings: 15		
Calories	132	Sodium	437 mg	PERCENT OF DAILY VALUE	
Calories from fat	67	Carbohydrates	17 g	Vitamin A	38 %
Fat	7 g	Fiber	1 g	Vitamin C	42 %
Saturated Fat	1 g	Protein	1 g	Calcium	4 %
Cholesterol	0 mg			Iron	7 %

Russian Salad

1 Tbs. oil	1 tsp. salt
3 onions, sliced	1 bay leaf
5 red peppers, cut in strips	½ tsp. oregano
8 carrots, shredded	½ tsp. basil
3 tomatoes, sliced	1 tsp. sugar

Put oil into a large pot, then layer onions, peppers, and carrots. Place tomato slices on top. Add seasonings. Cook over very low heat, covered, for about 1½ hours. Serve cold.

NUTRITIONAL INFORMATION PER SERVING:			Serving Size: 8 oz. Total Servings: 8		
Calories	104	Sodium	305 mg	PERCENT OF DAILY VALUE	
Calories from fat	19	Carbohydrates	20 g	Vitamin A	266 %
Fat	2 g	Fiber	4 g	Vitamin C	141 %
Saturated Fat	0 g	Protein	3 g	Calcium	6 %
Cholesterol	0 mg			Iron	20 %

Beet Salad

1 15-oz. can beets	¼ tsp. salt
⅓ cup beet juice	⅛ tsp. pepper
¼ cup sugar	¼ cup vinegar
½ Tbs. cornstarch	

Mix all ingredients together and chill.

NUTRITIONAL INFORMATION PER SERVING:				Serving Size: 4 oz. Total Servings: 4	
Calories	81	Sodium	414 mg	**PERCENT OF DAILY VALUE**	
Calories from fat	1	Carbohydrates	20 g	Vitamin C	7 %
Fat	0 g	Fiber	1 g	Calcium	2 %
Saturated Fat	0 g	Protein	1 g	Iron	5 %
Cholesterol	0 mg				

Broccoli Salad

1 bunch broccoli, cut into small pieces	½ cup unsalted cashews, chopped
1 carrot, diced	
½ red onion, chopped	*Dressing:*
1 zucchini, quartered and sliced	⅓ cup red wine vinegar
1 15-oz. can baby corn, drained	¾ cup mayonnaise
½ cup sunflower seeds	½ cup (or less) sugar, to taste

Combine vegetables and nuts in a salad bowl. Mix dressing ingredients and pour over vegetables. Toss until coated. Amount of dressing can be proportionately increased or decreased to taste.

NUTRITIONAL INFORMATION PER SERVING:				Serving Size: 5½ oz. Total Servings: 10	
Calories	315	Sodium	226 mg	**PERCENT OF DAILY VALUE**	
Calories from fat	212	Carbohydrates	24 g	Vitamin A	28 %
Fat	24 g	Fiber	4 g	Vitamin C	76 %
Saturated Fat	4 g	Protein	7 g	Calcium	5 %
Cholesterol	10 mg			Iron	14 %

Three-Bean Salad

1 16-oz. can red kidney
   beans
1 16-oz. can green beans
1 16-oz. can yellow wax
   beans
1 16-oz. can garbanzo
   beans (chickpeas)
   (optional)

½ cup chopped onion
½ cup minced green pepper
½ cup chopped celery
½ cup salad oil
½ cup cider vinegar
¾ cup sugar
1 tsp. salt
1 tsp. pepper

Drain beans well, then mix together. Toss vegetables together with beans. Blend oil, vinegar, sugar, salt, and pepper well. Pour over beans and vegetables. Best if marinated for 24 hours before serving.

NUTRITIONAL INFORMATION PER SERVING:		Serving Size: 6 oz. Total Servings: 10			
Calories	224	Sodium	565 mg	PERCENT OF DAILY VALUE	
Calories from fat	102	Carbohydrates	30 g	Vitamin A	7 %
Fat	11 g	Fiber	5 g	Vitamin C	184 %
Saturated Fat	1 g	Protein	4 g	Calcium	5 %
Cholesterol	0 mg			Iron	15 %

Deviled Eggs

6 hard-boiled eggs, peeled
¼ cup mayonnaise
1 tsp. mustard

1 tsp. vinegar
paprika for garnish

Halve eggs lengthwise and remove yolks. Mash yolks with a fork. Add mayonnaise, mustard, and vinegar. Mix well. Stuff halves with yolk mixture. Garnish with paprika.

NUTRITIONAL INFORMATION PER SERVING:		Serving Size: 2 halves Total Servings: 6			
Calories	144	Sodium	115 mg	PERCENT OF DAILY VALUE	
Calories from fat	113	Carbohydrates	1 g	Vitamin A	12 %
Fat	13 g	Fiber	0 g	Calcium	3 %
Saturated Fat	3 g	Protein	7 g	Iron	5 %
Cholesterol	218 mg				

Potato Salad

4 potatoes
¼ green pepper
1 stalk celery

2 dill pickles
½ cup mayonnaise (approx.)
1 tsp. salt, or to taste

Cook potatoes in jackets, then cool, peel, and dice. Dice green pepper, celery, and pickles. Mix vegetables together and add in enough mayonnaise to keep the mixture together. Add salt to taste and chill. Let sit overnight before serving.

NUTRITIONAL INFORMATION PER SERVING:				Serving Size: 4 oz. Total Servings: 8	
Calories	153	Sodium	583 mg	**PERCENT OF DAILY VALUE**	
Calories from fat	100	Carbohydrates	12 g	Vitamin A	2 %
Fat	11 g	Fiber	2 g	Vitamin C	28 %
Saturated Fat	2 g	Protein	2 g	Calcium	2 %
Cholesterol	8 mg			Iron	5 %

Vegetable Trifle

1-lb. bag shredded purple
    cabbage
1-lb. bag shredded lettuce
1-lb. bag frozen peas
2–3 small cucumbers, sliced

1 red pepper, sliced
1 yellow pepper, sliced
1 green pepper, sliced
1 container cherry tomatoes

In a clear glass bowl with straight sides, layer vegetables in the following order: purple cabbage, lettuce, frozen peas, cucumbers, red pepper, yellow pepper, green pepper, and cherry tomatoes. Make a dressing from our Dressing Section or any dressing of your choice and pour it over and in between vegetables.

NUTRITIONAL INFORMATION PER SERVING:				Serving Size: 7 oz. Total Servings: 12	
Calories	63	Sodium	50 mg	**PERCENT OF DAILY VALUE**	
Calories from fat	4	Carbohydrates	12 g	Vitamin A	11 %
Fat	0 g	Fiber	3 g	Vitamin C	76 %
Saturated Fat	0 g	Protein	4 g	Calcium	4 %
Cholesterol	0 mg			Iron	9 %

Almond Mandarin Salad

Dressing:
½ cup oil
3 Tbs. vinegar
1 Tbs. lemon juice
2 Tbs. sugar
½ tsp. salt
½ tsp. mustard
½ tsp. onion powder

Salad:
1 8-oz. can mandarin
   oranges
1 head lettuce, shredded
1 red onion, sliced
½ cup almonds

Mix dressing ingredients together well in a bowl. Combine salad ingredients with dressing. Super!

NUTRITIONAL INFORMATION PER SERVING:				Serving Size: 5 oz. Total Servings: 8	
Calories	218	Sodium	144 mg	PERCENT OF DAILY VALUE	
Calories from fat	166	Carbohydrates	11 g	Vitamin A	4 %
Fat	18 g	Fiber	2 g	Vitamin C	24 %
Saturated Fat	2 g	Protein	3 g	Calcium	6 %
Cholesterol	0 mg			Iron	9 %

Tal's Potato Salad

10 medium potatoes
6 Tbs. mayonnaise (not low-
   fat — it will make salad
   mushy)

3 half-sour pickles, diced
approx. 5–6 Tbs. pickle juice
1 tsp. garlic salt
fresh dill

Microwave or conventionally bake potatoes until soft, and peel off skin. Cut with a fork and place potato pieces in a bowl. Mix in the mayonnaise, pickles, pickle juice, and garlic salt. Garnish with fresh dill.

NUTRITIONAL INFORMATION PER SERVING:				Serving Size: 5 oz. Total Servings: 12	
Calories	108	Sodium	264 mg	PERCENT OF DAILY VALUE	
Calories from fat	22	Carbohydrates	19 g	Vitamin C	36 %
Fat	2 g	Fiber	2 g	Calcium	2 %
Saturated Fat	0 g	Protein	3 g	Iron	9 %
Cholesterol	3 mg				

Purple Cabbage Salad

½ cup oil
3 Tbs. vinegar
dash of salt
dash of pepper
4 Tbs. brown sugar

1 cup raisins
½ cup walnuts
1 purple cabbage (4 cups shredded)
2 apples

Combine oil, vinegar, salt, pepper, brown sugar, raisins, and walnuts. Add shredded cabbage. Peel and dice apples and add to mixture. Mix everything together and chill.

NUTRITIONAL INFORMATION PER SERVING:				Serving Size: 4 oz. Total Servings: 8	
Calories	271	Sodium	275 mg	**PERCENT OF DAILY VALUE**	
Calories from fat	165	Carbohydrates	28 g	Vitamin C	36 %
Fat	18 g	Fiber	3 g	Calcium	4 %
Saturated Fat	2 g	Protein	3 g	Iron	6 %
Cholesterol	0 mg				

String Bean Salad

1–1½ lbs. string beans
4 tomatoes, cubed
1 onion, diced
2 stalks celery, finely chopped

⅓ cup oil
¼ cup vinegar or lemon juice, or to taste
1 tsp. salt
pepper, to taste

Steam string beans about 5 minutes, until just crisp. Rinse with cold water so they do not overcook. Add remaining ingredients and toss. Marinate a few hours before serving.

NUTRITIONAL INFORMATION PER SERVING:				Serving Size: 6½ oz. Total Servings: 8	
Calories	131	Sodium	292 mg	**PERCENT OF DAILY VALUE**	
Calories from fat	89	Carbohydrates	8 g	Vitamin A	16 %
Fat	10 g	Fiber	2 g	Vitamin C	61 %
Saturated Fat	2 g	Protein	3 g	Calcium	8 %
Cholesterol	0 mg			Iron	12 %

Helen's Pink Salad

1 16-oz. can pineapple chunks	1 16-oz. can cubed beets
	½ cup mayonnaise

Combine all ingredients and refrigerate for a few hours or overnight. Delicious with a heavy meat meal or spicy chicken.

NUTRITIONAL INFORMATION PER SERVING:				Serving Size: 4½ oz. Total Servings: 8	
Calories	153	Sodium	94 mg	**PERCENT OF DAILY VALUE**	
Calories from fat	100	Carbohydrates	13 g	Vitamin A	1 %
Fat	11 g	Fiber	1 g	Vitamin C	18 %
Saturated Fat	2 g	Protein	1 g	Calcium	6 %
Cholesterol	8 mg			Iron	7 %

Cabbage Salad

1 green pepper	*Dressing:*
1 red onion	½ cup sugar
1 carrot	¾ cup apple cider vinegar
1 cucumber	½ cup salad oil
1 medium cabbage (2½–3 lbs.)	¼ cup water
	3 tsp. salt

Dice pepper. Slice onion very thin. Slice carrot and cucumber on an angle. Shred cabbage. Mix together dressing ingredients and pour over vegetables. Let stand — the longer it stands, the better it tastes.

Variation: For more color and eye appeal, add 1 or more of the following: red peppers, scallions, purple cabbage, more cucumbers, and/or carrots.

NUTRITIONAL INFORMATION PER SERVING:				Serving Size: 5 oz. Total Servings: 15	
Calories	115	Sodium	444 mg	**PERCENT OF DAILY VALUE**	
Calories from fat	67	Carbohydrates	13 g	Vitamin A	18 %
Fat	7 g	Fiber	2 g	Vitamin C	78 %
Saturated Fat	1 g	Protein	2 g	Calcium	5 %
Cholesterol	0 mg			Iron	5 %

Marinated Vegetable Salad

any vegetables on hand,
   such as:
2 carrots
1 bunch broccoli
½ lb. snow peas
2 zucchini squash
mushrooms, 1 cup chopped
½ lb. yellow beans

1 Spanish onion

Dressing:
⅓ cup water
1 cup vinegar
¼ cup sugar
½ tsp. oil

Slice vegetables. Heat dressing ingredients till boiling. Pour over vegetables. Marinate for 1 day before serving.

NUTRITIONAL INFORMATION PER SERVING:		Serving Size: 4½ oz. Total Servings: 10			
Calories	51	Sodium	17 mg	**PERCENT OF DAILY VALUE**	
Calories from fat	4	Carbohydrates	11 g	Vitamin A	53 %
Fat	0 g	Fiber	2 g	Vitamin C	45 %
Saturated Fat	0 g	Protein	2 g	Calcium	4 %
Cholesterol	0 mg			Iron	8 %

Georgi's Salad

1 bunch celery
1 lb. carrots
2 green peppers
1 red onion
1 white onion

½ cup sugar
½ cup lemon juice
¾ cup oil
¾ cup mayonnaise

Slice vegetables in food processor. Add remaining ingredients and mix well. Amount of dressing can be altered to taste.

NUTRITIONAL INFORMATION PER SERVING:		Serving Size: 6 oz. Total Servings: 10			
Calories	344	Sodium	140 mg	**PERCENT OF DAILY VALUE**	
Calories from fat	268	Carbohydrates	21 g	Vitamin A	163 %
Fat	30 g	Fiber	2 g	Vitamin C	52 %
Saturated Fat	4 g	Protein	1 g	Calcium	4 %
Cholesterol	10 mg			Iron	10 %

Jennifer's Broccoli Salad

2 bunches of broccoli
(florets only)
½ cup mayonnaise
3 Tbs. red wine vinegar

1 tsp. lemon juice
2–3 tsp. sugar (optional)
1 red bell pepper
1 bunch of scallions

In a small bowl, combine mayonnaise, wine vinegar, lemon juice, and sugar, and set aside. Cut broccoli florets into bite-size pieces. Dice pepper and scallions. In a separate bowl, mix broccoli together with peppers and scallions. Pour the dressing over the vegetables and mix well. Marinate in a covered bowl for several hours or overnight. Serve cold.

NUTRITIONAL INFORMATION PER SERVING:				Serving Size: 3½ oz. Total Servings: 8	
Calories	120	Sodium	99 mg	**PERCENT OF DAILY VALUE**	
Calories from fat	101	Carbohydrates	5 g	Vitamin A	4 %
Fat	11 g	Fiber	2 g	Vitamin C	108 %
Saturated Fat	2 g	Protein	2 g	Calcium	3 %
Cholesterol	8 mg			Iron	4 %

French Dressing

¼ tsp. dry mustard
⅛ tsp. pepper
½ tsp. salt
4 Tbs. vinegar

¼ tsp. paprika
1 tsp. sugar
¾ cup oil

Combine all ingredients in a bowl and mix thoroughly, or put in a glass jar and shake.

NUTRITIONAL INFORMATION PER SERVING:				Serving Size: 2 tsp. Total Servings: 30	
Calories	49	Saturated Fat	1 g	Carbohydrates	0 g
Calories from fat	49	Cholesterol	0 mg	Fiber	0 g
Fat	5 g	Sodium	36 mg	Protein	0 g

Garlic Dressing

1 cup vegetable oil
1 clove garlic, minced
¼ cup distilled white vinegar
1 tsp. salt

½ tsp. white pepper
½ tsp. celery salt
¼ tsp. cayenne pepper
¼ tsp. dry mustard

Combine ingredients in a jar. Cover and refrigerate 2 to 3 hours. Shake well before using.

NUTRITIONAL INFORMATION PER SERVING:		Serving Size: 1 Tbs. Total Servings: 30			
Calories	66	Saturated Fat	1 g	Carbohydrates	0 g
Calories from fat	66	Cholesterol	0 mg	Fiber	0 g
Fat	7 g	Sodium	71 mg	Protein	0 g

Italian Dressing

1 cup pure olive oil
⅓ cup distilled white vinegar
½ cup finely chopped onion
¼ cup finely chopped
      parsley
2 tsp. salt

1 tsp. garlic powder
1 tsp. oregano
½ tsp. pepper
¼ tsp. thyme
¼ tsp. rosemary

Combine all ingredients in a tightly covered jar. Allow to stand 24 hours. Shake well before using.

NUTRITIONAL INFORMATION PER SERVING:		Serving Size: 1 Tbs. Total Servings: 30			
Calories	66	Sodium	143 mg	**PERCENT OF DAILY VALUE**	
Calories from fat	65	Carbohydrates	1 g	Vitamin C	1 %
Fat	7 g	Fiber	0 g	Iron	1 %
Saturated Fat	1 g	Protein	0 g		
Cholesterol	0 mg				

Lemon Vinaigrette Dressing

¼ cup lemon juice
2 tsp. brown rice vinegar
3 tsp. tamari soy sauce

2 tsp. sesame oil (optional)
¼ cup water
½ tsp. thyme

Mix ingredients well and serve with salad. This dressing is especially tasty over Noodle Salad (p. 138, 158) and Sunflower Rice Salad (p. 153).

NUTRITIONAL INFORMATION PER SERVING:				Serving Size: 1 Tbs. Total Servings: 6	
Calories	17	Cholesterol	0 mg	**PERCENT OF DAILY VALUE**	
Calories from fat	14	Sodium	174 mg	Vitamin C	4 %
Fat	2 g	Carbohydrates	1 g	Iron	1 %
Saturated Fat	0 g				

Savory Salad Dressing

1 tsp. oil
1 Tbs. onion powder
½ cup sugar

¼ cup wine vinegar or apple
    cider vinegar
1 cup oil
⅓ cup ketchup

Mix first 4 ingredients together. Add oil and ketchup, and mix together well.

NUTRITIONAL INFORMATION PER SERVING:				Serving Size: 1 Tbs. Total Servings: 30	
Calories	82	Saturated Fat	1 g	Carbohydrates	4 g
Calories from fat	67	Cholesterol	0 mg		
Fat	7 g	Sodium	31 mg		

Russian Dressing

½ cup mayonnaise
⅓ cup ketchup

½ tsp. garlic powder
½ tsp. paprika

Combine ingredients in a bowl and mix well.

NUTRITIONAL INFORMATION PER SERVING:		Serving Size: 1 Tbs. Total Servings: 15			
Calories	60	Cholesterol	4 mg	**PERCENT OF DAILY VALUE**	
Calories from fat	53	Sodium	106 mg	Vitamin A	1 %
Fat	6 g	Carbohydrates	2 g	Vitamin C	1 %
Saturated Fat	1 g				

Yogurt-Nut Dip

¼ cup pecans or walnuts,
     chopped
1 clove of garlic, crushed
1 Tbs. olive oil

¾ cup yogurt
½ cup diced cucumber
1 tsp. lemon juice

Combine nuts, garlic, and oil. Add yogurt, cucumber, and lemon juice. Stir together and chill. Serve with crisp vegetables.

NUTRITIONAL INFORMATION PER SERVING:		Serving Size: 1 Tbs. Total Servings: 20			
Calories	22	Sodium	6 mg	**PERCENT OF DAILY VALUE**	
Calories from fat	15	Carbohydrates	1 g	Calcium	2 %
Fat	2 g	Fiber	0 g		
Saturated Fat	0 g	Protein	1 g		
Cholesterol	1 mg				

Tangy Avocado Dip

1 ripe avocado
1 bunch of scallions
4 Tbs. mayonnaise
2 Tbs. pickle juice

1 tsp. salt
1 tsp. white pepper
1 clove of garlic

Peel avocado. Remove and discard pit. Place all ingredients into blender and process until smooth.

NUTRITIONAL INFORMATION PER SERVING:				Serving Size: 1 Tbs. Total Servings: 25	
Calories	48	Sodium	184 mg	PERCENT OF DAILY VALUE	
Calories from fat	29	Carbohydrates	4 g	Vitamin A	1 %
Fat	3 g	Fiber	1 g	Vitamin C	2 %
Saturated Fat	0 g	Protein	1 g	Calcium	5 %
Cholesterol	1 mg			Iron	2 %

Creamy Avocado Dip

1 avocado
½ cup mayonnaise
1 Tbs. lemon juice

1 small onion
½ tsp. salt, or to taste
¼ tsp. pepper, or to taste

Peel avocado. Remove and discard pit. Blend all ingredients together in blender until smooth, or mash well with a fork.

NUTRITIONAL INFORMATION PER SERVING:				Serving Size: 2 Tbs. Total Servings: 15	
Calories	75	Sodium	186 mg	PERCENT OF DAILY VALUE	
Calories from fat	72	Carbohydrates	1 g	Vitamin C	3 %
Fat	8 g	Fiber	2 g	Iron	2 %
Saturated Fat	1 g				
Cholesterol	4 mg				

Tofu Dip

1 16-oz. pkg. soft tofu
⅓ cup vegetable oil
¼ cup apple cider vinegar or
    lemon juice
1 tsp. salt

2 cloves garlic, chopped
1 bunch of dill or scallions,
    or any fresh herbs,
    chopped

Combine all ingredients in a food processor and blend until smooth. This dip goes well with raw vegetables, crackers, or challah.

NUTRITIONAL INFORMATION PER SERVING:			Serving Size: 2 Tbs. Total Servings: 20	
Calories	45	Sodium	109 mg	**PERCENT OF DAILY VALUE**
Calories from fat	38	Carbohydrates	1 g	Vitamin C	2 %
Fat	4 g	Protein	1 g	Calcium	1 %
Saturated Fat	1 g			Iron	1 %
Cholesterol	0 mg				

Creamy Dip

1 cup mayonnaise
2 sprigs dill
2 sprigs parsley

2 scallions
1 clove garlic
1 tsp. salt, or to taste

Blend all ingredients together. Chill until ready to serve. Serve with crisp vegetable sticks.

NUTRITIONAL INFORMATION PER SERVING:			Serving Size: 1 Tbs. Total Servings: 20	
Calories	81	Sodium	170 mg	**PERCENT OF DAILY VALUE**
Calories from fat	79	Carbohydrates	1 g	Vitamin A	1 %
Fat	9 g			Vitamin C	1 %
Saturated Fat	1 g			Calcium	1 %
Cholesterol	6 mg			Iron	2 %

Spinach Salad Dip

1 10-oz. box frozen spinach
½ cup finely chopped
   scallions

2 cups mayonnaise
dash of pepper

Defrost and drain spinach. Put all ingredients into food processor. Mix thoroughly with steel blade. Chill before serving.

NUTRITIONAL INFORMATION PER SERVING:		Serving Size: 1 Tbs. Total Servings: 50			
Calories	65	Sodium	55 mg	**PERCENT OF DAILY VALUE**	
Calories from fat	63	Carbohydrates	1 g	Vitamin A	6 %
Fat	7 g			Vitamin C	1 %
Saturated Fat	1 g			Calcium	1 %
Cholesterol	5 mg			Iron	1 %

Fresh Cranberry Relish

1 lb. fresh cranberries
2 medium red apples,
   unpeeled

2 medium oranges, peeled
⅔ cup honey

Put all ingredients, except honey, in blender or food processor. Process coarsely. Add honey and mix.

NUTRITIONAL INFORMATION PER SERVING:		Serving Size: 2 Tbs. Total Servings: 40			
Calories	28	Sodium	0 mg	**PERCENT OF DAILY VALUE**	
Calories from fat	1	Carbohydrates	7 g	Vitamin C	12 %
Fat	0 g	Fiber	1 g		
Saturated Fat	0 g				
Cholesterol	0 mg				

Sweet and Sour Sauce
Compliments of Monsey Glatt, Monsey, NY

1 20-oz. can pineapple
    chunks
½ cup vinegar
½ cup brown sugar

1 green pepper, cut into
    chunks
1 tsp. salt
2 Tbs. soy sauce
1½ Tbs. cornstarch

Drain pineapple chunks, reserving juice. Put vinegar, brown sugar, green pepper, pineapple chunks, salt, and soy sauce in a saucepan and bring to a boil. To reserved pineapple juice, add enough water to measure 1 cup. Mix in cornstarch. Add to boiling mixture in saucepan and continue cooking till thickened. Serve with batter-dipped chicken or batter-dipped fish.

NUTRITIONAL INFORMATION PER SERVING:			Serving Size: 4 Tbs. Total Servings: 15	
Calories	71	Sodium	296 mg	**PERCENT OF DAILY VALUE**
Calories from fat	2	Carbohydrates	17 g	Vitamin A 5 %
Fat	0 g	Fiber	2 g	Vitamin C 238 %
Saturated Fat	0 g	Protein	2 g	Calcium 2 %
Cholesterol	0 mg			Iron 7 %

Dill Sauce

1 pickle, thinly sliced
1 cup mayonnaise
1 tsp. dried dill

1 tsp. sugar
1 tsp. lemon juice
¼ tsp. salt

Combine all ingredients and chill. Serve with fish.

NUTRITIONAL INFORMATION PER SERVING:			Serving Size: 1 Tbs. Total Servings: 20	
Calories	80	Cholesterol	6 mg	**PERCENT OF DAILY VALUE**
Calories from fat	79	Sodium	136 mg	Vitamin A 1 %
Fat	9 g	Carbohydrates	1 g	
Saturated Fat	1 g			

Pepper Relish

10 firm green peppers
3 large red tomatoes
1 full head garlic (whole
    head, not just a clove!)

oil for sautéing
2 Tbs. hot pepper sauce, or
    to taste

Halve and seed peppers. Cut tomatoes in half. Put tomatoes and peppers, cut-side down, on a cookie sheet and broil until skins turn black and blister. (Do this in 2 shifts if necessary.) When cool, remove and discard skins, and cut or mash vegetables into smaller pieces. Meanwhile, chop garlic and sauté in oil until tender. Add tomatoes and peppers, with all of their liquid, and simmer together until most of the liquid is absorbed. Add hot pepper sauce. Serve as a side dish with poultry, meat, or just plain bread!

NUTRITIONAL INFORMATION PER SERVING:			Serving Size: 2 Tbs. Total Servings: 50	
Calories	8	Cholesterol	0 mg	**PERCENT OF DAILY VALUE**
Calories from fat	1	Sodium	2 mg	Vitamin A 3 %
Fat	0 g	Carbohydrates	2 g	Vitamin C 37 %
Saturated Fat	0 g			Iron 1 %

Fish Sauce

1 cup mayonnaise
¼ cup dill pickle juice
1 small dill pickle, minced
1 tsp. dried dill weed

½ tsp. dried parsley
3 Tbs. sugar
½ tsp. lemon juice

Mix all ingredients well. Refrigerate 6 to 12 hours to allow flavors to blend. Makes approximately 1½ cups of sauce.

NUTRITIONAL INFORMATION PER SERVING:			Serving Size: 2 tsp. Total Servings: 30	
Calories	58	Saturated Fat	1 g	Carbohydrates 2 g
Calories from fat	53	Cholesterol	4 mg	
Fat	6 g	Sodium	67 mg	

Cranberry with Character

**1 16-oz. can whole-berry
  cranberry sauce**

**1 20-oz. can crushed
  pineapple, drained**
1 fresh orange, diced

Combine all ingredients. This is a festive, colorful accompaniment to meat or chicken. It is light, refreshing, mildly tart, and not overly sweet.

NUTRITIONAL INFORMATION PER SERVING:		Serving Size: 2 Tbs. Total Servings: 40			
Calories	25	Cholesterol	0 mg	**PERCENT OF DAILY VALUE**	
Calories from fat	0	Sodium	3 mg	Vitamin C	7 %
Fat	0 g	Carbohydrates	7 g		
Saturated Fat	0 g				

Cranberry Fruit Sauce

**1 16-oz. can whole-berry
  cranberry sauce**
**1 8-oz. can mandarin
  oranges**
**1 20-oz. can crushed
  pineapple**

1 box red jello
½ cup boiling water
**2 apples, peeled and
  chopped**

Drain cans well. Mix all ingredients together and refrigerate. Goes well with chicken.

NUTRITIONAL INFORMATION PER SERVING:		Serving Size: 2 Tbs. Total Servings: 50			
Calories	33	Cholesterol	0 mg	**PERCENT OF DAILY VALUE**	
Calories from fat	2	Sodium	6 mg	Vitamin C	5 %
Fat	0 g	Carbohydrates	8 g		
Saturated Fat	0 g				

Fruit Sauce

½ cup apple juice
¼ cup sugar
2 Tbs. lemon juice

2 tsp. cornstarch
4 cups chopped (fresh or
    frozen) fruit of any kind

In a heavy saucepan, whisk together the apple juice, sugar, lemon juice, and cornstarch. Stir over medium heat until slightly thickened — about 4 minutes. Add the fruit (such as strawberries, blueberries, raspberries, or peeled peaches), cover, and simmer until the fruit looks like a thick sauce — about 10 minutes. Remove from heat and cool. Stir often to prevent lumps from forming. Chill before serving (about 3 hours). Pour over pancakes, waffles, or mix into yogurt.

NUTRITIONAL INFORMATION PER SERVING:				Serving Size: 3½ oz. Total Servings: 12	
Calories	74	Sodium	2 mg	**PERCENT OF DAILY VALUE**	
Calories from fat	1	Carbohydrates	20 g	Vitamin C	57 %
Fat	0 g	Fiber	2 g	Calcium	1 %
Saturated Fat	0 g			Iron	2 %
Cholesterol	0 mg				

Tomato Relish

2 large tomatoes, sliced
3 cloves garlic, peeled and
    finely chopped
½ Tbs. apple cider vinegar

pinch of salt
1 tsp. oil
½ red pepper, finely
    chopped

Blend all ingredients together in a food processor.

Optional: For a sharper taste, 1 small hot red pepper can be used instead of ½ red pepper.

NUTRITIONAL INFORMATION PER SERVING:				Serving Size: ⁴/5 oz. Total Servings: 16	
Calories	8	Cholesterol	0 mg	**PERCENT OF DAILY VALUE**	
Calories from fat	3	Sodium	34 mg	Vitamin A	1 %
Fat	0 g	Carbohydrates	1 g	Vitamin C	10 %
Saturated Fat	0 g				

In Good Taste...

Fish and Dairy Dishes

Fish, Mushroom, and Rice Pie	Salmon with Spaghetti and Garlic
Sweet and Sour Salmon	Linguine with Salmon & Cream Sauce
Marinated Fish	Dairy Mushroom Quiche
Tuna Noodle Casserole	Pasta and Broccoli
Tropical Tuna Salad	Eggplant Parmesan
Mushroom Tuna Chow Mein	Easy Lasagna
Tuna Chow Mein	Macaroni and Cheese
Tuna Cutlets	Stuffed Shells
Fish Cakes	Taco-Dip Pizza
Salmon Loaf	Lentil Cheese Pie
Russian Salmon Loaf	Spinach Lasagna
Fried Fish	Cheese Blintzes
Sweet and Sour Fish	Noodle Cheese Kugel
Baked Fish à la Gittel	No-Yeast Pizza
Tuna Stir-Fry	Potato Cheese Casserole
Stuffed Baked Whitefish	Broccoli-Spinach Quiche
Baked Salmon	Vegetable Casserole
Fish Florentine	Herb Omelet
Tuna Rolls	Vegetable Cheese Quiche
Easy Gefilte Fish	Cheese Latkes
Smoked Salmon Rolls	Pancakes
Salmon Wellington	Whole-Wheat Pancakes
Almond Baked Halibut	Oat Bran and Wheat Germ Pancakes
Baked Fish with Veggies	Broccoli and Cheese
Baked Gefilte Fish Loaf	Baked Ziti
Zesty Sweet and Sour Salmon	Pizza
Baked Halibut	Cheese Kugel
Baked Whitefish	Tomato with Pasta and Cheese

Fish and Dairy Dishes

Fish, Mushroom, and Rice Pie

Crust:
1 Tbs. finely minced onion
2 cups cooked brown rice
2 Tbs. olive or peanut oil
½ tsp. dried or 1 Tbs. fresh
  thyme
1 egg, beaten

Filling:
¾ lb. cooked fish, flaked, or
  a 7-oz. can of tuna or
  salmon
1 cup sliced mushrooms
1 Tbs. olive, canola, or
  peanut oil
3 eggs, beaten
1 cup milk
dash of pepper
1 Tbs. finely minced onion

Crust: Combine all ingredients and press into bottom and sides of a greased, 8- or 9-inch pie plate.

Filling: Spread flaked fish over rice shell. Sauté mushrooms lightly in oil and combine with remaining ingredients. Pour over fish. Bake at 350° for 50 to 55 minutes. Serve hot. Brown rice makes a delicious, crunchy crust for this tasty, satisfying meal.

NUTRITIONAL INFORMATION PER SERVING:[*]				Serving Size: 6½ oz. Total Servings: 8	
Calories	215	Sodium	214 mg	**PERCENT OF DAILY VALUE**	
Calories from fat	88	Carbohydrates	15 g	Vitamin A	7 %
Fat	10 g	Fiber	1 g	Vitamin C	4 %
Saturated Fat	2 g	Protein	16 g	Calcium	8 %
Cholesterol	139 mg			Iron	6 %

* Analysis done with olive oil and baked flounder.

Sweet and Sour Salmon

2 onions
1 large lemon
¼ cup brown sugar
¼ cup raisins

1 bay leaf
1½–2 tsp. salt
6 slices (2½ lb.) salmon
2 cups water

Slice onions thinly and place on bottom of pot. Peel and slice lemon, remove seeds, and place slices on top of onion. Layer sugar, raisins, bay leaf, and salt. Put fish on top. Add water. Cook over low flame for 1 hour.

NUTRITIONAL INFORMATION PER SERVING:				Serving Size: 6 oz. Total Servings: 6	
Calories	353	Sodium	435 mg	PERCENT OF DAILY VALUE	
Calories from fat	143	Carbohydrates	20 g	Vitamin A	10 %
Fat	16 g	Fiber	1 g	Vitamin C	19 %
Saturated Fat	4 g	Protein	31 g	Calcium	8 %
Cholesterol	100 mg			Iron	12 %

Marinated Fish

1 Tbs. sesame oil
1 Tbs. soy sauce
1 Tbs. mirin or sherry
1 Tbs. honey

2 garlic cloves, minced
4 slices halibut, salmon, or
    other fish

Stir together oil, soy sauce, mirin, honey, and garlic. Marinate fish in this mixture for 2 hours in the refrigerator. Bake at 350° about ½ hour or until fish flakes easily with a fork.

NUTRITIONAL INFORMATION PER SERVING:[*]				Serving Size: 6½ oz. Total Servings: 4	
Calories	352	Sodium	338 mg	PERCENT OF DAILY VALUE	
Calories from fat	191	Carbohydrates	4 g	Vitamin A	12 %
Fat	21 g	Protein	35 g	Vitamin C	12 %
Saturated Fat	5 g			Calcium	5 %
Cholesterol	112 mg			Iron	8 %

* Analysis done with salmon.

FISH AND DAIRY DISHES

Tuna Noodle Casserole

1 lb. medium noodles
2 6⅛-oz. cans tuna, drained
   and flaked
1 8-oz. can mushrooms

Sauce:
6 Tbs. butter

onion powder, to taste
garlic powder, to taste
pepper, to taste
4 Tbs. flour
3 cups milk
8 oz. American cheese,
   grated

Cook noodles as directed on package, and drain. Meanwhile, in a saucepan, melt butter and add spices. Add flour and, while stirring, gradually mix in milk, then cheese. Stir until sauce thickens. Mix tuna and mushrooms with noodles and place in a 9x13-inch pan. Pour sauce over mixture. Bake at 375° for 25 minutes.

NUTRITIONAL INFORMATION PER SERVING:				Serving Size: 5 oz. Total Servings: 10	
Calories	392	Sodium	568 mg	**PERCENT OF DAILY VALUE**	
Calories from fat	152	Carbohydrates	39 g	Vitamin A	11 %
Fat	17 g	Fiber	1 g	Calcium	19 %
Saturated Fat	9 g	Protein	21 g	Iron	20 %
Cholesterol	82 mg				

Tropical Tuna Salad

1 6⅛-oz. can tuna, drained
   and flaked
1 8-oz. can mandarin
   oranges, drained

1 small onion, diced
¼ cup mayonnaise
1 tsp. Dijon mustard

Mix all ingredients together. Serve over lettuce or with bread.

NUTRITIONAL INFORMATION PER SERVING:				Serving Size: 4 oz. Total Servings: 6	
Calories	174	Sodium	330 mg	**PERCENT OF DAILY VALUE**	
Calories from fat	74	Carbohydrates	7 g	Vitamin A	3 %
Fat	8 g	Fiber	0 g	Vitamin C	18 %
Saturated Fat	1 g	Protein	17 g	Calcium	2 %
Cholesterol	13 mg			Iron	5 %

Mushroom Tuna Chow Mein

1 10½ oz. can mushroom
   soup
¼ cup water
1 6⅛-oz. can tuna, drained
   and flaked

1 cup diced celery
¼ cup chopped onion
pepper to taste
2 cups chow mein noodles

Combine mushroom soup and water. Mix remaining ingredients, except for noodles. Turn into a 1½-quart baking dish and bake at 375° for 30 minutes. Add noodles and bake an additional 15 minutes.

NUTRITIONAL INFORMATION PER SERVING:		Serving Size: 7 oz. Total Servings: 4		
Calories	270	Sodium	737 mg	**PERCENT OF DAILY VALUE**
Calories from fat	131	Carbohydrates	19 g	Vitamin A	1 %
Fat	15 g	Fiber	2 g	Vitamin C	3 %
Saturated Fat	3 g	Protein	16 g	Calcium	4 %
Cholesterol	9 mg			Iron	13 %

Tuna Chow Mein

2 stalks celery, chopped
2 large onions, chopped
4 Tbs. oil for sautéing
2 6⅛-oz. cans tuna, drained
   and flaked

paprika, to taste
garlic powder, to taste
2 Tbs. soy sauce, or to taste
1 Tbs. cornstarch
½ cup cold water

Sauté celery and onion in oil until golden. Add tuna, spices, and soy sauce. Mix well. Dissolve cornstarch in cold water and add to the pan. Stir and cook over medium flame to thicken and heat all ingredients well. Serve over hot rice.

NUTRITIONAL INFORMATION PER SERVING:		Serving Size: 4½ oz. Total Servings: 6		
Calories	228	Sodium	657 mg	**PERCENT OF DAILY VALUE**
Calories from fat	128	Carbohydrates	6 g	Vitamin A	1 %
Fat	14 g	Fiber	1 g	Vitamin C	6 %
Saturated Fat	2 g	Protein	19 g	Calcium	3 %
Cholesterol	11 mg			Iron	7 %

FISH AND DAIRY DISHES

3 oz. tuna
1 egg
2 tsp. flour
1½ Tbs. matzah meal
2 tsp. baking powder

½ carrot, grated
2 tsp. minced onion
1 tsp. onion powder
2 tsp. oil

Drain and flake tuna and mix with rest of ingredients, except oil. Spread oil in a baking dish. Form patties and bake at 350° on one side only for 30 minutes or until brown.

NUTRITIONAL INFORMATION PER SERVING:				Serving Size: 4 oz. Total Servings: 2	
Calories	215	Sodium	205 mg	PERCENT OF DAILY VALUE	
Calories from fat	96	Carbohydrates	12 g	Vitamin A	70 %
Fat	11 g	Fiber	1 g	Vitamin C	4 %
Saturated Fat	2 g	Protein	17 g	Calcium	7 %
Cholesterol	114 mg			Iron	9 %

Fish Cakes

1 lb. frozen flounder fillets
5 potatoes, sliced
1 onion, sliced
1 large carrot, sliced
3 eggs

1 tsp. salt
¾ cup matzah meal or bread
   crumbs
oil for frying

In a pot, place fish, potatoes, onion, and carrot. Fill with water to cover, bring to a boil, and cook for 40 minutes over a low-medium flame. Drain, then mash in food processor. Add remaining ingredients. Form balls and flatten. Dip into matzah meal or bread crumbs and fry on both sides until light brown.

NUTRITIONAL INFORMATION PER SERVING:				Serving Size: 6 oz. Total Servings: 8	
Calories	258	Sodium	355 mg	PERCENT OF DAILY VALUE	
Calories from fat	88	Carbohydrates	22 g	Vitamin A	37 %
Fat	10 g	Fiber	2 g	Vitamin C	26 %
Saturated Fat	2 g	Protein	19 g	Calcium	4 %
Cholesterol	118 mg			Iron	9 %

Salmon Loaf

1 onion, diced
4 Tbs. oil
1 16-oz. can salmon,
    undrained
¾ cup bread crumbs

1 cup milk
2 eggs
2 Tbs. chopped parsley
crushed cornflakes (about 2
    cups)

Sauté onion in oil. Mix together salmon, bread crumbs, milk, eggs, onion, and parsley. Grease a loaf pan. Turn mixture into pan. Cover with cornflakes. Bake at 350° for 1 hour and 15 minutes.

NUTRITIONAL INFORMATION PER SERVING:				Serving Size: 4 oz. Total Servings: 9	
Calories	206	Sodium	429 mg	**PERCENT OF DAILY VALUE**	
Calories from fat	94	Carbohydrates	14 g	Vitamin A	2 %
Fat	10 g	Fiber	1 g	Vitamin C	2 %
Saturated Fat	2 g	Protein	13 g	Calcium	19 %
Cholesterol	31 mg			Iron	14 %

Russian Salmon Loaf

Pastry:
1 cup margarine
⅓ cup shortening
4 cups flour
1 tsp. salt
10–12 Tbs. water

Filling:
1 cup water
1 tsp. parve instant chicken
    bouillon
½ cup rice
¼ cup margarine

8 oz. mushrooms, thinly
    sliced   •
3 large onions, finely diced
3 hard-boiled eggs, chopped
2 Tbs. fresh or 1 Tbs. dried
    dill
1 15½-oz. can salmon,
    drained, boned, and
    flaked
1 tsp. salt

1 egg yolk
1 Tbs. water

Pastry: Cut margarine and shortening into flour and salt, until it forms balls the size of peas. Sprinkle water slowly over this and toss with fork, until pastry almost cleans the sides of the bowl. Gather into a ball; cut in half. Cover and refrigerate 3 hours.

Filling: Boil water. Add bouillon and rice. Cover and simmer 15 minutes. Remove from heat. Heat margarine. Sauté mushrooms and onion till tender. Gently combine rice with sautéed vegetables, eggs, dill, and salmon. Sprinkle with salt.

Heat oven to 400°. On a floured board, roll out half the dough to 16x7 inches. Trim edges. Pile filling onto pastry, leaving a 1-inch space around the edges. Roll out second dough to 18x9 inches. Moisten edges of first pastry with water. Cover with second pastry and seal by pressing edges together with the tines of a fork. Cut out a 1-inch hole in the center for steam leakage. Use remaining pastry for a floral design on the top. Mix egg yolk with water; brush on pastry. Bake on an ungreased cookie sheet for 1 hour or until golden.

NUTRITIONAL INFORMATION PER SERVING:				Serving Size: 7 oz. Total Servings: 10	
Calories	568	Sodium	1062 mg	**PERCENT OF DAILY VALUE**	
Calories from fat	325	Carbohydrates	45 g	Vitamin A	44 %
Fat	36 g	Fiber	3 g	Vitamin C	4 %
Saturated Fat	7 g	Protein	15 g	Calcium	16 %
Cholesterol	95 mg			Iron	19 %

Fried Fish

¾ cup bread crumbs
½ tsp. garlic powder
½ tsp. onion powder

1 lb. pkg. frozen flounder
    fillets, thawed
1 egg, beaten
oil for frying

Mix bread crumbs and spices. Dip fish in egg, then in bread crumb mixture. Fry in oil on both sides until brown.

NUTRITIONAL INFORMATION PER SERVING:				Serving Size: 5 oz. Total Servings: 4	
Calories	311	Sodium	252 mg	**PERCENT OF DAILY VALUE**	
Calories from fat	144	Carbohydrates	14 g	Vitamin A	1 %
Fat	16 g	Fiber	1 g	Vitamin C	5 %
Saturated Fat	2 g	Protein	26 g	Calcium	5 %
Cholesterol	65 mg			Iron	6 %

Sweet and Sour Fish

2 carrots, sliced diagonally
½ cup water
½ cup brown sugar
⅓ cup vinegar
2 Tbs. cornstarch
2 Tbs. soy sauce
1 13-oz. can pineapple
    chunks
1 green pepper, cut into 1-
    inch cubes

1½ lbs. fish fillets, cut into
    1-inch pieces

Batter:
¾ cup water
⅔ cup flour
1¼ tsp. salt
½ tsp. baking powder

Bring carrots and water to a boil in a pot. Cook 8 to 10 minutes. Mix next 4 ingredients in a saucepan. Add carrots with liquid, pineapple with syrup, and pepper. Bring to a boil and stir 1 minute. Turn off heat, but keep sauce warm. In a large frying pan, heat 1½ inches oil to 360°. Stir together batter ingredients, being sure to remove all lumps. Pat fish dry and dip into batter with tongs. Drip off excess. Fry a few pieces at a time — don't overcrowd pan! When golden, drain on paper towels. Arrange on serving platter. Pour warm sauce over fish.

NUTRITIONAL INFORMATION PER SERVING:		Serving Size: 7 oz. Total Servings: 8			
Calories	243	Sodium	756 mg	**PERCENT OF DAILY VALUE**	
Calories from fat	14	Carbohydrates	34 g	Vitamin A	65 %
Fat	2 g	Fiber	1 g	Vitamin C	31 %
Saturated Fat	0 g	Protein	22 g	Calcium	5 %
Cholesterol	58 mg			Iron	11 %

Baked Fish à la Gittel

8 slices (about 3 lb.) fresh
    carp, salmon, whitefish,
    or flounder
½ cup olive oil
¼ cup tamari soy sauce

2 medium onions, sliced
    into rings
⅛ tsp. powdered ginger
⅛ tsp. basil and/or thyme

Mix oil and tamari in a bowl. Layer baking pan with half the onion rings. Dip fish slices (on both sides) in the oil and tamari mixture and lay on onions. Sprinkle with ginger, basil, and/or thyme, and layer remaining onion rings on top. Bake uncovered in hot oven (400°–500°) for 15 minutes. Broil for 2 minutes to brown. Can be served cold.

NUTRITIONAL INFORMATION PER SERVING:[*]				Serving Size: 8 oz. Total Servings: 8	
Calories	353	Sodium	675 mg	**PERCENT OF DAILY VALUE**	
Calories from fat	178	Carbohydrates	4 g	Vitamin A	1 %
Fat	20 g	Protein	40 g	Vitamin C	3 %
Saturated Fat	4 g			Calcium	11 %
Cholesterol	65 mg			Iron	18 %

* Analysis done with salmon.

Tuna Stir-Fry

1½ Tbs. oil
1 large onion, diced
1 16-oz. bag frozen
   vegetables (oriental or
   any other assortment,
   such as carrots, pea
   pods, broccoli,
   cauliflower, mushrooms,
   corn, or green beans)

1 large clove of garlic,
   minced
4½ Tbs. tamari or shoyu
   soy sauce
2 6⅛-oz. cans tuna, drained
   and flaked
2 Tbs. arrowroot flour
   (optional)

Heat oil in a large skillet or wok. Stir-fry onion, vegetables, garlic, and soy sauce. Add water to barely cover; stir-fry until crisp and tender. For a thick sauce, mix arrowroot flour with less than ¼ cup cold water, and add to vegetables. Add tuna and stir-fry 5 more minutes. Serve over hot rice.

Note: Vegetable mixture tastes better if it sits awhile when done. Tuna almost tastes like chicken.

NUTRITIONAL INFORMATION PER SERVING:				Serving Size: 7 oz. Total Servings: 5	
Calories	257	Sodium	1162 mg	**PERCENT OF DAILY VALUE**	
Calories from fat	88	Carbohydrates	20 g	Vitamin A	1 %
Fat	10 g	Fiber	2 g	Vitamin C	5 %
Saturated Fat	1 g	Protein	21 g	Calcium	3 %
Cholesterol	10 mg			Iron	17 %

Stuffed Baked Whitefish

3 lb. whitefish, gutted and
   cleaned
½ tsp. salt
⅛ tsp. pepper
¼ tsp. dill weed
⅛ tsp. parsley
1 small onion, chopped
1 4-oz. can mushrooms,
   sliced
3 Tbs. margarine

3 cups soft bread cubes
3 Tbs. water
1 Tbs. snipped parsley
lemon slices for garnish

Basting Sauce:
¼ cup melted margarine
2 Tbs. lemon juice
1 large clove of garlic,
   minced

Wash off fish. Rub cavity with next 4 ingredients. Gently sauté onion
and mushrooms in margarine until tender. Remove from heat. Mix
with bread cubes, water, and parsley. Stuff fish. Close with skewers or
sew. Place in a not-too-shallow pan. Mix together ingredients for
sauce, and spoon over fish. Bake at 350° for 1 hour or until golden,
basting fish with sauce occasionally. Garnish with lemon slices. This
recipe is also good with salmon, trout, bass, and pike.

NUTRITIONAL INFORMATION PER SERVING:		Serving Size: 5 oz. Total Servings: 10			
Calories	236	Sodium	303 mg	**PERCENT OF DAILY VALUE**	
Calories from fat	123	Carbohydrates	5 g	Vitamin A	11 %
Fat	14 g	Fiber	0 g	Vitamin C	4 %
Saturated Fat	2 g	Protein	22 g	Calcium	4 %
Cholesterol	68 mg			Iron	4 %

Baked Salmon

½ cup French dressing
2 Tbs. lemon juice
¼ tsp. salt
2 lbs. salmon

1 15-oz. can French-fried
   onions
¼ cup grated Parmesan
   cheese

Combine dressing, lemon juice, and salt. Pour over fish and marinate
for 30 minutes or more. Remove fish from sauce and place in a

greased pan. Crush onions. Combine with cheese and place in pan along with salmon. Bake in moderate oven at 350° for 25 to 30 minutes.

NUTRITIONAL INFORMATION PER SERVING:				Serving Size: 7½ oz. Total Servings: 6	
Calories	433	Sodium	383 mg	**PERCENT OF DAILY VALUE**	
Calories from fat	274	Carbohydrates	6 g	Vitamin A	12 %
Fat	30 g	Fiber	1 g	Vitamin C	16 %
Saturated Fat	7 g	Protein	33 g	Calcium	12 %
Cholesterol	104 mg			Iron	8 %

Fish Florentine

1 10-oz. pkg. frozen
    chopped spinach, thawed
    and drained well
1 egg, beaten
1 small onion, diced
½ tsp. garlic, or to taste
1 16-oz. pkg. frozen
    flounder fillets, thawed
    and separated

¼ cup white wine
1 tsp. lemon juice
1 stick butter
paprika
1–2 tomatoes, sliced

Combine spinach, egg, onion, and garlic. Spread some spinach mixture on each fish fillet. Roll up and tack closed with a toothpick. Leave ends open. Place in a baking pan. Pour ¼ cup wine (or more, if desired) over fish. Sprinkle lemon juice over fish. Slice butter and place pats between the fish rolls and sprinkle paprika on top. Place tomato slices over butter. Bake at 350° for 25 minutes or until fish flakes easily with a fork.

NUTRITIONAL INFORMATION PER SERVING:				Serving Size: 10 oz. Total Servings: 4	
Calories	393	Sodium	358 mg	**PERCENT OF DAILY VALUE**	
Calories from fat	230	Carbohydrates	10 g	Vitamin A	87 %
Fat	26 g	Fiber	2 g	Vitamin C	44 %
Saturated Fat	15 g	Protein	28 g	Calcium	17 %
Cholesterol	180 mg			Iron	14 %

Tuna Rolls

2 6⅛-oz. cans tuna, drained
    and flaked
2 eggs
4 Tbs. matzah meal
pepper

½ tsp. salt, or to taste
1 large onion, finely
    chopped
1 lb. ready-made puff pastry
1 egg for brushing

Mix tuna with eggs, matzah meal, pepper, salt, and onion to make a soft mixture. Roll out pastry into 4-inch-wide, 12-inch-long strips. Dampen edges. Place filling along one half of pastry. Fold pastry and pinch together edges to seal. Brush with egg. Cut into 1-inch slices. Bake for 20 minutes in hot oven.
Variation: Salmon can be used in place of tuna.

NUTRITIONAL INFORMATION PER SERVING:				Serving Size: 4 oz. Total Servings: 10	
Calories	229	Sodium	465 mg	PERCENT OF DAILY VALUE	
Calories from fat	59	Carbohydrates	25 g	Vitamin A	4 %
Fat	7 g	Fiber	0 g	Vitamin C	1 %
Saturated Fat	2 g	Protein	16 g	Calcium	3 %
Cholesterol	72 mg			Iron	12 %

Easy Gefilte Fish

1 lb. ground fish (white and
    pike *or* white and mullet)
1 egg
3 Tbs. grated onion
1 scant tsp. salt
2 shakes of white or black
    pepper

¼ cup sugar
1 onion, sliced
1 carrot, sliced
¼ tsp. salt
dash of pepper
½ Tbs. sugar
onion powder (optional)

Combine ground fish, egg, and grated onion. Add salt, pepper, and sugar. Fill pot (any size) ⅓ of the way up with water. Add sliced onion and carrot. Season water with additional salt, pepper, and sugar. Onion powder may be added for flavor. Bring water to a boil. Shape fish mixture into balls, drop gently into water, and cook 2 hours on a very low flame. Check periodically to see that water has not boiled out.

P. S. Gefilte fish gets perfected by trial and error!

NUTRITIONAL INFORMATION PER SERVING:[*]				Serving Size: 4 oz. Total Servings: 8	
Calories	102	Sodium	301 mg	PERCENT OF DAILY VALUE	
Calories from fat	10	Carbohydrates	11 g	Vitamin A	34 %
Fat	1 g	Fiber	1 g	Vitamin C	8 %
Saturated Fat	0 g	Protein	12 g	Calcium	5 %
Cholesterol	49 mg			Iron	3 %

* Analysis based on ground pike.

Smoked Salmon Rolls
Compliments of Jerusalem Plaza, Monsey, NY

1 14¾-oz. can salmon
¼ tsp. liquid smoke
1 9-inch pastry circle
¼ tsp. black pepper, or to taste

1 Tbs. chopped scallions or chives
1 egg
1 tsp. cold water

Preheat oven to 425°. Drain salmon. Add liquid smoke. Cover with foil and refrigerate overnight. Drain liquid, flake salmon, and sprinkle over pastry circle. Sprinkle with pepper and scallions. Cut pastry circle into 8 wedge-shaped pieces and roll each wedge tightly from outside edge to center. Arrange on a baking sheet. Beat egg with water and brush onto rolls. Bake for 15 to 20 minutes, until golden.

NUTRITIONAL INFORMATION PER SERVING:				Serving Size: 2½ oz. Total Servings: 8	
Calories	96	Sodium	232 mg	PERCENT OF DAILY VALUE	
Calories from fat	41	Carbohydrates	3 g	Vitamin A	2 %
Fat	5 g	Fiber	1 g	Vitamin C	1 %
Saturated Fat	1 g	Protein	10 g	Calcium	13 %
Cholesterol	17 mg			Iron	3 %

Salmon Wellington

2 7½-oz. cans salmon
1 medium onion, grated
1 egg, beaten
¼ cup water

1 Tbs. matzah meal
3 heaping Tbs. mayonnaise
half of a 1-lb. 10 oz. pkg.
   flaky dough

Mash salmon in a bowl. Add onion and egg. Then add water and matzah meal, and mix well. Gently fold in mayonnaise, making sure that mixture remains fluffy. Roll out dough into a large rectangle. Spread salmon filling over dough and roll carefully, like a jelly roll. (Brush with additional beaten egg for a glossy look.) Place roll on a greased pan. Bake at 350° for 30 to 45 minutes. Serve warm or cold.

NUTRITIONAL INFORMATION PER SERVING:				Serving Size: 3 oz. Total Servings: 12	
Calories	199	Sodium	384 mg	**PERCENT OF DAILY VALUE**	
Calories from fat	90	Carbohydrates	16 g	Vitamin A	3 %
Fat	10 g	Fiber	0 g	Vitamin C	1 %
Saturated Fat	2 g	Protein	10 g	Calcium	12 %
Cholesterol	36 mg			Iron	8 %

Almond Baked Halibut

3 lbs. halibut steaks
1 Tbs. salt
½ tsp. pepper
juice of 3 limes
2 cloves garlic, crushed

¼ cup oil
½ cup sliced almonds
1 Tbs. butter or margarine
lime wedges

Preheat oven to 500°. Put fish in a shallow baking pan. Season with salt and pepper. Blend together lime juice, garlic, and oil, and brush over fish. Bake for 10 minutes, turn over and baste with juice. Lower oven to 425° and bake 15 to 20 minutes longer or until fish flakes easily with fork. Baste several times during cooking. Sauté almonds in butter or margarine until golden brown. Serve fish with almonds sprinkled on top and garnished with lime wedges.

NUTRITIONAL INFORMATION PER SERVING::		Serving Size: 7½ oz. Total Servings: 8		
Calories	374	Sodium	375 mg	**PERCENT OF DAILY VALUE**
Calories from fat	197	Carbohydrates	5 g	Vitamin A 12 %
Fat	22 g	Fiber	2 g	Vitamin C 10 %
Saturated Fat	2 g	Protein	41 g	Calcium 19 %
Cholesterol	54 mg			Iron 16 %

Baked Fish with Veggies

1 lb. fish fillets (flounder or sole)
1 tsp. + 2 tsp. oil
½ cup chopped carrots
½ cup chopped celery
½ cup chopped scallions

1 clove garlic, crushed
1 large, ripe tomato, chopped
1 Tbs. fresh chopped parsley
½ tsp. grated lemon peel
pepper to taste

Heat oven to 350°. Grease a baking pan with 1 tsp. oil. Arrange fish fillets in the pan. In a skillet, heat 2 tsp. oil. Add carrots, celery, scallions, and garlic. Cook about 3 minutes, until vegetables are tender and crisp. Remove from heat. Stir in tomato, parsley, lemon peel, and pepper. Spoon mixture over fillets. Bake about 15 minutes, until fish is tender.

NUTRITIONAL INFORMATION PER SERVING:		Serving Size: 6 oz. Total Servings: 5		
Calories	148	Sodium	115 mg	**PERCENT OF DAILY VALUE**
Calories from fat	38	Carbohydrates	4 g	Vitamin A 63 %
Fat	4 g	Fiber	1 g	Vitamin C 34 %
Saturated Fat	1 g	Protein	23 g	Calcium 4 %
Cholesterol	61 mg			Iron 5 %

Baked Gefilte Fish Loaf

½ bag frozen mixed
  vegetables
1 loaf frozen gefilte fish
1 onion, chopped (optional)

1 8-oz. can tomato sauce
½ cup water
salt, pepper, and garlic
  powder, to taste

Put frozen vegetables and onion on bottom of a rectangular baking dish. Take gefilte fish out of its wrappings and place on vegetables. Pour tomato sauce and water over fish and vegetables. Season to taste. Cover well with aluminum foil and bake at 350° for 1½–2 hours. Slice. Serve hot or cold. Makes a fast and easy supper.

NUTRITIONAL INFORMATION PER SERVING:				Serving Size: 5 oz. Total Servings: 8	
Calories	159	Sodium	465 mg	**PERCENT OF DAILY VALUE**	
Calories from fat	12	Carbohydrates	23 g	Vitamin A	24 %
Fat	1 g	Fiber	2 g	Vitamin C	5 %
Saturated Fat	1 g	Protein	14 g	Calcium	6 %
Cholesterol	67 mg			Iron	6 %

Zesty Sweet and Sour Salmon

4 slices salmon (about
  1¾ lb.)
1 cup water

¼ cup lemon juice
2–3 Tbs. sugar
1 Tbs. pickling spices

Put fish in a pot. Mix water, lemon juice, and sugar, and pour over fish. Make sure fish is covered with mixture — make more mixture if necessary. Cover pot and cook 40 minutes. When fish is cooked, transfer juice mixture to a bowl and add pickling spices. Strain this mixture over the fish immediately. Serve cold.

NUTRITIONAL INFORMATION PER SERVING:				Serving Size: 6 oz. Total Servings: 4	
Calories	320	Sodium	77 mg	**PERCENT OF DAILY VALUE**	
Calories from fat	147	Carbohydrates	10 g	Vitamin A	11 %
Fat	16 g	Fiber	0 g	Vitamin C	16 %
Saturated Fat	4 g	Protein	31 g	Calcium	4 %
Cholesterol	103 mg			Iron	7 %

FISH AND DAIRY DISHES

Baked Halibut

2 large onions, diced
3 Tbs. oil
3 small halibut steaks
½ tsp. salt, or to taste

pepper to taste
3 Tbs. sour cream
3 Tbs. mayonnaise

Sauté onions in oil until soft. Place fish in baking dish and top with onions. Season with salt and pepper. Cover and bake 1 hour. Before serving, make a dressing by mixing sour cream and mayonnaise and serve over fish.

NUTRITIONAL INFORMATION PER SERVING::				Serving Size: 7 oz. Total Servings: 3	
Calories	375	Sodium	491 mg	**PERCENT OF DAILY VALUE**	
Calories from fat	267	Carbohydrates	8 g	Vitamin A	10 %
Fat	30 g	Fiber	1 g	Vitamin C	11 %
Saturated Fat	5 g	Protein	19 g	Calcium	9 %
Cholesterol	41 mg			Iron	6 %

Baked Whitefish

1 whitefish (head and tail
    removed)
1½ cups water
1 onion, cut into eighths
1 carrot, sliced

2 Tbs. sugar
1½ tsp. salt
½ tsp. pepper
¾ tsp. onion powder

Put fish into a shallow baking pan. Add water and vegetables. Sprinkle seasonings over fish, and adjust to taste. Cover and bake at 350° for about 50 minutes.

NUTRITIONAL INFORMATION PER SERVING:				Serving Size: 4 oz. Total Servings: 6	
Calories	143	Sodium	581 mg	**PERCENT OF DAILY VALUE**	
Calories from fat	45	Carbohydrates	7 g	Vitamin A	43 %
Fat	5 g	Fiber	1 g	Vitamin C	6 %
Saturated Fat	1 g	Protein	17 g	Calcium	3 %
Cholesterol	51 mg			Iron	2 %

Salmon with Spaghetti and Garlic

1 lb. whole-wheat spaghetti
¼ cup olive oil
10 garlic cloves, halved or
    quartered

15½ oz. water-packed red
    salmon
3 Tbs. minced parsley
1 egg, lightly beaten

Fill a large pot halfway with water, bring to a boil and cook spaghetti for 10 minutes. Meanwhile, put oil in a skillet over low heat. Add garlic and cook, stirring, until slightly tender (about 2 to 3 minutes). Remove from heat. Drain salmon, add to garlic with parsley, and heat. Drain cooked spaghetti and toss immediately with egg. Add salmon mixture and toss again. Serve hot.

NUTRITIONAL INFORMATION PER SERVING:				Serving Size: 7 oz. Total Servings: 10	
Calories	296	Sodium	193 mg	**PERCENT OF DAILY VALUE**	
Calories from fat	100	Carbohydrates	36 g	Vitamin A	2 %
Fat	11 g	Fiber	4 g	Calcium	15 %
Saturated Fat	2 g	Protein	15 g	Iron	12 %
Cholesterol	32 mg				

Linguine with Salmon and Cream Sauce
Compliments of Cyrk Cafe, Monsey, NY

12 oz. fresh salmon
2 cups sour cream
½ cup tomato sauce
¼ tsp. dried basil
¼ tsp. salt

pinch cayenne pepper
    (optional)
¼ cup water
8 oz. linguine noodles
fresh parsley

Cut salmon into 4 pieces. For sauce, mix all remaining ingredients except linguine and parsley over medium flame. Increase to high, add salmon, and continue cooking until sauce thickens and salmon is cooked through (about 8 minutes). Do not overcook. Prepare linguine as directed on package. Pour sauce over cooked linguine. Sprinkle with fresh parsley.

NUTRITIONAL INFORMATION PER SERVING:				Serving Size: 8 oz. Total Servings: 4	
Calories	424	Sodium	521 mg	**PERCENT OF DAILY VALUE**	
Calories from fat	324	Carbohydrates	9 g	Vitamin A	42 %
Fat	36 g	Fiber	1 g	Vitamin C	15 %
Saturated Fat	18 g	Protein	17 g	Calcium	22 %
Cholesterol	92 mg			Iron	6 %

Dairy Mushroom Quiche

pie dough for a 9-inch pie
1 onion, chopped
4 Tbs. oil for sautéing
1   8-oz. can mushrooms or
     1 pkg. fresh mushrooms
3 oz. American cheese,
     shredded
2 oz. Muenster cheese,
     shredded

Sauce:
½ cup milk
⅓ cup flour
2 eggs
½ tsp. baking powder
(½ tsp. salt if using fresh
     mushrooms)
⅛ tsp. black pepper

Press pie dough into a 9-inch round pie pan. Bake for 10 minutes. Remove from oven. Sauté onion in oil until soft and light brown. Add mushrooms and cook for 5 minutes on low flame. Add cheeses. Stir. Put this mixture on top of dough. Mix together ingredients for sauce by hand. Pour over mushroom mixture. Bake for 35 minutes at 350°.

NUTRITIONAL INFORMATION PER SERVING:*				Serving Size: 3½ oz. Total Servings: 8	
Calories	182	Sodium	331 mg	**PERCENT OF DAILY VALUE**	
Calories from fat	121	Carbohydrates	9 g	Vitamin A	10 %
Fat	13 g	Fiber	1 g	Vitamin C	2 %
Saturated Fat	5 g	Protein	7 g	Calcium	18 %
Cholesterol	69 mg			Iron	5 %

* Analysis done without pie dough.

Pasta and Broccoli

8 oz. noodles
16 oz. milk
4 Tbs. butter
1 tsp. garlic powder
2 oz. tomato sauce

2 oz. frozen chopped
  broccoli
½ cup grated Parmesan
  cheese
salt and pepper, to taste

Cook noodles until halfway done. Drain, and return noodles to pot. Add milk, butter, garlic powder, tomato sauce, and broccoli. Bring to a boil. When noodles are fully cooked, remove from heat; add Parmesan cheese. Add salt and pepper. Toss and serve.

NUTRITIONAL INFORMATION PER SERVING:				Serving Size: 8 oz. Total Servings: 4	
Calories	435	Sodium	517 mg	**PERCENT OF DAILY VALUE**	
Calories from fat	171	Carbohydrates	48 g	Vitamin A	29 %
Fat	19 g	Fiber	2 g	Vitamin C	26 %
Saturated Fat	11 g	Protein	18 g	Calcium	43 %
Cholesterol	100 mg			Iron	20 %

Eggplant Parmesan

1 large eggplant, peeled
2 eggs, beaten
½ cup matzah meal or bread
  crumbs

¼ cup oil for frying
8–10 slices yellow cheese of
  your choice
2 8-oz. cans tomato sauce

Slice eggplant into ¼-inch slices. Dip slices in egg, then in matzah meal or bread crumbs. Fry in oil until light brown. In a 9x13-inch pan, place a layer of eggplant, a layer of cheese, and a layer of tomato sauce. Repeat until eggplant is used up. Top with cheese. Bake at 350°, uncovered, for 30 minutes.

NUTRITIONAL INFORMATION PER SERVING:				Serving Size: 5 oz. Total Servings: 12	
Calories	166	Sodium	609 mg	**PERCENT OF DAILY VALUE**	
Calories from fat	92	Carbohydrates	13 g	Vitamin A	17 %
Fat	10 g	Fiber	1 g	Vitamin C	17 %
Saturated Fat	4 g	Protein	7 g	Calcium	16 %
Cholesterol	47 mg			Iron	7 %

Easy Lasagna

1 32-oz. jar marinara sauce
1 1-lb. box lasagna noodles
1 lb. cottage cheese

2 6-oz. pkgs. hard cheese:
American, Muenster, or
mozzarella

Cover the bottom of a 9x13-inch pan with a thin layer of marinara sauce. Into the pan, place a layer of uncooked noodles, then a layer of cottage cheese, then a layer of marinara sauce, then a layer of hard cheese. Repeat this pattern 2 to 3 times; the last layer should be noodles, sauce, then hard cheese. Pour a little water between the sides of the pan and the noodles. Bake, covered, at 350° for 1 to 1½ hours. For a firmer lasagna, uncover for last 5 minutes of baking.

NUTRITIONAL INFORMATION PER SERVING:				Serving Size: 6½ oz. Total Servings: 12	
Calories	329	Sodium	1016 mg	**PERCENT OF DAILY VALUE**	
Calories from fat	108	Carbohydrates	40 g	Vitamin A	22 %
Fat	12 g	Fiber	1 g	Vitamin C	17 %
Saturated Fat	6 g	Protein	16 g	Calcium	25 %
Cholesterol	24 mg			Iron	18 %

Macaroni and Cheese

1 lb. elbow macaroni
3 Tbs. butter
2 Tbs. flour
2 cups milk

2 cups American cheese,
grated
1 tsp. salt

Cook macaroni. Meanwhile, make sauce as follows: Melt butter and blend in flour. Slowly stir in milk. Add cheese and salt, and stir until smooth. Drain macaroni, add sauce and stir well. Place in a baking dish and bake uncovered at 350° for 30 minutes.

NUTRITIONAL INFORMATION PER SERVING:				Serving Size: 4 oz. Total Servings: 12	
Calories	280	Sodium	566 mg	**PERCENT OF DAILY VALUE**	
Calories from fat	98	Carbohydrates	33 g	Vitamin A	16 %
Fat	11 g	Fiber	0 g	Calcium	27 %
Saturated Fat	6 g	Protein	12 g	Iron	11 %
Cholesterol	27 mg				

Stuffed Shells

1 lb. box jumbo shells
2 16-oz. containers cottage
    cheese
8 oz. shredded mozzarella
    cheese

2 eggs
½ tsp. salt
¼ tsp. pepper
1 32-oz. jar marinara sauce

Cook shells and drain. Combine cheeses, eggs, salt, and pepper. Cover bottom of a 9x13-inch pan with some sauce. Fill shells with cheese mixture and arrange in pan in a single layer. Pour remaining sauce over shells. Bake uncovered at 350° for 30 minutes.

NUTRITIONAL INFORMATION PER SERVING:		Serving Size: 7½ oz. Total Servings: 12		
Calories	322	Sodium	984 mg	**PERCENT OF DAILY VALUE**
Calories from fat	84	Carbohydrates	39 g	Vitamin A	15 %
Fat	9 g	Fiber	0 g	Vitamin C	16 %
Saturated Fat	3 g	Protein	22 g	Calcium	8 %
Cholesterol	53 mg			Iron	15 %

Taco-Dip Pizza

2 8-oz. pkgs. cream cheese,
    softened
30 (approx.) small green
    olives with pimentos,
    chopped fine
1 small jar spicy tomato
    sauce or salsa sauce
½ green pepper, diced

½ red pepper, diced
½ yellow pepper, diced
1 tomato, diced
8 oz. mozzarella cheese,
    shredded
8 oz. cheddar cheese,
    shredded
taco chips

Blend together cream cheese, olives, and a little juice from the olives to a very soft consistency (like a dip). On a large round tray, drop cream cheese mixture by spoonfuls in a circular motion, starting at center of tray. Using spoon, spread mixture ¼-inch thick, leaving a 2- to 3-inch border around tray. Spread tomato or salsa sauce over mixture, and sprinkle with diced vegetables. Alternating mozzarella and cheddar, sprinkle cheeses on top. Place taco chips around dip mixture on the remaining 2 to 3 inches of tray. It should look like pizza. Take tacos and dig into the dip!

NUTRITIONAL INFORMATION PER SERVING:*				Serving Size: 5 oz. Total Servings: 10		
Calories	277	Sodium	558 mg	**PERCENT OF DAILY VALUE**		
Calories from fat	213	Carbohydrates	6 g	Vitamin A	37 %
Fat	24 g	Fiber	1 g	Vitamin C	57 %
Saturated Fat	13 g	Protein	14 g	Calcium	16 %
Cholesterol	70 mg			Iron	7 %

* Analysis does not include taco chips.

Lentil Cheese Pie

¾ oz. low-fat mozzarella
  cheese, shredded
¼ oz. Parmesan cheese,
  grated
4 oz. lentils, cooked* and
  drained
½ cup each: cooked sliced
  carrots, cooked cut green
  beans, and cooked sliced
  mushrooms

¼ cup tomato sauce
½ tsp. onion flakes
¼ tsp. salt
3 slices tomato
¼ tsp. oregano

Preheat oven to 325°. Combine cheeses. Put half the cheese mixture into a bowl. Mix in lentils, vegetables, tomato sauce, onion flakes, and salt. Lightly grease or spray a pie plate and spread lentil mixture evenly into it. Top with tomato slices. Sprinkle with remaining cheese mixture and oregano. Bake 20 to 30 minutes.

* To cook lentils, soak overnight in enough water to cover. Drain and cover again with water. Bring to a boil and simmer until tender.

NUTRITIONAL INFORMATION PER SERVING:				Serving Size: 2½ oz. Total Servings: 8		
Calories	40	Sodium	146 mg	**PERCENT OF DAILY VALUE**		
Calories from fat	5	Carbohydrates	7 g	Vitamin A	48 %
Fat	1 g	Fiber	2 g	Vitamin C	6 %
Saturated Fat	0 g	Protein	3 g	Calcium	2 %
Cholesterol	1 mg			Iron	6 %

Spinach Lasagna

1 lb. frozen spinach	1 tsp. salt
1 lb. cottage cheese	¾ tsp. oregano
1 lb. grated Muenster or	⅛ tsp. pepper
mozzarella cheese	32 oz. marinara sauce
1 egg	1 lb. lasagna noodles

Thaw and drain spinach. Mix with cottage cheese and half the grated cheese. Add egg and seasonings. In a greased 9x13-inch pan, layer marinara sauce, raw noodles, and spinach mixture. Repeat. Top with remaining grated cheese. Pour water between edges of pan and noodles (approx. ¼ cup water or less). Cover tightly. Bake at 350° for about 1 hour and 15 minutes.

NUTRITIONAL INFORMATION PER SERVING:		Serving Size: 8½ oz. Total Servings: 12			
Calories	331	Sodium	1093 mg	PERCENT OF DAILY VALUE	
Calories from fat	87	Carbohydrates	41 g	Vitamin A	36 %
Fat	10 g	Fiber	1 g	Vitamin C	42 %
Saturated Fat	2 g	Protein	23 g	Calcium	7 %
Cholesterol	37 mg			Iron	27 %

Cheese Blintzes

Batter:	*Filling:*
1 cup flour	1 7-oz. pkg. farmer cheese
1 cup milk	½ cup cottage cheese
4 eggs	1 large egg
½ tsp. salt	3 Tbs. sugar
2 Tbs. sugar	
	oil for greasing

Batter: Slowly mix together flour and milk. Add eggs, salt, and sugar. Stir until no lumps remain. Lightly grease a frying pan and heat it. Pour a little of the batter into the hot oil (enough to form a thin pancake). When edges begin to dry, turn over to the other side and fry another minute. Turn out onto a towel and cool. Continue frying pancakes using remaining batter.

Filling: Combine ingredients and place a tablespoon of mixture in center of each pancake. Fold sides in and roll.

Variation: For parve potato blintzes, substitute water for milk in dough. Fill with mashed potatoes and serve with mushroom sauce.

NUTRITIONAL INFORMATION PER SERVING:			Serving Size: 3 oz. Total Servings: 12		
Calories	169	Sodium	236 mg	**PERCENT OF DAILY VALUE**	
Calories from fat	71	Carbohydrates	15 g	Vitamin A	10 %
Fat	8 g	Fiber	0 g	Calcium	21 %
Saturated Fat	1 g	Protein	9 g	Iron	5 %
Cholesterol	108 mg				

Noodle Cheese Kugel

12 oz. medium egg noodles
1 8-oz. pkg. farmer cheese
6 oz. whipped cream cheese,
    at room temperature
1½ Tbs. + 1–2 Tbs. butter
8 oz. sour cream

½ cup sugar
2–3 eggs
½ cup cornflake crumbs
½ tsp. cinnamon, or to taste
2 Tbs. sugar

Cook noodles, drain, and rinse in warm water. Mix immediately with cheeses and 1½ Tbs. butter until melted. Add sour cream, sugar, and eggs. Pour into 2 greased loaf pans or a 9x13-inch pan. Mix cornflake crumbs with cinnamon and sugar and sprinkle over kugel. Dot with remaining butter. Bake uncovered at 350° for 1¼ hours.

NUTRITIONAL INFORMATION PER SERVING:			Serving Size: 4 oz. Total Servings: 12		
Calories	364	Sodium	218 mg	**PERCENT OF DAILY VALUE**	
Calories from fat	181	Carbohydrates	34 g	Vitamin A	25 %
Fat	20 g	Fiber	0 g	Calcium	24 %
Saturated Fat	8 g	Protein	12 g	Iron	13 %
Cholesterol	131 mg				

No-Yeast Pizza

2 cups flour
1 tsp. baking powder
½ tsp. salt
⅓ cup oil
⅓ cup milk
1 large egg
1 8-oz. can tomato sauce

1 tsp. salt
dash of pepper
1 tsp. oregano
2 Tbs. oil
1 8-oz. pkg. shredded
    mozzarella cheese

Combine the first 6 ingredients to make dough, and knead until soft. Roll out dough and spread into 2 round baking pans or one 9x13-inch pan. Combine tomato sauce, salt, pepper, oregano, and oil. Spread on dough. Sprinkle cheese on top. Bake at 350° for 20 minutes.

Variation: Apple juice can be substituted for milk.

NUTRITIONAL INFORMATION PER SERVING:				Serving Size: 1 slice Total Servings: 12	
Calories	255	Sodium	499 mg	**PERCENT OF DAILY VALUE**	
Calories from fat	112	Carbohydrates	29 g	Vitamin A	16 %
Fat	12 g	Fiber	1 g	Vitamin C	2 %
Saturated Fat	2 g	Protein	10 g	Calcium	31 %
Cholesterol	24 mg			Iron	51 %

Potato Cheese Casserole

6 medium potatoes, peeled
    and diced
¼ cup minced onion
1 Tbs. oil for sautéing
2 tsp. salt
½ tsp. black pepper

2 Tbs. chopped parsley
1 cup cottage cheese
½ cup grated American
    cheese (other hard
    cheeses may be used)
¾ cup milk

Cook and drain potatoes. Sauté onion in oil. Line a 2-quart casserole dish with half the potatoes and onion. Sprinkle with half the salt, pepper, and parsley. Spoon on half the cottage cheese. Add a second layer of potatoes, onions, seasonings, and cottage cheese. Sprinkle hard cheese on top, then pour milk over the casserole. Bake at 350° for 30 to 35 minutes.

NUTRITIONAL INFORMATION PER SERVING:				Serving Size: 6½ oz. Total Servings: 8	
Calories	168	Sodium	807 mg	**PERCENT OF DAILY VALUE**	
Calories from fat	49	Carbohydrates	20 g	Vitamin A	8 %
Fat	5 g	Fiber	2 g	Vitamin C	37 %
Saturated Fat	3 g	Protein	9 g	Calcium	15 %
Cholesterol	17 mg			Iron	9 %

Broccoli-Spinach Quiche

1 10-oz. pkg. frozen broccoli
1 10-oz. pkg. frozen spinach
1 onion, chopped
2 Tbs. oil for sautéing
6 eggs, beaten

10 slices (8 oz.) American or Muenster cheese, grated or cut up
1 red pepper, diced
1 tsp. onion soup mix
1 9-inch pie shell

Cook broccoli and spinach as directed on package and combine. Meanwhile, sauté onion in oil. Add onion, eggs, cheese, red pepper, and soup mix to broccoli and spinach. Bake pie shell for 5 minutes. Turn mixture into pie shell and bake for 45 minutes at 350°.

NUTRITIONAL INFORMATION PER SERVING:*				Serving Size: 6 oz. Total Servings: 8	
Calories	212	Sodium	582 mg	**PERCENT OF DAILY VALUE**	
Calories from fat	129	Carbohydrates	9 g	Vitamin A	62 %
Fat	14 g	Fiber	1 g	Vitamin C	46 %
Saturated Fat	6 g	Protein	13 g	Calcium	32 %
Cholesterol	178 mg			Iron	10 %

* Analysis does not include pie shell.

Vegetable Casserole

1 Tbs. oil
1½ tsp. paprika
½ tsp. oregano
½ tsp. salt
3 potatoes, cubed
1 large onion, cut into 6
    wedges

3 zucchini
1 green pepper, cut into 6
    wedges
1 red pepper, cut into 6
    wedges
8 oz. low-fat mozzarella
    cheese, shredded

In a 3-quart pot, mix oil, paprika, oregano, and salt. Add potatoes and onion. Cut zucchini in half lengthwise and then crosswise. Add zucchini and peppers to pot. Cover and simmer on low flame until vegetables get soft but not mushy. Drain excess liquid. Sprinkle with cheese and cover pot until cheese melts.

NUTRITIONAL INFORMATION PER SERVING:		Serving Size: 7 oz. Total Servings: 8			
Calories	144	Sodium	270 mg	**PERCENT OF DAILY VALUE**	
Calories from fat	59	Carbohydrates	13 g	Vitamin A	14 %
Fat	7 g	Fiber	3 g	Vitamin C	75 %
Saturated Fat	3 g	Protein	9 g	Calcium	26 %
Cholesterol	16 mg			Iron	7 %

Herb Omelet

1 tsp. chopped fresh parsley
1 tsp. chopped fresh basil
1 tsp. chopped onion

1 egg
1 Tbs. milk
1 tsp. margarine

In a small bowl, combine first 3 ingredients. In a larger bowl, beat egg with milk. In a small skillet or omelet pan, melt margarine over a medium-high flame. Add egg mixture and cook for 30 seconds. Slip a spatula under the egg, tilt pan, and allow any uncooked egg to flow under cooked portion. Spoon herbs down center of omelet. With a spatula, loosen one side of the omelet and fold it one-third over the remainder. Loosen folded portion and fold over again in the same direction. Slide omelet onto a serving plate.

NUTRITIONAL INFORMATION PER SERVING:		Serving Size: 2½ oz. Total Servings: 1			
Calories	121	Sodium	116 mg	**PERCENT OF DAILY VALUE**	
Calories from fat	84	Carbohydrates	2 g	Vitamin A	19 %
Fat	9 g	Fiber	0 g	Vitamin C	3 %
Saturated Fat	2 g	Protein	7 g	Calcium	7 %
Cholesterol	215 mg			Iron	6 %

Vegetable Cheese Quiche

2 10-oz. pkgs. frozen
    chopped broccoli
1 cup part-skim ricotta
    cheese or low-fat cottage
    cheese
4 oz. cheddar cheese, cubed
    or shredded

4 eggs
2 tsp. minced onion
1 bouillon cube
1 Tbs. flour
dash of garlic powder

Cook broccoli until soft, and drain liquid. Arrange on bottom of 2-qt. casserole dish. Blend remaining ingredients and pour over vegetables. Bake for 50 minutes or until brown at 350°.

Variation: Other vegetables may be substituted in place of broccoli.

NUTRITIONAL INFORMATION PER SERVING:		Serving Size: 5 oz. Total Servings: 8			
Calories	141	Sodium	359 mg	**PERCENT OF DAILY VALUE**	
Calories from fat	68	Carbohydrates	6 g	Vitamin A	28 %
Fat	8 g	Fiber	3 g	Vitamin C	47 %
Saturated Fat	4 g	Protein	13 g	Calcium	21 %
Cholesterol	123 mg			Iron	6 %

Cheese Latkes

3 eggs
½ cup sugar
1½ tsp. vanilla extract
1 lb. cottage cheese

¼ cup flour, or as needed to
    thicken
oil or margarine for frying

Combine all ingredients, beating lightly with a fork as each item is added. Lightly grease a frying pan and heat it well. Drop cheese mixture by tablespoonfuls into the pan and fry each side until golden. Remember to regrease the pan with each batch.
Yield: 30-45 latkes when done in batches of 5.

NUTRITIONAL INFORMATION PER SERVING:				Serving Size: 3 latkes Total Servings: 12	
Calories	144	Sodium	169 mg	**PERCENT OF DAILY VALUE**	
Calories from fat	68	Carbohydrates	12 g	Vitamin A	5 %
Fat	8 g	Fiber	0 g	Calcium	3 %
Saturated Fat	2 g	Protein	7 g	Iron	2 %
Cholesterol	59 mg				

Pancakes

1½ cups milk
1–2 eggs, well beaten
1 Tbs. oil
2 cups flour

3 tsp. baking powder
½ tsp. salt
1 Tbs. sugar
6 Tbs. oil for frying

Combine milk, eggs, and oil. Add dry ingredients and mix until smooth. Pour by spoonfuls onto hot, lightly greased griddle. Cook until bubbles begin to break on surface, turn, and fry other side until golden brown.

NUTRITIONAL INFORMATION PER SERVING:*				Serving Size: 2 oz. Total Servings: 12	
Calories	143	Sodium	119 mg	**PERCENT OF DAILY VALUE**	
Calories from fat	49	Carbohydrates	19 g	Vitamin A	3 %
Fat	5 g	Fiber	1 g	Calcium	6 %
Saturated Fat	1 g	Protein	4 g	Iron	6 %
Cholesterol	40 mg				

* Calculated with 2 eggs.

Whole-Wheat Pancakes

2 cups 1% milk
2 eggs
2½ cups whole-wheat flour
2 tsp. baking powder

½ tsp. salt
3 Tbs. molasses
¼ cup oil for frying

Beat milk and eggs together. Mix in flour, baking powder, salt, and molasses in order, and continue to mix until well blended. Heat a little of the oil in a large skillet. Drop spoonfuls of batter into pan. Turn pancake when bubbles form at the top. Serve with 100% pure maple syrup. Yum!

NUTRITIONAL INFORMATION PER SERVING:				Serving Size: 2 oz. Total Servings: 18	
Calories	111	Sodium	86 mg	**PERCENT OF DAILY VALUE**	
Calories from fat	38	Carbohydrates	16 g	Vitamin A	3 %
Fat	4 g	Fiber	2 g	Calcium	8 %
Saturated Fat	1 g	Protein	4 g	Iron	8 %
Cholesterol	25 mg				

Oat Bran and Wheat Germ Pancakes

½ cup enriched white flour
½ cup oat bran
½ cup wheat germ
2 tsp. baking powder
1 Tbs. brown sugar

⅔ cup 1% milk
1 egg
1 Tbs. oil
1 tsp. vanilla
margarine to grease pan

In a large bowl, mix flour, oat bran, wheat germ, baking powder, and sugar. In a measuring cup, combine milk, egg, oil, and vanilla. Mix with dry ingredients. Heat skillet and melt margarine. Pour in 1 Tbs. batter for each pancake. Fry over medium heat until brown, then turn and fry other side.

NUTRITIONAL INFORMATION PER SERVING:				Serving Size: 1½ oz. Total Servings: 12	
Calories	140	Sodium	48 mg	**PERCENT OF DAILY VALUE**	
Calories from fat	92	Carbohydrates	10 g	Vitamin A	4 %
Fat	10 g	Fiber	1 g	Calcium	3 %
Saturated Fat	2 g	Protein	4 g	Iron	3 %
Cholesterol	18 mg				

Broccoli and Cheese

2 10-oz. pkgs. frozen
   broccoli spears
9 slices (approx.) American
   cheese

1 10-oz. can cream of
   mushroom soup
1 cup cornflake crumbs

Cook broccoli as directed on package. In a 1½-qt. Pyrex dish, layer broccoli and then cheese slices to cover broccoli. Spread soup on top and sprinkle with cornflake crumbs. Bake at 350° for approximately 25 minutes, or until bubbling.

NUTRITIONAL INFORMATION PER SERVING:				Serving Size: 6 oz. Total Servings: 6	
Calories	192	Sodium	720 mg	PERCENT OF DAILY VALUE	
Calories from fat	96	Carbohydrates	15 g	Vitamin A	35 %
Fat	11 g	Fiber	4 g	Vitamin C	63 %
Saturated Fat	6 g	Protein	10 g	Calcium	28 %
Cholesterol	27 mg			Iron	13 %

Baked Ziti

1 lb. ziti noodles, cooked
   and drained
1 17-oz. jar salsa sauce

White Sauce:
1½ cups milk

2 Tbs. flour
1 tsp. salt
¼ tsp. pepper
½ tsp. paprika
3 Tbs. butter
8 oz. American cheese

Bring milk and flour to a slow boil. Add salt, pepper, paprika, butter, and cheese. Stir until cheese is completely melted, then remove from flame. Combine ziti with salsa sauce and top with white sauce. Bake at 350° in an 8x10-inch greased pan, for 1 hour.

NUTRITIONAL INFORMATION PER SERVING:				Serving Size: 4 oz. Total Servings: 12	
Calories	266	Sodium	628 mg	PERCENT OF DAILY VALUE	
Calories from fat	94	Carbohydrates	34 g	Vitamin A	20 %
Fat	10 g	Fiber	1 g	Vitamin C	21 %
Saturated Fat	6 g	Protein	11 g	Calcium	20 %
Cholesterol	27 mg			Iron	16 %

FISH AND DAIRY DISHES

Pizza

2 oz. fresh yeast
¼ cup water
⅛ cup sugar
1 tsp. salt
2 Tbs. oil
3½ cups flour

1 cup apple juice
8 oz. marinara sauce or
    tomato sauce
1 8-oz. pkg. shredded
    mozzarella cheese

Mix yeast and water in a bowl. In a separate bowl, mix the next 5 ingredients. Add yeast mixture. Mix to form dough. Roll out dough in a pizza pan, spread on sauce, and sprinkle cheese on top. Bake at 350° for 15 minutes.

NUTRITIONAL INFORMATION PER SERVING:				Serving Size: 1 slice Total Servings: 8	
Calories	343	Sodium	616 mg	**PERCENT OF DAILY VALUE**	
Calories from fat	72	Carbohydrates	53 g	Vitamin A	3 %
Fat	8 g	Fiber	2 g	Vitamin C	7 %
Saturated Fat	1 g	Protein	15 g	Calcium	2 %
Cholesterol	10 mg			Iron	19 %

Cheese Kugel

1 lb. farmer cheese
3 eggs
½ cup sugar
4 oz. fine noodles, crushed

½ pt. sour cream
1 20-oz. can crushed
    pineapple

Combine all ingredients except pineapple. Turn into a casserole dish. Drain pineapple and spoon over top of mixture. Bake at 350° until firm, about 1 hour.

NUTRITIONAL INFORMATION PER SERVING:				Serving Size: 6 oz. Total Servings: 8	
Calories	412	Sodium	300 mg	**PERCENT OF DAILY VALUE**	
Calories from fat	221	Carbohydrates	30 g	Vitamin A	27 %
Fat	25 g	Fiber	1 g	Vitamin C	2 %
Saturated Fat	4 g	Protein	19 g	Calcium	61 %
Cholesterol	159 mg			Iron	7 %

Tomato with Pasta and Cheese

1-lb. box spaghetti	½ cup olive oil
2 tomatoes, thinly sliced	8 oz. shredded mozzarella
1 Tbs. minced garlic	cheese
2 Tbs. basil	

Cook spaghetti as directed on package and drain. Combine remaining ingredients and let sit while spaghetti is cooking. Pour mixture over cooked spaghetti.

NUTRITIONAL INFORMATION PER SERVING:				Serving Size: 8⅓ oz. Total Servings: 6	
Calories	525	Sodium	209 mg	**PERCENT OF DAILY VALUE**	
Calories from fat	210	Carbohydrates	59 g	Vitamin A	2 %
Fat	23 g	Fiber	0 g	Vitamin C	7 %
Saturated Fat	3 g	Protein	21 g	Calcium	2 %
Cholesterol	13 mg			Iron	20 %

Poultry and Stuffings

Poultry and Stuffings

Honey-Mustard Chicken

2 tsp. dry mustard
2 tsp. water
¼ cup honey
1 Tbs. soy sauce
1 Tbs. hot water
1 tsp. cornstarch
1 Tbs. cold water
2 Tbs. oil
6 cloves of garlic, peeled
   and chopped

1 tsp. ground ginger
   (optional)
dash of hot pepper sauce
1 lb. chicken breast, cut into
   bite-size pieces
⅓ cup cashews or toasted
   pignolia nuts (pine nuts)
   (optional)

Combine dry mustard with water. Let stand 10 minutes. Add honey, soy sauce, hot water, and cornstarch dissolved in 1 Tbs. cold water. Stir to combine. Heat oil in frying pan over medium-high heat. Add garlic cloves (and ground ginger, if using) and hot pepper sauce. Heat 7 to 10 seconds; remove pan from flame. Add chicken (and nuts, if using). Put pan back on flame and heat 2½ to 3 minutes. Add honey-mustard sauce and cook another 3 to 4 minutes.

NUTRITIONAL INFORMATION PER SERVING:				Serving Size: 4 oz. Total Servings: 4	
Calories	315	Sodium	322 mg	**PERCENT OF DAILY VALUE**	
Calories from fat	181	Carbohydrates	5 g	Vitamin A	6 %
Fat	20 g	Fiber	1 g	Vitamin C	2 %
Saturated Fat	4 g	Protein	29 g	Calcium	4 %
Cholesterol	72 mg			Iron	10 %

Raspberry Chicken

Compliments of Cyrk Cafe, Monsey, NY

1 pt. CYRK Raspberry Sorbet **2 2½-lb. chickens, cut into pieces**

Empty sorbet container into a saucepan and melt over medium flame. Continue to cook until reduced by ⅔. Place chicken pieces flat on broiling pan. Brush or spoon on raspberry sauce to coat. Bake at 400° for approximately 40 minutes, or until juices flow clear from chicken when pierced with a knife. Serve over rice.

NUTRITIONAL INFORMATION PER SERVING:		Serving Size: ¼ chicken Total Servings: 8			
Calories	515	Sodium	176 mg	**PERCENT OF DAILY VALUE**	
Calories from fat	250	Carbohydrates	10 g	Vitamin A	46 %
Fat	28 g	Fiber	0 g	Vitamin C	14 %
Saturated Fat	7 g	Protein	53 g	Calcium	3 %
Cholesterol	212 mg			Iron	35 %

Queen Victoria Chicken Breast

Compliments of Jerusalem Plaza, Monsey, NY

1½ lbs. ground veal
¼ lb. mushrooms, sautéed
2 large eggs, beaten
½ tsp. onion powder
2 Tbs. seasoned bread crumbs
8 chicken cutlets (approx. 3¼ lbs.)
1 1-lb. pkg. puff pastry dough squares

Cherry Jubilee Sauce:
1 16-oz. can dark sweet cherries, pitted (reserve syrup)
1 Tbs. cornstarch
1 Tbs. sugar
1 Tbs. brandy or rum
[1 Tbs. cold water can be added to sauce to increase amount.]

Combine ground veal and mushrooms. Add eggs, onion powder, and bread crumbs. Mix well. Heat oven to 400°. Grease a baking pan. Pound each cutlet to flatten. Spoon some filling across the center of each cutlet and roll up. Roll out each puff pastry square to accommodate the chicken roll. Roll pastry around chicken. Arrange in pan and bake for 10 minutes. Lower heat to 325° and bake an additional 45 to 50 minutes, until golden brown.

Sauce: Take 1 cup of syrup from cherries and dissolve cornstarch and sugar in it. Blend in remaining syrup. Cook on low heat, stirring until it bubbles (about 1 minute). Stir in cherries. Before serving, add brandy or rum. Pour sauce over chicken.

NUTRITIONAL INFORMATION PER SERVING:			Serving Size: 13 oz. Total Servings: 8	
Calories	662	Sodium	411 mg	**PERCENT OF DAILY VALUE**
Calories from fat	221	Carbohydrates	26 g	Vitamin A 2 %
Fat	25 g	Fiber	1 g	Vitamin C 3 %
Saturated Fat	6 g	Protein	79 g	Calcium 5 %
Cholesterol	233 mg			Iron 22 %

Okobuko

2 large turkey drumsticks, sliced into rounds by the butcher
6 Tbs. (approx.) flour
1 onion, chopped
1 tsp. crushed garlic
4 Tbs. (approx.) oil

1 carrot, shredded
1 stalk celery, diced
1 tsp. Italian seasoning
1 26-oz. can crushed tomatoes
½ cup dry wine

Coat drumstick slices in flour and sear quickly on all sides in a hot skillet. Sauté onion and garlic in oil, followed by carrot, celery, and seasoning. Add tomatoes and wine last. Lay out turkey meat on bottom of a baking dish. Spread vegetable mixture on meat. Bake, covered, for 2 hours at 350°.

NUTRITIONAL INFORMATION PER SERVING:*			Serving Size: 13 oz. Total Servings: 4	
Calories	569	Sodium	378 mg	**PERCENT OF DAILY VALUE**
Calories from fat	276	Carbohydrates	14 g	Vitamin A 79 %
Fat	31 g	Fiber	1 g	Vitamin C 39 %
Saturated Fat	7 g	Protein	50 g	Calcium 12 %
Cholesterol	145 mg			Iron 36 %

* Serving size includes bones and sauce.

Chicken Continental

1 cup flour
½ tsp. salt
½ tsp. paprika
⅛ tsp. pepper
1 2-lb. broiling chicken
3 Tbs. oil

1 large onion, sliced
10 fresh mushrooms or 1
   small can button
   mushrooms
½–1 cup dry white wine

Mix flour, salt, paprika, and pepper, coat chicken, and lightly brown in hot oil. Remove from oil and drain on a paper towel. Add onion and mushrooms to skillet, and brown lightly. Stir in wine. Arrange chicken in casserole dish. Pour onion/mushroom mixture on top. Cover. Bake at 350° for 1 hour. If you want, you can slice potatoes and place them at the bottom of the casserole, and then place chicken and onion/mushroom mixture on top. Nice for *Yom Tov.*

NUTRITIONAL INFORMATION PER SERVING:		Serving Size: ¼ chicken Total Servings: 4			
Calories	578	Sodium	403 mg	**PERCENT OF DAILY VALUE**	
Calories from fat	297	Carbohydrates	15 g	Vitamin A	40 %
Fat	33 g	Fiber	1 g	Vitamin C	4 %
Saturated Fat	8 g	Protein	48 g	Calcium	4 %
Cholesterol	182 mg			Iron	23 %

Chicken Cacciatore

½ cup flour
1 tsp. salt
¼ tsp. pepper
1 2½-lb. chicken, cut up
¼ cup olive oil
1 lb. (approx.) fresh
   tomatoes, chopped
1 8-oz. can tomato sauce

1 lb. mushrooms, sliced
¼ cup water
1–2 onions, chopped
2 cloves of garlic, crushed
1 tsp. salt
1 tsp. oregano, crushed
¼ tsp. pepper
1 large bay leaf

Mix flour, salt, and pepper. Coat chicken with flour mixture. In a large frying pan, heat oil. Brown chicken on all sides (approximately 15 minutes). Remove chicken to a warming pan and drain most of the fat. In the same fry pan, combine remaining ingredients. Heat to boiling, then reduce to simmer. Place chicken gently on top of sauce. Cover and simmer until the thickest pieces are done, about 30 minutes. Remove bay leaf. Serve over hot spaghetti or linguine.

NUTRITIONAL INFORMATION PER SERVING:*				Serving Size: 9½ oz. Total Servings: 8	
Calories	367	Sodium	542 mg	**PERCENT OF DAILY VALUE**	
Calories from fat	191	Carbohydrates	14 g	Vitamin A	36 %
Fat	21 g	Fiber	1 g	Vitamin C	30 %
Saturated Fat	5 g	Protein	31 g	Calcium	4 %
Cholesterol	106 mg			Iron	20 %

* Serving size includes sauce.

Orange Juice Chicken for Friday Night

4 chicken thighs (bottoms), approx. 2½ lbs. altogether
garlic powder, to taste
onion powder, to taste

paprika, to taste
dash of salt
1½ Tbs. oil
1½ cups (approx.) orange juice

Remove skin and fat from chicken. Arrange pieces in an aluminum baking pan, and season with garlic powder, onion powder, paprika, and salt. Spread oil on chicken. Pour enough orange juice into pan to cover ⅓ of chicken. Bake at 350° for 1 hour, skin side up. Remove from oven and turn each piece of chicken over. Place pan on *blech*, over flame, until remaining orange juice cooks into chicken. Then remove it from flame so chicken doesn't dry out.

NUTRITIONAL INFORMATION PER SERVING:				Serving Size: ¼ chicken Total Servings: 4	
Calories	399	Sodium	423 mg	**PERCENT OF DAILY VALUE**	
Calories from fat	175	Carbohydrates	7 g	Vitamin A	4 %
Fat	19 g	Fiber	0 g	Vitamin C	40 %
Saturated Fat	5 g	Protein	46 g	Calcium	3 %
Cholesterol	159 mg			Iron	15 %

Chinese Chicken

2 lbs. chicken cutlets
3 stalks of celery, sliced
4 carrots, sliced
1 large pkg. fresh
    mushrooms, sliced

oil (approx. 4 Tbs. total)
¼ cup water
4 Tbs. soy sauce
½ cup cornstarch
3 Tbs. minced scallions

Cut chicken cutlets into cubes and set aside. In a frying pan, sauté celery, carrots, and mushrooms in a small amount of oil until tender. Cover bottom of a 5-quart pot with some oil, and place sautéed vegetables into pot. Add the water, cover, and steam vegetables for 5 minutes. Dip chicken pieces into soy sauce and then coat with cornstarch. Shake off excess, and brown in hot oil in the frying pan. Transfer chicken to vegetable pot. Add scallions. Cook until chicken is tender, about 30 minutes. More soy sauce may be added for flavor. Serve over rice.

NUTRITIONAL INFORMATION PER SERVING:				Serving Size: 7 oz. Total Servings: 8	
Calories	290	Sodium	729 mg	**PERCENT OF DAILY VALUE**	
Calories from fat	129	Carbohydrates	13 g	Vitamin A	130 %
Fat	14 g	Fiber	1 g	Vitamin C	8 %
Saturated Fat	3 g	Protein	27 g	Calcium	4 %
Cholesterol	72 mg			Iron	10 %

Chicken Waikiki

1 2½-lb. chicken, cut in
    quarters
½ cup flour
4 Tbs. (approx.) oil

Sauce:
1 20-oz. can sliced
    pineapple

½ cup sugar (optional)
2 tsp. cornstarch
¾ cup cider vinegar
1 Tbs. soy sauce
¼ tsp. ginger
1 chicken bouillon cube
1 large green pepper, cut
    crosswise in circles

Rinse chicken; pat dry with paper towels. Coat chicken with flour. Heat oil in a large skillet and add the chicken, a few pieces at a time, to brown. Remove to a shallow roasting pan, arranging pieces skin side up. Preheat oven to 350°.

Sauce: Drain pineapple, pouring syrup into a measuring cup. Add water to make 1¼ cups. In a saucepan, combine pineapple syrup, sugar (if using), cornstarch, vinegar, soy sauce, ginger, and bouillon cube. Bring to a boil, stirring constantly. Boil for 2 minutes. Pour sauce over chicken. Bake uncovered for 30 minutes. Add pineapple slices and green pepper. Bake 30 minutes longer or until chicken is tender. Serve with white rice.

NUTRITIONAL INFORMATION PER SERVING:*		Serving Size: ¼ chicken Total Servings: 4			
Calories	781	Sodium	1055 mg	**PERCENT OF DAILY VALUE**	
Calories from fat	334	Carbohydrates	63 g	Vitamin A	42 %
Fat	37 g	Fiber	2 g	Vitamin C	63 %
Saturated Fat	8 g	Protein	49 g	Calcium	8 %
Cholesterol	183 mg			Iron	30 %

* Analysis includes sauce.

Pineapple-Orange Duck

2 4-lb. ducklings
2 tsp. salt
1 cup orange juice
¼ cup honey
2 Tbs. soy sauce

2 Tbs. lemon juice
1 20-oz. can pineapple
   tidbits, drained
2 tsp. cornstarch

Rub ducklings with salt and place in a roasting pan. Bake uncovered for 45 minutes at 400°. Stir together all remaining ingredients and pour over ducklings. Cover and bake an additional 2 hours.

NUTRITIONAL INFORMATION PER SERVING:*		Serving Size: ¼ duck Total Servings: 4			
Calories	722	Sodium	906 mg	**PERCENT OF DAILY VALUE**	
Calories from fat	489	Carbohydrates	20 g	Vitamin A	15 %
Fat	54 g	Fiber	1 g	Vitamin C	30 %
Saturated Fat	18 g	Protein	37 g	Calcium	4 %
Cholesterol	160 mg			Iron	37 %

* Serving size is without bones.

CROCK-POT Chicken with Rice

1 2½-lb. chicken, quartered
3 Tbs. olive oil
1 onion, sliced
4 potatoes, sliced
3 carrots, sliced
2 stalks celery, chopped
garlic powder, to taste

paprika, to taste
MRS. DASH Onion and Herb
    Mix, to taste
4 bay leaves
rosemary leaves, to taste
1 cup uncooked rice,
    preferably Basmati

Line CROCK-POT with olive oil and onion. Add potatoes, carrots, and celery. Put chicken in the pot and sprinkle on garlic powder, paprika, and MRS. DASH, and add bay leaves and rosemary. Pour in rice and add enough water to cover ingredients. Cook on high heat for 2 hours, then cook on low heat until ready to serve. This can cook for several hours.

NUTRITIONAL INFORMATION PER SERVING:				Serving Size: 8 oz. Total Servings: 10	
Calories	375	Sodium	90 mg	PERCENT OF DAILY VALUE	
Calories from fat	134	Carbohydrates	32 g	Vitamin A	96 %
Fat	15 g	Fiber	3 g	Vitamin C	27 %
Saturated Fat	4 g	Protein	26 g	Calcium	27 %
Cholesterol	85 mg			Iron	21 %

Chicken Capon

Mixture #1:
¾ lb. fresh mushrooms
2 onions
½ stick margarine
¼ cup bread crumbs
¼ tsp. salt
2 egg yolks

Mixture #2:
1 10-oz. pkg. frozen
    chopped broccoli
¼ cup mayonnaise
1 egg white
1 tsp. minced onion
½ tsp. salt
⅛ tsp. pepper

1 pkg. frozen flaky dough
2 lb. chicken cutlets

Mixture #1: Fry together mushrooms and onions in margarine. Add bread crumbs, salt, and egg yolks.

Mixture #2: In a separate pot, cook broccoli. When cooled, mix in mayonnaise, egg white, onion, salt, and pepper.

Roll dough out into 8 squares, 8x8 inches each. Place one spoonful of Mixture #1 on each piece of dough. Then place a piece of chicken cutlet on top. Spoon on one spoonful of Mixture #2. Fold dough over and press sides shut. Place on a baking sheet. Brush with egg and bake at 350° for 40 minutes.

NUTRITIONAL INFORMATION PER SERVING:*			Serving Size: 10 oz. Total Servings: 8		
Calories	463	Sodium	664 mg	**PERCENT OF DAILY VALUE**	
Calories from fat	220	Carbohydrates	36 g	Vitamin A	21 %
Fat	24 g	Fiber	1 g	Vitamin C	7 %
Saturated Fat	5 g	Protein	27 g	Calcium	5 %
Cholesterol	143 mg			Iron	18 %

* Serving size includes sauce and dough.

Baked Crispy Chicken

3 Tbs. prepared mustard
2 Tbs. honey
1 tsp. lemon juice
1 clove of garlic, crushed, or
    1 tsp. garlic powder

1 2½-lb. chicken, cut up, or
    1 pkg. thighs (bottoms)
1½ cups (approx.) bread
    crumbs
½ tsp. salt
⅛ tsp. pepper

Mix first 4 ingredients. Roll chicken in mixture. Combine bread crumbs, salt, and pepper, and coat chicken. (Suggestion: Put bread crumbs, salt, and pepper in a plastic bag and shake chicken pieces inside.) Bake in a greased baking pan at 400° for 45 minutes or until golden brown.

NUTRITIONAL INFORMATION PER SERVING:			Serving Size: ¼ chicken Total Servings: 4		
Calories	644	Sodium	1119 mg	**PERCENT OF DAILY VALUE**	
Calories from fat	261	Carbohydrates	34 g	Vitamin A	46 %
Fat	29 g	Fiber	1 g	Vitamin C	2 %
Saturated Fat	8 g	Protein	59 g	Calcium	11 %
Cholesterol	212 mg			Iron	32 %

Lemon Chicken

1 2½-lb. chicken
½ cup olive oil
½ cup lemon juice
2 Tbs. dried oregano

3 cloves of garlic, minced
1 tsp. salt, or to taste
pepper, to taste

Mix first 6 ingredients together. Pour over chicken and marinate in refrigerator for several hours. Bake uncovered at 350°–375° until done.

NUTRITIONAL INFORMATION PER SERVING:		Serving Size: ¼ chicken Total Servings: 4		
Calories	537	Sodium	764 mg	PERCENT OF DAILY VALUE
Calories from fat	358	Carbohydrates	2 g	Vitamin C 12 %
Fat	40 g	Fiber	0 g	Calcium 8 %
Saturated Fat	11 g	Protein	44 g	Iron 38 %
Cholesterol	174 mg			

Lemon Hunan Chicken

4 large whole chicken
    breasts (approx. 2 lb.)
¼ cup oil for frying

Batter:
¼ cup flour
¼ cup water
1 egg
2 Tbs. cornstarch
2 Tbs. oil
1 tsp. salt
1 tsp. soy sauce
¼ tsp. baking soda

Lemon Sauce:
½ cup water
½ tsp. grated lemon peel
¼ cup lemon juice
¼ cup honey
1 Tbs. ketchup
½ tsp. chicken bouillon
½ tsp. salt
1 clove garlic, minced
1 Tbs. cornstarch mixed
    with 2 Tbs. cold water

Split chicken breasts in half to make 8 pieces. Mix together batter ingredients. Dip chicken pieces into batter one at a time. Drain and fry in oil, 2 or 3 at a time, in a frying pan until golden on both sides.

Keep on a warm platter until all the chicken is done.

Lemon Sauce: heat all ingredients *except* cornstarch and cold water. When sauce is at a full boil, add starch and water. Stir and cook to thicken (30 to 60 seconds). Pour sauce over chicken. Garnish with lemon slices if desired.

NUTRITIONAL INFORMATION PER SERVING:		Serving Size: 10 oz. Total Servings: 4		
Calories	840	Sodium	1139 mg	**PERCENT OF DAILY VALUE**
Calories from fat	496	Carbohydrates	23 g	Vitamin A 10 %
Fat	55 g	Fiber	1 g	Vitamin C 7 %
Saturated Fat	10 g	Protein	61 g	Calcium 5 %
Cholesterol	219 mg			Iron 18 %

Chicken Chow Mein

2 cups celery, chopped
1 large onion, chopped
4 Tbs. oil
1 4-oz. can mushrooms
2 cups diced, cooked
    chicken
1 15-oz. can baby corn

1 15-oz. can mixed Chinese
    vegetables
1 Tbs. + 2 Tbs. soy sauce
1½ cups water
3 Tbs. cornstarch
2 Tbs. brown sugar

Sauté celery and onion in oil until transparent. Add mushrooms and sauté until tender. Add chicken, corn, vegetables, 1 Tbs. soy sauce, and water. Cover and cook for 20 minutes over a medium flame. Mix cornstarch, brown sugar, and 2 Tbs. soy sauce into a paste. Add to chicken, stirring constantly until sauce becomes thick and it boils. Serve on rice; top with Chinese noodles.

NUTRITIONAL INFORMATION PER SERVING:		Serving Size: 10 oz. Total Servings: 6		
Calories	290	Sodium	895 mg	**PERCENT OF DAILY VALUE**
Calories from fat	120	Carbohydrates	28 g	Vitamin A 2 %
Fat	13 g	Fiber	2 g	Vitamin C 54 %
Saturated Fat	3 g	Protein	17 g	Calcium 5 %
Cholesterol	42 mg			Iron 22 %

Chicken Patties

3–4 slices challah
1 lb. ground chicken
1 egg, beaten

½ pkg. onion soup mix
pepper, to taste
oil for frying (approx. 4 Tbs.)

Briefly soak challah in water; drain. Mix with ground chicken, egg, onion soup mix, and pepper. Form into patties and fry in oil until brown on both sides.

NUTRITIONAL INFORMATION PER SERVING:				Serving Size: 4½ oz. Total Servings: 6	
Calories	395	Sodium	1865 mg	PERCENT OF DAILY VALUE	
Calories from fat	243	Carbohydrates	21 g	Vitamin A	7 %
Fat	27 g	Fiber	1 g	Vitamin C	3 %
Saturated Fat	6 g	Protein	17 g	Calcium	5 %
Cholesterol	105 mg			Iron	11 %

Chicken with Vegetables

1 red pepper, sliced
1 green pepper, sliced
1 8-oz. can mushrooms
3 stalks celery, diced
½ cup chicken soup

½ cup white wine
dash of white pepper
leftover chicken from
    chicken soup (2 lbs.)

Poach vegetables in chicken soup and white wine, until vegetables are tender. Add white pepper. Add pieces of soup chicken and cook until everything is hot. Serve over rice.

Variation: Any other vegetables may be added, except tomato.

NUTRITIONAL INFORMATION PER SERVING:				Serving Size: 7½ oz. Total Servings: 8	
Calories	273	Sodium	228 mg	PERCENT OF DAILY VALUE	
Calories from fat	128	Carbohydrates	4 g	Vitamin A	26 %
Fat	14 g	Fiber	1 g	Vitamin C	45 %
Saturated Fat	4 g	Protein	29 g	Calcium	3 %
Cholesterol	110 mg			Iron	14 %

Chicken in Wine Sauce

1 small onion, grated	1 Tbs. oil
1 Tbs. frozen orange juice	dash of pepper
concentrate	½ cup dry white wine
1 Tbs. sugar	1 2½-lb. chicken, whole or
1 tsp. salt	quartered

Mix grated onion, orange juice, sugar, salt, oil, and pepper, by hand or in a food processor. Add wine. Rub mixture onto chicken and place in a single layer in a roasting pan. Cover tightly and bake at 350° for approximately 1½ hours. A crisper skin and darker glaze can be obtained by uncovering for the last 15 minutes or so.

NUTRITIONAL INFORMATION PER SERVING:		Serving Size: ¼ chicken Total Servings: 4			
Calories	331	Sodium	728 mg	**PERCENT OF DAILY VALUE**	
Calories from fat	129	Carbohydrates	7 g	Vitamin C	11 %
Fat	14	Fiber	1 g	Calcium	8 %
Saturated Fat	7 g	Protein	38 g	Iron	32 %
Cholesterol	149 mg				

Chicken Salad

2 scallions, chopped	½ tsp. salt, or to taste
1 stalk celery, diced	¼ tsp. pepper, or to taste
2 cups diced chicken	½ cup (approx.) mayonnaise

Mix vegetables with chicken. Season to taste. Moisten with mayonnaise.

NUTRITIONAL INFORMATION PER SERVING:		Serving Size: 4 oz. Total Servings: 4			
Calories	333	Sodium	492 mg	**PERCENT OF DAILY VALUE**	
Calories from fat	245	Carbohydrates	1 g	Vitamin A	6 %
Fat	27 g	Fiber	0 g	Vitamin C	3 %
Saturated Fat	5 g	Protein	21 g	Calcium	2 %
Cholesterol	79 mg			Iron	7 %

Sweet Chicken I

1 2½-lb. chicken, quartered   ¼ cup French dressing
¼ cup apricot jelly or jam   1 Tbs. OSEM onion soup mix

Arrange chicken in pan. Mix apricot jelly or jam, dressing, and soup mix. Spoon over chicken. Bake covered for 1 hour at 350° and then uncovered for 15 minutes.

NUTRITIONAL INFORMATION PER SERVING:		Serving Size: ¼ chicken Total Servings: 4			
Calories	486	Sodium	673 mg	**PERCENT OF DAILY VALUE**	
Calories from fat	263	Carbohydrates	7 g	Vitamin A	40 %
Fat	29 g	Fiber	0 g	Vitamin C	1 %
Saturated Fat	8 g	Protein	46 g	Calcium	4 %
Cholesterol	184 mg			Iron	19 %

Pickled or Fresh Turkey Roast
Compliments of Monsey Glatt, Monsey, NY

4 lbs. pickled or fresh light   1 cup ketchup
    meat turkey roast   1 cup apricot jam
1 onion, diced   2 Tbs. soy sauce
1 clove of garlic, minced

Place turkey in a roasting pan on top of diced onion and garlic. Mix ketchup, jam, and soy sauce. Brush roast with mixture. Bake in 325° oven, covered, for 1½ to 2 hours. Baste and rotate during baking. If using a thermometer, bake until temperature reaches 160°.

NUTRITIONAL INFORMATION PER SERVING:[*]		Serving Size: 7 oz. Total Servings: 10			
Calories	252	Sodium	588 mg	**PERCENT OF DAILY VALUE**	
Calories from fat	26	Carbohydrates	30 g	Vitamin A	3 %
Fat	3 g	Fiber	1 g	Vitamin C	7 %
Saturated Fat	1 g	Protein	26 g	Calcium	3 %
Cholesterol	59 mg			Iron	11 %

* Nutritional values based on light meat: turkey breast, no skin.

Sweet Chicken II

1 2½-lb. chicken, quartered
3 Tbs. apricot jam or
   marmalade

3 Tbs. Russian dressing
2 oz. (approx.) onion soup
   mix

Put chicken pieces into pan. Combine apricot jam or marmalade, Russian dressing, and soup mix. Spoon over chicken. Marinate for a few hours or overnight in refrigerator. Bake at 350° for 1 hour, basting chicken occasionally with the sauce.

NUTRITIONAL INFORMATION PER SERVING:		Serving Size: ¼ chicken Total Servings: 4			
Calories	533	Sodium	1526 mg	**PERCENT OF DAILY VALUE**	
Calories from fat	263	Carbohydrates	18 g	Vitamin A	43 %
Fat	29 g	Fiber	1 g	Vitamin C	7 %
Saturated Fat	7 g	Protein	47 g	Calcium	6 %
Cholesterol	183 mg			Iron	21 %

Apricot Duck
Compliments of Monsey Glatt, Monsey, NY

1 cup apricot preserves
3 Tbs. soy sauce
3 Tbs. mustard

3 Tbs. chopped garlic
1 medium-large duck
   (approx. 4 lb.)

Stir together preserves, soy sauce, mustard, and garlic. Brush duck with mixture. Roast covered for 2 hours at 350°. Uncover, baste, and continue baking uncovered for 30 minutes or until brown.

NUTRITIONAL INFORMATION PER SERVING:[*]		Serving Size: 6 oz. Total Servings: 8			
Calories	502	Sodium	534 mg	**PERCENT OF DAILY VALUE**	
Calories from fat	293	Carbohydrates	29 g	Vitamin A	8 %
Fat	33 g	Fiber	0 g	Calcium	3 %
Saturated Fat	11 g	Protein	22 g	Iron	24 %
Cholesterol	95 mg				

* Serving size is without bones.

Garlic Chicken

2 2½-lb. chickens, cut in
   quarters or eighths
3 Tbs. margarine
¼ cup oil
30 cloves of garlic (approx.
   4 bulbs), peeled

10 shallots, peeled and
   diced
⅔ cup white wine
1 tsp. salt, or to taste
pepper, to taste

In a large skillet, sauté chicken in margarine and oil (combined) until slightly browned. Add garlic and shallots and sauté for an additional 10 minutes. Add wine and seasonings and bring to a boil. Remove from skillet and transfer to an 11x16-inch roasting pan. Bake uncovered at 350° for 45 to 50 minutes.

NUTRITIONAL INFORMATION PER SERVING:		Serving Size: ¼ chicken Total Servings: 8			
Calories	584	Sodium	474 mg	PERCENT OF DAILY VALUE	
Calories from fat	337	Carbohydrates	2 g	Vitamin A	69 %
Fat	37 g	Fiber	0 g	Vitamin C	3 %
Saturated Fat	9 g	Protein	54 g	Calcium	4 %
Cholesterol	212 mg			Iron	23 %

Spicy Barbecued Chicken
Compliments of Monsey Glatt, Monsey, NY

1 small onion, diced
2 Tbs. oil
2 8-oz. cans tomato sauce
½ cup brown sugar
⅓ cup soy sauce

3 Tbs. ketchup
1 Tbs. prepared mustard
2 2½-lb. chickens, cut in
   quarters

In a saucepan, sauté onion in oil until tender. Stir in next 5 ingredients and simmer for 5 minutes. Cool sauce. Place chicken parts in large roasting pan. Pour sauce over chicken and marinate for 1 hour at room temperature, or overnight in refrigerator. Bake uncovered at 350° for 1 hour or until done. Baste frequently with sauce.

NUTRITIONAL INFORMATION PER SERVING:*		Serving Size: ¼ chicken Total Servings: 8			
Calories	517	Sodium	1232 mg	PERCENT OF DAILY VALUE	
Calories from fat	236	Carbohydrates	19 g	Vitamin A	47 %
Fat	26 g	Fiber	1 g	Vitamin C	18 %
Saturated Fat	7 g	Protein	48 g	Calcium	8 %
Cholesterol	182 mg			Iron	32 %

* Analysis includes sauce.

Chinese Chicken Cutlets

4 chicken cutlets (approx. 2 lbs.)
¼ cup oil for frying
1 20-oz. can pineapple chunks (drain and reserve juice)

½ cup ketchup
4 Tbs. brown sugar
4 Tbs. red cooking wine
1 8-oz. can mushrooms

Fry chicken cutlets in oil and place in a single layer in a 9x13-inch pan. Mix together pineapple juice, ketchup, brown sugar, and wine, and bring to a boil. Pour sauce over chicken, then pour pineapple chunks and mushrooms over all. Bake uncovered for 30 minutes, until liquid is absorbed.

NUTRITIONAL INFORMATION PER SERVING:*		Serving Size: 14 oz. Total Servings: 4			
Calories	663	Sodium	738 mg	PERCENT OF DAILY VALUE	
Calories from fat	264	Carbohydrates	38 g	Vitamin A	11 %
Fat	29 g	Fiber	2 g	Vitamin C	20 %
Saturated Fat	6 g	Protein	60 g	Calcium	8 %
Cholesterol	166 mg			Iron	23 %

* Serving size includes sauce.

Chinese Rice and Chicken

1 cup rice
2 cups boiling water
leftover Shabbos chicken
(approx. 1 lb.)

½ cup (approx.) chicken
soup
4 Tbs. soy sauce, or to taste

Add rice to boiling water and cook until fluffy. Cut up chicken into bite-size pieces and mix with rice. Moisten rice and chicken with soup. Add soy sauce until brown. Heat and serve.

NUTRITIONAL INFORMATION PER SERVING:				Serving Size: 8 oz. Total Servings: 4	
Calories	401	Sodium	1128 mg	**PERCENT OF DAILY VALUE**	
Calories from fat	78	Carbohydrates	40 g	Vitamin A	2 %
Fat	9 g	Fiber	0 g	Calcium	3 %
Saturated Fat	2 g	Protein	37 g	Iron	25 %
Cholesterol	101 mg				

Tangy Chicken

½ onion, diced
½ cup ketchup
⅓ cup oil
½ cup water
2 Tbs. sugar

1½ tsp. mustard
1½ tsp. salt
¼ tsp. pepper
1 2½-lb. chicken, quartered

Mix all ingredients together and pour over chicken. Bake uncovered at 375° for 1½ hours.

NUTRITIONAL INFORMATION PER SERVING:				Serving Size: ¼ chicken Total Servings: 4	
Calories	637	Sodium	1365 mg	**PERCENT OF DAILY VALUE**	
Calories from fat	368	Carbohydrates	20 g	Vitamin A	44 %
Fat	41 g	Fiber	1 g	Vitamin C	15 %
Saturated Fat	9 g	Protein	47 g	Calcium	6 %
Cholesterol	182 mg			Iron	21 %

Easy Shabbos Chicken

1 2½-lb. chicken, cut in
    quarters or eighths
½ tsp. garlic powder

1 tsp. LAWRY'S Seasoned
    Salt
½ cup cornflake crumbs

Place chicken in roasting pan. Sprinkle with garlic powder and seasoned salt. Pour cornflake crumbs over chicken. Cover and bake at 350° for about 1¾ hours.

NUTRITIONAL INFORMATION PER SERVING:		Serving Size: ¼ chicken Total Servings: 4			
Calories	425	Sodium	603 mg	PERCENT OF DAILY VALUE	
Calories from fat	203	Carbohydrates	6 g	Vitamin A	40 %
Fat	23 g	Fiber	0 g	Vitamin C	1 %
Saturated Fat	6 g	Protein	46 g	Calcium	3 %
Cholesterol	182 mg			Iron	25 %

Stuffing

4 cups leftover challah,
    cubed
2 onions, diced
1 cup celery, chopped
¼ cup oil

2 eggs
¼ tsp. pepper
1 tsp. salt
¼ tsp. garlic powder
½ tsp. paprika

Soak challah briefly in warm water. Squeeze out water. Sauté onions and celery in oil until golden brown. Mix challah, onions, celery, eggs, and spices well. Makes 4 cups of stuffing. Use to stuff veal or poultry.

NUTRITIONAL INFORMATION PER SERVING:		Serving Size: 2½ oz. Total Servings: 10			
Calories	174	Sodium	408 mg	PERCENT OF DAILY VALUE	
Calories from fat	80	Carbohydrates	20 g	Vitamin A	1 %
Fat	9 g	Fiber	1 g	Vitamin C	4 %
Saturated Fat	1 g	Protein	4 g	Calcium	2 %
Cholesterol	11 mg			Iron	13 %

Meat and Sauces

A Guide to Meats

Beef

BRISKET Use in potted dishes for stews, or bone and use for corned beef.

CHUCK Use for soups, stews, or braised dishes, or bone and roll for pot roast.

CHUCK STEAKS Use for potted, stewed, or braised dishes.

NECK OF BEEF Use for soups and stews. Bone and use for ground meat.

RIB CUTS Use for steaks.

SHOULDER OF BEEF Use for roasts. Slice thin for steaks or to stuff and roll.

Lamb

BREAST Cut up and use in stews, or use unboned for roasted or potted dishes.

NECK Use in stews.

SHANK Use in soups, bone for ground meat, or use unboned for pot roast or braised dishes.

SHOULDER CHOPS Broil, pan broil, or grill.

Veal

BREAST Cut up and use in stews, or use unboned for roasted or potted dishes.

RIB OR SHOULDER CHOPS Pan-fry.

FORESHANK For ground meat, or use unboned for pot roast or braised dishes.

SHOULDER Slice for cutlets or steaks. Use for pot roast or roast.

Meat and Sauces

Brisket

3½ lb. brisket	**garlic powder, to taste**
onion powder, to taste	**paprika, to taste**

Mix generous amounts of seasoning in a bowl. Add drops of water to form a paste. Place meat in a pan and rub on seasoning. Add some water to cover the bottom of the pan. Cover pan tightly with aluminum foil. Bake at 350° for 1½ to 2 hours. Open foil and test with a fork. If brisket is not tender, cover and continue cooking. Test periodically. When tender and fork goes in easily, remove foil and cook a little longer until meat is browned. Do not let water cook out. Add more water if necessary to make gravy.

NUTRITIONAL INFORMATION PER SERVING:				Serving Size: 5½ oz. Total Servings: 7	
Calories	536	Cholesterol	122 mg	**PERCENT OF DAILY VALUE**	
Calories from fat	424	Sodium	106 mg	Calcium	1 %
Fat	47 g	Protein	26 g	Iron	16 %
Saturated Fat	19 g				

Roast Veal in Duck Sauce

3 lb. rolled veal roast	**1 tsp. onion powder**
1 cup duck sauce	**¼ cup sweet red wine**
1 tsp. garlic powder	

Pierce veal roast all over with a fork. Mix together duck sauce, garlic and onion powders, and wine. Pour over veal roast. Marinate in refrigerator for several hours or overnight. Bake, covered, at 350° until meat is tender (about 1½ hours).

NUTRITIONAL INFORMATION PER SERVING:				Serving Size: 6 oz. Total Servings: 8	
Calories	310	Cholesterol	153 mg	**PERCENT OF DAILY VALUE**	
Calories from fat	105	Sodium	231 mg	Vitamin C	7 %
Fat	12 g	Carbohydrates	12 g	Calcium	4 %
Saturated Fat	5 g	Protein	36 g	Iron	11 %

Moussaka

1 large eggplant, sliced
   lengthwise
4 Tbs. oil, divided
2 large onions, chopped
4–5 garlic cloves, minced
1 lb. ground beef

2 tsp. salt, or to taste
pepper, to taste
paprika, to taste
1 15-oz. can tomato sauce
4 eggs
3 Tbs. flour

Brown eggplant in some oil. In a separate pan, sauté onions and all but 1 clove of garlic until soft, and add to ground beef. Add seasonings. Combine reserved garlic with tomato sauce. In a 9x13-inch pan, layer eggplant, meat, and tomato sauce, ending with eggplant. Bake uncovered for 1 hour at 350°. Beat together eggs and flour and spread on top of eggplant. Bake an additional 15 minutes or as needed.

NUTRITIONAL INFORMATION PER SERVING:				Serving Size: 8 oz. Total Servings: 6	
Calories	293	Sodium	1040 mg	**PERCENT OF DAILY VALUE**	
Calories from fat	141	Carbohydrates	14 g	Vitamin A	13 %
Fat	16 g	Fiber	1 g	Vitamin C	30 %
Saturated Fat	6 g	Protein	23 g	Calcium	7 %
Cholesterol	203 mg			Iron	34 %

French Roast Meat

4 lb. French roast, deckel, or
   brisket
ginger, to taste
4 Tbs. oil
4 cups boiling water
2 Tbs. onion soup mix
1 bay leaf
1 clove

Gravy:
1 Tbs. cornstarch
2 Tbs. cold water
a dash of black pepper or
   other spices (optional)

Rub ginger on all sides of meat. In a large skillet, heat oil. Brown meat on all sides. Remove from pan and place in a CROCK-POT. To drippings in frying pan, add water, soup mix, bay leaf, and clove. Boil until liquid is reduced by half and nicely thickened. Pour over meat in crock. Cover and cook on low, 8 to 10 hours. (I like to make this on Friday before Shabbos, then eat it for the second *seudah*.) If you cook it during the week, refrigerate the cooked meat until chilled, then slice. The juices may be used for (or as) gravy.

Gravy: Bring meat juices to a boil, then add a mixture of cornstarch, cold water, and spices. Simmer gently and stir constantly until thick.

NUTRITIONAL INFORMATION PER SERVING:		Serving Size: 7 oz. Total Servings: 7			
Calories	716	Cholesterol	147 mg	**PERCENT OF DAILY VALUE**	
Calories from fat	579	Sodium	127 mg	Calcium	1 %
Fat	64 g	Carbohydrates	1 g	Iron	19 %
Saturated Fat	24 g	Protein	31 g		

Beef Stew

3 carrots, sliced	2 cloves of garlic, sliced
3 celery stalks, sliced	2 pkgs. beef stew meat,
1 bunch kohlrabi, sliced (2	about 2 lbs. each
cups)	1 18-oz. can tomato juice
3 zucchini squash, sliced	⅓ cup water

Place all vegetables at the bottom of a 14x16-inch roasting pan. Spread beef stew meat evenly over the vegetables. Mix tomato juice and water, and pour over meat and vegetables. Cover pan with parchment paper and then aluminum foil. Bake in 325° oven for about 3½ to 4 hours or until meat is soft.

NUTRITIONAL INFORMATION PER SERVING:		Serving Size: 9 oz. Total Servings: 10			
Calories	517	Sodium	300 mg	**PERCENT OF DAILY VALUE**	
Calories from fat	350	Carbohydrates	7 g	Vitamin A	80 %
Fat	39 g	Fiber	2 g	Vitamin C	64 %
Saturated Fat	15 g	Protein	33 g	Calcium	4 %
Cholesterol	125 mg			Iron	25 %

Shepherd's Pie

1 large onion, diced	1 lb. chopped meat or
1 carrot, grated	turkey or a mixture of
1–2 tomatoes, chopped	both
1 clove garlic	1 Tbs. ketchup
1 stalk celery, diced	1 lb. potatoes, cooked
4 Tbs. oil for sautéing	½ tsp. paprika

Sauté onion, carrot, tomatoes, garlic, and celery in oil. Add chopped meat and ketchup, and stir to brown the meat. Place into a 9-inch round baking tin. Mash potatoes and place on top of meat and vegetable mixture. Sprinkle paprika on top. Bake, uncovered, at 350° for approximately 45 minutes until the potatoes are brown.

NUTRITIONAL INFORMATION PER SERVING:		Serving Size: 6 oz. Total Servings: 6	
Calories	318	Sodium 71 mg	**PERCENT OF DAILY VALUE**
Calories from fat	193	Carbohydrates 12 g	Vitamin A 47 %
Fat	21 g	Fiber 2 g	Vitamin C 31 %
Saturated Fat	6 g	Protein 18 g	Calcium 3 %
Cholesterol	61 mg		Iron 21 %

Stuffed Cabbage

1 large head of cabbage	2 eggs, beaten
1 14-oz. bottle of ketchup	2 tsp. salt, or to taste
1 16-oz. can jellied	pepper, garlic powder, to
cranberry sauce	taste
14 oz. water	½ cup rice, uncooked
2 lbs. chopped meat	(optional)

Cabbage: Freeze cabbage overnight and defrost thoroughly. Remove core. Carefully take leaves off cabbage and lay them flat on a table, on paper towels. (Freezing cabbage enables easy removal of leaves after defrosting.)

Sauce: Mix ketchup, cranberry sauce, and water in pot over low flame.

Meat: Combine chopped meat with eggs, and season to taste. Add rice (optional) and mix together.

Put some meat in the middle of each cabbage leaf. Fold right and left sides over meat, and then roll up tightly. Insert wooden toothpick to hold closed. Place rolled cabbage into sauce, bring to a boil, then lower flame and simmer in a covered pot for 2 hours.

NUTRITIONAL INFORMATION PER SERVING:		Serving Size: 8½ oz. Total Servings: 14		
Calories	395	Sodium	404 mg	**PERCENT OF DAILY VALUE**
Calories from fat	225	Carbohydrates	25 g	Vitamin A 1 %
Fat	25 g	Fiber	3 g	Vitamin C 82 %
Saturated Fat	10 g	Protein	18 g	Calcium 6 %
Cholesterol	79 mg			Iron 15 %

Sweet and Saucy Corned Beef

1 3½-lb. corned beef
1 12-oz. jar apricot
   preserves

1 20-oz. can pineapple
   chunks

Put corned beef in a large pot. Fill pot with water until meat is covered and bring to a boil. Pour off the water and refill the pot. Boil and cook for 1 hour. Remove corned beef and put it in a baking pan. Drain can of pineapple chunks and reserve juice. Mix juice with apricot preserves and pour over meat. Cover and bake at 350° for 1½ to 2 hours, depending on size of meat. Add pineapple chunks for the last 15 minutes of baking.

NUTRITIONAL INFORMATION PER SERVING:*		Serving Size: 9 oz. Total Servings: 7		
Calories	490	Sodium	1840 mg	**PERCENT OF DAILY VALUE**
Calories from fat	277	Carbohydrates	23 g	Vitamin A 13 %
Fat	31 g	Fiber	2 g	Vitamin C 51 %
Saturated Fat	10 g	Protein	30 g	Calcium 3 %
Cholesterol	158 mg			Iron 26 %

* Serving size includes sauce.

Marinated Veal Chops

6 veal chops (approx. 3 lbs.)   2 Tbs. ketchup
5 Tbs. soy sauce   ½ cup brown sugar
2 cloves garlic   ½ cup water

Arrange veal chops in a single layer in a large oven-proof glass dish. Mix together all of the remaining ingredients in food processor or blender. Pour over veal chops. Marinate in refrigerator for 1 hour. Bake, covered, at 350° until meat is tender (about 45 minutes to 1 hour).

NUTRITIONAL INFORMATION PER SERVING:				Serving Size: 7 oz. Total Servings: 6	
Calories	455	Cholesterol	214 mg	**PERCENT OF DAILY VALUE**	
Calories from fat	155	Sodium	885 mg	Calcium	9 %
Fat	17 g	Carbohydrates	17 g	Iron	20 %
Saturated Fat	6 g	Protein	55 g		

Grandma's Lamb

1 lamb shank per person   salt, pepper, and garlic
1 28-oz. can crushed or   powder to taste
   whole tomatoes

Brown (sear) meat in a pot. Add tomatoes and season to taste. Cover pot and let cook for 2 hours on medium heat, until tender. Serve over white rice.

NUTRITIONAL INFORMATION PER SERVING:[*]				Serving Size: 12 oz. Total Servings: 4	
Calories	574	Sodium	358 mg	**PERCENT OF DAILY VALUE**	
Calories from fat	276	Carbohydrates	5 g	Vitamin A	9 %
Fat	31 g	Fiber	1 g	Vitamin C	19 %
Saturated Fat	13 g	Protein	65 g	Calcium	9 %
Cholesterol	240 mg			Iron	37 %

* Serving size includes the bone.

Meat Loaf

2 lbs. lean ground beef
2 cups instant oats
1 egg
¼ tsp. pepper

1 Tbs. onion powder
½ Tbs. garlic powder
1 tsp. paprika
1 8-oz. can tomato sauce

Preheat oven to 350°. Combine all ingredients and mix well. Press into a loaf pan and bake for 1 hour.

NUTRITIONAL INFORMATION PER SERVING:				Serving Size: 4 oz. Total Servings: 8	
Calories	275	Sodium	228 mg	**PERCENT OF DAILY VALUE**	
Calories from fat	127	Carbohydrates	15 g	Vitamin A	5 %
Fat	14 g	Fiber	1 g	Vitamin C	7 %
Saturated Fat	5 g	Protein	21 g	Calcium	2 %
Cholesterol	88 mg			Iron	19 %

Sweet and Sour Corned Beef

1 3½-lb. corned beef
1 Tbs. mustard
5 tsp. ketchup
1 cup brown sugar

1 Tbs. cider vinegar
1 20-oz. can pineapple
   chunks with half of the
   juice

Place corned beef in an 8-quart pot with enough water to cover. Cook until soft, 1½ to 2 hours, testing with a fork to see if meat is tender. Slice beef and transfer to a baking pan. Combine remaining ingredients and pour over meat. Bake, uncovered, at 350° for 30 minutes.

NUTRITIONAL INFORMATION PER SERVING:*				Serving Size: 6 oz. Total Servings: 10	
Calories	373	Sodium	1325 mg	**PERCENT OF DAILY VALUE**	
Calories from fat	194	Carbohydrates	23 g	Vitamin C	38 %
Fat	22 g	Protein	21 g	Calcium	3 %
Saturated Fat	7 g			Iron	17 %
Cholesterol	111 mg				

* Serving size includes sauce.

Fricassee

2 carrots, diced
3 stalks celery, diced
4 garlic cloves, minced
1 onion, diced
2 tomatoes, diced
2 zucchini, diced
3 lbs. ground beef

2 eggs, beaten
¾ cup oatmeal
⅓ cup water
onion powder, to taste
 (optional)
garlic powder, to taste
 (optional)

In a 6-quart heavy pot, combine vegetables. Add enough water to pot to cover vegetables and simmer slowly for about 10 minutes. Combine ground beef, eggs, oatmeal, and water (and onion powder and garlic powder, if using). Mix until smooth. Form small meatballs and place in pot over vegetables. A little water may have to be added to reach level of meatballs. Let simmer for about 2½ hours. Move pot back and forth occasionally to prevent vegetables from sticking to bottom of pot.

NUTRITIONAL INFORMATION PER SERVING:		Serving Size: 9 oz. Total Servings: 8		
Calories	514	Sodium	138 mg	**PERCENT OF DAILY VALUE**
Calories from fat	355	Carbohydrates	11 g	Vitamin A 102 %
Fat	39 g	Fiber	2 g	Vitamin C 19 %
Saturated Fat	16 g	Protein	27 g	Calcium 5 %
Cholesterol	173 mg			Iron 25 %

Tongue Polonaise
Compliments of Sabel's Catering, Monsey, NY

Tongue:
2 lb. pickled tongue
2 large onions, sliced
½ cup pickling spice

Sauce:
2 qts. water

½ of a 40-oz. bottle of
 ketchup
½ cup brown sugar, or to
 taste
½ cup raisins
2 Tbs. cornstarch

Place tongue in an 8-quart pot, cover with water, and add onion and pickling spice. Cook for 2 hours over medium to low flame. Remove tongue from pot, let cool, then slice.

Sauce: Put water, ketchup, brown sugar, and raisins in a pot and bring to a boil. Lower fire and simmer for 15 minutes. Stir a little cold water into the cornstarch and add to mixture. Continue to cook for 2 more minutes.

Serving suggestion: Place slices of tongue and sauce over a serving of noodle kugel or mashed potatoes.

NUTRITIONAL INFORMATION PER SERVING:				Serving Size: 6 oz. Total Servings: 10	
Calories	325	Sodium	602 mg	**PERCENT OF DAILY VALUE**	
Calories from fat	125	Carbohydrates	35 g	Vitamin A	3 %
Fat	14 g	Fiber	1 g	Vitamin C	13 %
Saturated Fat	7 g	Protein	15 g	Calcium	5 %
Cholesterol	64 mg			Iron	22 %

Veal Spareribs

Compliments of Monsey Glatt, Monsey, NY

3 lbs. beef or veal spareribs
1 20-oz. jar Gold's Saucy
    Rib Sauce
1 15-oz. jar regular style
    barbecue sauce

¼ cup soy sauce
3 Tbs. ketchup
dash of hot pepper sauce
    (optional)

Arrange spareribs in one layer in a large oven-safe glass dish. Mix together remaining ingredients and pour over ribs. Marinate overnight in refrigerator. Bake, uncovered, at 325° for 2 hours or until very tender, basting frequently with sauce.

NUTRITIONAL INFORMATION PER SERVING:				Serving Size: 9 oz. Total Servings: 7	
Calories	445	Sodium	1492 mg	**PERCENT OF DAILY VALUE**	
Calories from fat	180	Carbohydrates	13 g	Vitamin A	12 %
Fat	20 g	Fiber	1 g	Vitamin C	12 %
Saturated Fat	7 g	Protein	50 g	Calcium	6 %
Cholesterol	202 mg			Iron	20 %

6 small minute steaks
2 Tbs. + 4 Tbs. oil
1 large onion, diced

2 4-oz. cans mushrooms
onion soup mix, to taste

Brown steaks in 2 Tbs. oil. In a separate pan, sauté onions and mushrooms in 4 Tbs. oil. Sprinkle some onion soup mix on each steak. Top each steak with onions and mushrooms. Place steaks in a 9x13-inch baking pan with ¼ inch water. Cover. Bake at 350° for 1½ to 2 hours.

NUTRITIONAL INFORMATION PER SERVING:				Serving Size: 8 oz. Total Servings: 6	
Calories	612	Sodium	231 mg	**PERCENT OF DAILY VALUE**	
Calories from fat	400	Carbohydrates	3 g	Vitamin A	20 %
Fat	44 g	Fiber	1 g	Vitamin C	12 %
Saturated Fat	15 g	Protein	48 g	Calcium	4 %
Cholesterol	153 mg			Iron	37 %

1 tongue, pickled (3 lb.)

Wash tongue well. Fill pot with water and place tongue in pot. Let boil 1 hour. Pour out water and refill pot. Boil again for about 2 hours or until tender. Let cold water run over tongue and peel off skin. Cool tongue and slice. Serve with sauce (suggested recipes follow).

NUTRITIONAL INFORMATION PER SERVING:				Serving Size: 5 oz. Total Servings: 8	
Calories	402	Sodium	85 mg	**PERCENT OF DAILY VALUE**	
Calories from fat	264	Carbohydrates	0 g	Vitamin C	1 %
Fat	29 g	Fiber	0 g	Calcium	1 %
Saturated Fat	13 g	Protein	31 g	Iron	32 %
Cholesterol	152 mg				

Tangy Tongue Sauce

2 cups brown sugar
4 Tbs. flour
1 tsp. salt
2 cups cold water

1 cup orange juice
12 Tbs. lemon juice
½ cup raisins

Mix first 4 ingredients and bring to a boil. Add orange juice, lemon juice, and raisins. Cook for 20 minutes over low to medium heat.

NUTRITIONAL INFORMATION PER SERVING:				Serving Size: 4 Tbs. Total Servings: 15	
Calories	121	Sodium	153 mg	**PERCENT OF DAILY VALUE**	
Calories from fat	1	Carbohydrates	31 g	Vitamin C	16 %
Fat	0 g	Fiber	1 g	Calcium	3 %
Saturated Fat	0 g	Protein	1 g	Iron	5 %
Cholesterol	0 mg				

Mustard Tongue Sauce

½ cup brown sugar
½ tsp. dry mustard
½ Tbs. flour

½ cup raisins
¼ cup vinegar
1¾ cups water

Combine dry ingredients. Add liquid ingredients and cook for 20 minutes over medium to low heat.

NUTRITIONAL INFORMATION PER SERVING:				Serving Size: 2 Tbs. Total Servings: 8	
Calories	74	Sodium	5 mg	**PERCENT OF DAILY VALUE**	
Calories from fat	3	Carbohydrates	18 g	Calcium	2 %
Fat	0 g	Fiber	1 g	Iron	3 %
Saturated Fat	0 g	Protein	1 g		
Cholesterol	0 mg				

Meat Lasagna

1 lb. ground beef	2 tsp. salt
¾ cup chopped onions	1 tsp. sugar
2 Tbs. oil	1 tsp garlic powder
1 16-oz. can tomatoes	½ tsp. pepper
2 6-oz. cans tomato paste	½ tsp. oregano
2 cups water	8 oz. lasagna noodles

Brown beef and onions in oil. Add tomatoes, tomato paste, water, salt, sugar, garlic powder, pepper, and oregano. Simmer, uncovered, for 30 minutes, stirring occasionally. Meanwhile, cook lasagna noodles as directed on package and drain. Spread 1 cup of beef mixture in a greased 9x13-inch pan. Alternate noodles and beef mixture, ending with beef mixture. Bake at 350° for 40 to 50 minutes.

NUTRITIONAL INFORMATION PER SERVING:				Serving Size: 7 oz. Total Servings: 8	
Calories	331	Sodium	1003 mg	**PERCENT OF DAILY VALUE**	
Calories from fat	122	Carbohydrates	35 g	Vitamin A	17 %
Fat	14 g	Fiber	3 g	Vitamin C	48 %
Saturated Fat	4 g	Protein	18 g	Calcium	6 %
Cholesterol	46 mg			Iron	34 %

Sweetbreads

2 lbs. beef sweetbreads	paprika, to taste
1 Tbs. vinegar	garlic powder, to taste
1 Tbs. salt	1 large tomato, diced
1 onion, diced	½ cup water
2–3 stalks celery, diced	2 Tbs. cornstarch or flour
1 6-oz. can sliced	½ 10½-oz. can mushroom
mushrooms	soup
salt, to taste	¾ cup frozen peas
pepper, to taste	

Boil sweetbreads, vinegar, and salt together in 2 quarts water for about 20 minutes. Save ¾ cup water and pour out the rest. Put sweetbreads in cold water, separate, cut, and peel off skin. In a separate pot, stew onion, celery, and mushrooms with salt, pepper, paprika, and garlic powder in the reserved ¾ cup water for about 15 minutes. Add cut up sweetbreads and water, and cook for 30 to 35 minutes over medium heat. Taste for seasoning. In the last 10 minutes add tomato. Mix water and cornstarch and stir until thick. Add to mixture along with mushroom soup. Before serving, add the frozen peas.

NUTRITIONAL INFORMATION PER SERVING:		Serving Size: 4½ oz. Total Servings: 12		
Calories	214	Sodium	365 mg	**PERCENT OF DAILY VALUE**
Calories from fat	132	Carbohydrates	6 g	Vitamin A	3 %
Fat	15 g	Fiber	1 g	Vitamin C	39 %
Saturated Fat	0 g	Protein	14 g	Calcium	2 %
Cholesterol	167 mg			Iron	12 %

Meatballs and Noodles

1 16-oz. pkg. noodles or
    spaghetti
½ cup boiling water
2 Tbs. mayonnaise

1 lb. ground meat
2 18-oz. cans tomato juice
2 Tbs. sugar

Cook noodles or spaghetti and set aside. Mix boiling water and mayonnaise into ground meat. Add 2 tablespoons of the tomato juice to mixture. Mix well. Form small to medium-size balls. In a skillet, bring to a boil remaining tomato juice with sugar. Add meatballs, cover, and cook on a medium-low flame for about 30 minutes. Remove cover and raise flame slightly. Allow all tomato juice to cook into meatballs so that each one is covered by the sauce. Turn off flame. Carefully add noodles or spaghetti into skillet, making sure they are covered with the sauce.

NUTRITIONAL INFORMATION PER SERVING:		Serving Size: 13 oz. Total Servings: 5		
Calories	644	Sodium	825 mg	**PERCENT OF DAILY VALUE**
Calories from fat	185	Carbohydrates	81 g	Vitamin A	14 %
Fat	21 g	Fiber	5 g	Vitamin C	62 %
Saturated Fat	7 g	Protein	33 g	Calcium	5 %
Cholesterol	77 mg			Iron	50 %

Cranberry Sweet and Sour Meatballs

2 lbs. ground beef (or
　chicken or turkey)
2 eggs, beaten
1 cup cooked rice
½ cup bread crumbs
1 pkg. onion soup mix
¼ cup sugar

Sauce:
1 16-oz. can jellied
　cranberry sauce
1½ cups ketchup
½ cup brown sugar
3 tsp. lemon juice

In a large bowl, combine all meatball ingredients. Mix well and roll into
1-inch balls.

Sauce: In a large saucepan, combine cranberry sauce, ketchup,
brown sugar, and lemon juice. Cook over low flame, 25 to 30
minutes. Stir often. Add meatballs and simmer for 1 hour. Yields 4
dozen meatballs.

NUTRITIONAL INFORMATION PER SERVING:				Serving Size: 7 oz. Total Servings: 10	
Calories	459	Sodium	477 mg	**PERCENT OF DAILY VALUE**	
Calories from fat	145	Carbohydrates	56 g	Vitamin A	4 %
Fat	16 g	Fiber	1 g	Vitamin C	10 %
Saturated Fat	6 g	Protein	23 g	Calcium	4 %
Cholesterol	116 g			Iron	22 %

Glazed Corned Beef

any cut of pickled beef
　(3½ lb.)
2 whole onions, peeled
cloves
2 stalks celery
2 carrots
1 tsp. vinegar
2 to 3 cloves garlic
1 tsp. parsley

1 tsp. rosemary
1 tsp. thyme
4–5 peppercorns

Glaze:
1 Tbs. mustard
5 Tbs. ketchup
2 Tbs. vinegar
½ cup brown sugar

Place meat in an 8-quart pot with enough water to cover. Boil for 1
hour. Change water and boil again. Press cloves into onions, covering

sparsely. Add to meat along with remaining ingredients, except for glaze ingredients. Boil for a minimum of 1 hour or more, according to size of the meat. When cooled, put meat onto a large piece of aluminum foil. Reserve some liquid from pot and add to meat. Combine glaze ingredients together and pour onto meat. Bake in sealed foil for a minimum of 30 minutes at 350°. Test with a fork to see if meat is tender. Slice; serve hot or cold.

NUTRITIONAL INFORMATION PER SERVING:*		Serving Size: 6 oz. Total Servings: 7			
Calories	458	Sodium	1887 mg	**PERCENT OF DAILY VALUE**	
Calories from fat	276	Carbohydrates	14 g	Vitamin C	44 %
Fat	31 g	Fiber	0 g	Calcium	3 %
Saturated Fat	10 g	Protein	29 g	Iron	22 %
Cholesterol	158 mg				

* Serving size includes sauce.

Pot Roast

1 stalk celery	¾ cup red wine
1 onion	½ cup chopped tomato
3 cloves garlic	½ cup water
3 Tbs. oil	1 bay leaf
4 lb. brisket	1 tsp. salt
3 carrots, sliced	¼ tsp. pepper

Dice celery, onion, and garlic. Sauté in oil until soft. Add meat and brown on all sides. Add remaining ingredients. Cover and simmer 2½ to 3 hours until tender. Cool and slice meat. To serve, warm sliced beef in gravy.

NUTRITIONAL INFORMATION PER SERVING:*		Serving Size: 9 oz. Total Servings: 8			
Calories	650	Sodium	409 mg	**PERCENT OF DAILY VALUE**	
Calories from fat	492	Carbohydrates	6 g	Vitamin A	96 %
Fat	55 g	Fiber	1 g	Vitamin C	12 %
Saturated Fat	21 g	Protein	28 g	Calcium	4 %
Cholesterol	129 mg			Iron	26 %

* Serving size includes sauce.

Shoulder Steak Bake

Compliments of Monsey Glatt, Monsey, NY

4 shoulder steaks (approx. 2½ lb.)
1 pkg. onion soup mix
½ tsp. garlic powder
3 Tbs. honey

3 Tbs. orange juice
3 Tbs. soy sauce
1 Tbs. cider vinegar
¼ tsp. each: ginger and chili powder

Place meat in a single layer in a large oven-proof glass dish. Mix together all of the remaining ingredients. Pour over meat. Bake, covered, at 350° for 1½ to 2 hours or until tender.

NUTRITIONAL INFORMATION PER SERVING:				Serving Size: 8 oz. Total Servings: 4	
Calories	622	Sodium	891 mg	**PERCENT OF DAILY VALUE**	
Calories from fat	374	Carbohydrates	11 g	Vitamin C	7 %
Fat	42 g	Fiber	0 g	Calcium	7 %
Saturated Fat	17 g	Protein	48 g	Iron	32 %
Cholesterol	143 mg				

Cholent

½ cup baby lima beans
½ cup kidney beans
½ cup barley
3 Tbs. oil
1 onion, sliced
3 potatoes
2 sweet potatoes
honey, to taste
2 lbs. beef stew meat or flanken

ketchup, to taste
½ Tbs. salt, or to taste
pepper, to taste
garlic powder, to taste
onion powder, to taste
paprika, to taste
MRS. DASH Table Blend

Soak beans and barley in water for 30 minutes. On the bottom of a CROCK-POT, pour oil and line with onion slices. Peel and cut potatoes and add to CROCK-POT. Pour a small amount of honey over potatoes.

Drain beans and barley and add to pot. Next, place meat in pot and pour a few drops of ketchup onto the meat. Add salt, pepper, garlic powder, onion powder, paprika, and MRS. DASH Table Blend. Add water to cover. Cook on high for 1 hour and then switch to low.

Variation: Put some peeled, hard-boiled eggs in CROCK-POT with cholent.

NUTRITIONAL INFORMATION PER SERVING:				Serving Size: 6 oz. Total Servings: 10		
Calories	338	Sodium	401 mg	**PERCENT OF DAILY VALUE**		
Calories from fat	130	Carbohydrates	27 g	Vitamin C		13 %
Fat	14 g	Fiber	4 g	Calcium		4 %
Saturated Fat	5 g	Protein	25 g	Iron		30 %
Cholesterol	50 mg					

Teriyaki Chuck Roast
Compliments of Monsey Glatt, Monsey, NY

4 lb. boneless chuck roast
1 tsp. garlic powder
½ cup oil
½ cup orange juice
½ cup cooking sherry

¼ cup soy sauce
1 Tbs. brown sugar
½ tsp. ginger
1 large onion, sliced

Place roast in a large oven-proof glass pan. Pierce meat all over with a fork. Combine garlic powder, oil, orange juice, sherry, soy sauce, brown sugar, and ginger. Pour over meat and marinate overnight, covered, in refrigerator, turning meat once. Drain most of marinade from meat, leaving about ½ cup in pan. Add sliced onion to pan. Cover tightly and bake at 325° for 2½ to 3 hours or until very tender. Cool for easier slicing, then reheat to serve.

NUTRITIONAL INFORMATION PER SERVING:				Serving Size: 5½ oz. Total Servings: 15		
Calories	382	Sodium	348 mg	**PERCENT OF DAILY VALUE**		
Calories from fat	265	Carbohydrates	4 g	Vitamin C		7 %
Fat	29 g	Fiber	0 g	Calcium		2 %
Saturated Fat	10 g	Protein	23 g	Iron		22 %
Cholesterol	82 mg					

5 medium potatoes	1 lb. chopped meat
2 medium carrots	1 egg
1 onion, chopped	½ cup matzah meal
3 Tbs. oil	1 Tbs. oil
2 tsp. salt, or to taste	

Peel potatoes and dice. Peel carrots and grate. Sauté onions in 3 Tbs. oil in a 3-quart saucepan and add vegetables. Stir. Add water to cover and some salt, and cook for approximately 10 minutes on a medium flame. Combine chopped meat, egg, matzah meal, some salt, and 1 Tbs. oil, and mix well. Form into balls. When vegetables are cooked, add meatballs to pot and cook an additional 30 minutes over medium-low flame.

NUTRITIONAL INFORMATION PER SERVING:				Serving Size: 10 oz. Total Servings: 5	
Calories	400	Sodium	910 mg	**PERCENT OF DAILY VALUE**	
Calories from fat	176	Carbohydrates	38 g	Vitamin A	57 %
Fat	20 g	Fiber	4 g	Vitamin C	47 %
Saturated Fat	6 g	Protein	17 g	Calcium	4 %
Cholesterol	84 mg			Iron	25 %

1 onion, quartered	2 Tbs. sugar
2–3 green peppers, in strips	1 pkg. onion soup mix
Oil for frying	1 cup water
2 lbs. pepper steak or flank steak	1 tsp. soy sauce (optional)
Garlic powder	1 4-oz. can mushrooms or
2 Tbs. flour	4 oz. fresh mushrooms

In a large skillet, brown onion and pepper in oil. Add meat, sliced into thin strips and seasoned with garlic. Separately, mix flour and sugar.

Then add soup mix and water to this mixture. Soy sauce may be added too. Pour over meat and cook over low heat for 1¼ hours or until meat is tender. Add mushrooms 30 minutes before end of cooking time. Serve over bed of rice.

NUTRITIONAL INFORMATION PER SERVING:				Serving Size: 15 oz. Total Servings: 4	
Calories	633	Sodium	1208 mg	**PERCENT OF DAILY VALUE**	
Calories from fat	283	Carbohydrates	24 g	Vitamin A	8 %
Fat	31 g	Fiber	3 g	Vitamin C	174 %
Saturated Fat	9 g	Protein	62 g	Calcium	5 %
Cholesterol	99 mg			Iron	53 %

Sweet and Sour Meatballs

1 15-oz. can tomato sauce
⅔ cup water
¾ cup brown sugar
2 Tbs. lemon juice
½ cup ketchup
2 lbs. ground meat
2 eggs, beaten

2 tsp. salt, or to taste
pepper, to taste
½ cup water
½ cup matzah meal
onion powder or grated
   onion, to taste

In a 3-quart saucepan, combine first 5 ingredients for sauce. Bring to a boil and simmer for 10 to 15 minutes. Mix together remaining ingredients, form meatballs, and add to sauce. Cover and cook on low heat for 1½ hours, stirring occasionally to keep sauce from sticking. Serve over rice or noodles as a main dish or just with its own sauce as a *Yom Tov* appetizer.

NUTRITIONAL INFORMATION PER SERVING:				Serving Size: 7 oz. Total Servings: 8	
Calories	416	Sodium	1087 mg	**PERCENT OF DAILY VALUE**	
Calories from fat	178	Carbohydrates	31 g	Vitamin A	11 %
Fat	20 g	Fiber	1 g	Vitamin C	18 %
Saturated Fat	8 g	Protein	28 g	Calcium	5 %
Cholesterol	145 mg			Iron	26 %

Tenderized Shoulder Roast

1 pkg. onion soup mix
3 lb. shoulder roast

1 16-oz. can jellied
cranberry sauce

Line bottom of a pan with half of the onion soup mix and then place roast in pan. Pour cranberry sauce and remaining soup mix on top of roast. Bake, covered, at 300° for 2½ hours. Slice roast into thin slices and bake, covered, for another hour.

NUTRITIONAL INFORMATION PER SERVING:				Serving Size: 7.0 oz. Total Servings: 7	
Calories	572	Sodium	139 mg	**PERCENT OF DAILY VALUE**	
Calories from fat	354	Carbohydrates	16 g	Vitamin C	2 %
Fat	39 g	Fiber	1 g	Calcium	1 %
Saturated Fat	16 g	Protein	37 g	Iron	25 %
Cholesterol	134 mg				

Unstuffed Cabbage

1 lb. ground beef
½ cup uncooked rice
1 12-oz. cabbage, shredded

1 16-oz. can whole-berry
cranberry sauce
1 14-oz. jar spaghetti sauce

Mix meat and rice and form meatballs. Line a 9x13-inch pan with cabbage and top with meatballs and a mixture of the cranberry sauce and spaghetti sauce. Bake, covered, at 350° for 45 minutes.

NUTRITIONAL INFORMATION PER SERVING:				Serving Size: 10 oz. Total Servings: 6	
Calories	458	Sodium	763 mg	**PERCENT OF DAILY VALUE**	
Calories from fat	176	Carbohydrates	57 g	Vitamin A	9 %
Fat	20 g	Fiber	2 g	Vitamin C	67 %
Saturated Fat	7 g	Protein	14 g	Calcium	6 %
Cholesterol	56 mg			Iron	21 %

In a Lighter Vein…

Vegetables, Tofu, Rice, and Pasta

Vegetables, Tofu, Rice, and Pasta

Parve Cholent

1 large onion, diced
1½ Tbs. sesame or
    vegetable oil
1 cup pinto beans
1 cup kidney beans
1 cup large lima beans
1 cup adzuki beans
1 cup barley
1 Tbs. salt, or to taste
2 tsp. garlic powder, or to
    taste

Optional:
2 carrots, peeled and diced
2 parsnips or potatoes,
    peeled and diced
2 strips kombu (a sea
    vegetable, available at
    health food stores)

Sauté onion in oil in an 8-quart pot. Add water to fill up ¾ of pot. Add beans, barley, and seasonings. Carrots, parsnips or potatoes, and kombu may also be added. Cook for 1¼ to 1½ hours on medium flame.

Note: Kombu is a rich source of minerals and vitamins. To prepare kombu, soak it in cold water (do not rinse under faucet) for about 10 to 15 minutes until it softens. Remove from water and run through your fingers to check for any bugs. Slice on a cutting board as you would any other vegetable.

NUTRITIONAL INFORMATION PER SERVING:		Serving Size: 7 oz. Total Servings: 12			
Calories	315	Sodium	591 mg	**PERCENT OF DAILY VALUE**	
Calories from fat	40	Carbohydrates	55 g	Vitamin A	42 %
Fat	4 g	Fiber	10 g	Vitamin C	14 %
Saturated Fat	1 g	Protein	15 g	Calcium	12 %
Cholesterol	0 mg			Iron	32 %

Butternut Squash Stew

1 large onion, chopped
1½ tsp. oil for sautéing
½ of a large butternut
    squash

2 large parsnips
3 carrots
1 tsp. arrowroot flour and
    cold water (optional)

Sauté onion in oil. Peel and cut up squash into chunks. Peel parsnips and carrots, and cut into ½-inch pieces. Fill frying pan with water, a quarter full, and add onion, squash, parsnip, and carrots. Cook, covered, on medium flame for 30 minutes. (Optional: Towards end of cooking, mix flour with some cold water and stir into stew to thicken it.) Serve over rice.

Variation: Zucchini squash can be substituted for parsnips, carrots, and onion.

NUTRITIONAL INFORMATION PER SERVING:		Serving Size: 6 oz. Total Servings: 5		
Calories	104	Sodium	24 mg	**PERCENT OF DAILY VALUE**
Calories from fat	15	Carbohydrates	22 g	Vitamin A	201 %
Fat	2 g	Fiber	5 g	Vitamin C	33 %
Saturated Fat	0 g	Protein	2 g	Calcium	7 %
Cholesterol	0 mg			Iron	12 %

Marduma

2 medium onions, diced or
    sliced into thin strips
2 Tbs. oil for sautéing
2 medium green peppers,
    diced or sliced into thin
    strips
1 16-oz. can tomato sauce
1 Tbs. vinegar

½ tsp. salt, or to taste
generous sprinkling of red
    pepper
light sprinkling of garlic
    powder

Sauté onions in oil. Add green peppers; stir and sauté until tender. Add tomato sauce, vinegar, salt, red pepper, and garlic powder.

Simmer, covered, over a low flame for 10 minutes, stirring occasionally. Delicious hot as a side dish, or cold, served as a spread on bread or challah. Great for *shalosh seudos.*

NUTRITIONAL INFORMATION PER SERVING:				Serving Size: 4 oz. Total Servings: 8	
Calories	69	Sodium	491 mg	**PERCENT OF DAILY VALUE**	
Calories from fat	32	Carbohydrates	8 g	Vitamin A	9 %
Fat	4 g	Fiber	2 g	Vitamin C	60 %
Saturated Fat	0 g	Protein	1 g	Calcium	2 %
Cholesterol	0 mg			Iron	13 %

Cauliflower Antipasto

⅓ cup oil
6 cloves of garlic, or to taste
2 heads cauliflower, cut in florets
4 carrots, sliced
4 stalks celery, cut in ½-inch strips

2 red peppers, cut in ½-inch strips
2 green peppers, cut in ½-inch strips
⅓ cup vinegar (wine or apple cider)
1 cup olives

Heat oil. Add vegetables in the following order, sautéing each kind for 2 minutes before adding the next vegetable: garlic, cauliflower, carrots, celery, and peppers. Then add vinegar and olives. Cover pot and cook for 2 minutes. Remove vegetables and liquid from pot and let marinate overnight in refrigerator (if they last that long!).

NUTRITIONAL INFORMATION PER SERVING:				Serving Size: 6 oz. Total Servings: 20	
Calories	70	Sodium	218 mg	**PERCENT OF DAILY VALUE**	
Calories from fat	43	Carbohydrates	6 g	Vitamin A	53 %
Fat	5 g	Fiber	4 g	Vitamin C	136 %
Saturated Fat	1 g	Protein	2 g	Calcium	4 %
Cholesterol	0 mg			Iron	4 %

Sweet Potato à la Pineapple

3 16-oz. cans sweet potato
   or 7 large, freshly cooked
   sweet potatoes
3 Tbs. margarine, melted
2 tsp. vanilla sugar

1 tsp. cinnamon
¼ cup brown sugar
1 20-oz. can pineapple
   slices, drained
1 jar maraschino cherries

Mash sweet potatoes. Add margarine, vanilla sugar, cinnamon, and brown sugar. Mix well. Place pineapple slices on a greased pan. Place a scoop of mashed sweet potato mixture on each slice. Put a cherry on top of each scoop of sweet potato. Bake at 350° until warmed and slightly browned. Extra sweet potato can be eaten plain or baked in individual pie crusts.

NUTRITIONAL INFORMATION PER SERVING:				Serving Size: 7 oz. Total Servings: 8	
Calories	210	Sodium	63 mg	**PERCENT OF DAILY VALUE**	
Calories from fat	40	Carbohydrates	42 g	Vitamin A	279 %
Fat	4 g	Fiber	4 g	Vitamin C	49 %
Saturated Fat	1 g	Protein	2 g	Calcium	6 %
Cholesterol	0 mg			Iron	7 %

Spicy Roasted Potatoes

½ cup olive oil
½ tsp. garlic powder
½ tsp. onion powder

½ tsp. paprika
2 16-oz. cans whole
   potatoes

Combine oil, garlic powder, onion powder, and paprika to make a paste. Roll potatoes in paste, covering all sides. Bake, uncovered, at 350° for 1 hour.

NUTRITIONAL INFORMATION PER SERVING:				Serving Size: 5 oz. Total Servings: 6	
Calories	240	Sodium	344 mg	**PERCENT OF DAILY VALUE**	
Calories from fat	165	Carbohydrates	18 g	Vitamin A	1 %
Fat	18 g	Fiber	3 g	Vitamin C	11 %
Saturated Fat	3 g	Protein	2 g	Calcium	1 %
Cholesterol	0 mg			Iron	11 %

Potato Knishes

1 large onion, chopped
2 Tbs. oil
4 large potatoes, cooked
  and mashed

2 eggs
1½ tsp. salt
dash of pepper
3 Tbs. matzah meal

Fry onion in oil. Mix all ingredients together. Wet hands. Form patties. Bake on greased cookie sheet at 350° for 15 minutes on each side.

NUTRITIONAL INFORMATION PER SERVING:		Serving Size: 4½ oz. Total Servings: 8			
Calories	134	Sodium	420 mg	**PERCENT OF DAILY VALUE**	
Calories from fat	43	Carbohydrates	18 g	Vitamin A	3 %
Fat	5 g	Fiber	2 g	Vitamin C	28 %
Saturated Fat	1 g	Protein	4 g	Calcium	3 %
Cholesterol	53 mg			Iron	13 %

Kishke

1 tsp. paprika
1¼ tsp. salt
½ tsp. pepper
2 stalks celery, sliced

1 large onion, sliced
½ cup oil
1½ cups flour

Blend first six ingredients in blender. Add flour. You might have to add a little more, if necessary, to be able to form a loaf, but not too much or it will become very hard. Make a loaf and place it on aluminum foil or parchment paper. Close the foil or paper and twist the ends, leaving room to expand. Place on a cookie sheet and bake at 350° for 1½ hours. Cool before opening foil or paper and slicing. After it's baked, the foil-wrapped kishke can be put into cholent.

NUTRITIONAL INFORMATION PER SERVING:		Serving Size: 2½ oz. slice Total Servings: 8			
Calories	220	Sodium	345 mg	**PERCENT OF DAILY VALUE**	
Calories from fat	125	Carbohydrates	21 g	Vitamin A	2 %
Fat	14 g	Fiber	1 g	Vitamin C	4 %
Saturated Fat	2 g	Protein	3 g	Calcium	2 %
Cholesterol	0 mg			Iron	14 %

Carrot Tzimmes

10 carrots
¼ cup brown sugar
2 Tbs. honey
¼ tsp. salt

2 Tbs. margarine
½ tsp. cinnamon
½ tsp. ginger (optional)

Peel and dice carrots. Place in a 3-quart saucepan with enough water to cover carrots. Combine remaining ingredients and add to carrots. Cover and cook over low heat until tender (test with fork).

Variation: Substitute some sweet potatoes for a few of the carrots.

NUTRITIONAL INFORMATION PER SERVING:				Serving Size: 4 oz. Total Servings: 8	
Calories	98	Sodium	135 mg	**PERCENT OF DAILY VALUE**	
Calories from fat	29	Carbohydrates	17 g	Vitamin A	317 %
Fat	3 g	Fiber	3 g	Vitamin C	14 %
Saturated Fat	1 g	Protein	1 g	Calcium	4 %
Cholesterol	0 mg			Iron	4 %

Breaded Cauliflower

½ cup wheat germ
1 tsp. garlic powder
1 extra-large egg

1 16-oz. bag frozen
    cauliflower florets

Combine wheat germ and garlic powder in a plastic bag or bowl. Beat egg in a smaller bowl. Dip florets into egg and then into wheat germ mixture. Place in an ungreased baking dish and bake at 350° for ½ hour.

NUTRITIONAL INFORMATION PER SERVING:				Serving Size: 4 oz. Total Servings: 5	
Calories	154	Sodium	47 mg	**PERCENT OF DAILY VALUE**	
Calories from fat	113	Carbohydrates	7 g	Vitamin A	2 %
Fat	13 g	Fiber	2 g	Vitamin C	47 %
Saturated Fat	2 g	Protein	5 g	Calcium	2 %
Cholesterol	43 mg			Iron	3 %

Butternut Squash

1 medium butternut squash	1 Tbs. brown sugar
1 Tbs. butter	⅛ tsp. cinnamon

Cut squash in half from top to bottom. Clean out seeds. With a knife, make 2 slits down the inside of the squash from top to bottom. Slice butter into 6 parts; put 3 parts of butter on each half of the squash. Sprinkle brown sugar, then cinnamon, evenly over halves. Place on a baking sheet and bake at 350° for 1 hour or until squash is soft. Enjoy!

NUTRITIONAL INFORMATION PER SERVING:				Serving Size: 11 oz. Total Servings: 2	
Calories	197	Sodium	57 mg	**PERCENT OF DAILY VALUE**	
Calories from fat	53	Carbohydrates	38 g	Vitamin A	270 %
Fat	6 g	Fiber	5 g	Vitamin C	77 %
Saturated Fat	4 g	Protein	3 g	Calcium	16 %
Cholesterol	16 mg			Iron	13 %

Red Cabbage

2 Tbs. oil	½ cup water
1 Tbs. chopped onion	2 Tbs. honey
2 sour apples, peeled and shredded	1 head red cabbage (4 cups shredded)
2 Tbs. lemon juice	1 tsp. salt

Heat oil in a large pan. Add onion and sauté until soft. Add remaining ingredients and simmer for 15 to 20 minutes, stirring occasionally. May be served hot or cold.

NUTRITIONAL INFORMATION PER SERVING:				Serving Size: 3 oz. Total Servings: 8	
Calories	72	Sodium	272 mg	**PERCENT OF DAILY VALUE**	
Calories from fat	32	Carbohydrates	10 g	Vitamin C	37 %
Fat	4 g	Fiber	1 g	Calcium	2 %
Saturated Fat	0 g	Protein	1 g	Iron	2 %
Cholesterol	0 mg				

Almond Green Beans

2 10-oz. pkgs. frozen green
  beans
1 tsp. garlic powder

1 tsp. oregano
1 Tbs. tamari soy sauce
1 Tbs. ground almonds

Cook green beans as directed on package. Do not drain. Add garlic powder, oregano, and soy sauce to them. Cover and simmer for another 10 minutes. Sprinkle almonds on top before serving.

NUTRITIONAL INFORMATION PER SERVING:				Serving Size: 5 oz. Total Servings: 4	
Calories	67	Sodium	276 mg	**PERCENT OF DAILY VALUE**	
Calories from fat	21	Carbohydrates	11 g	Vitamin A	9 %
Fat	2 g	Fiber	3 g	Vitamin C	19 %
Saturated Fat	0 g	Protein	3 g	Calcium	10 %
Cholesterol	0 mg			Iron	10 %

Marinated Mushrooms

¾ cup vegetable oil
½ cup apple cider vinegar
1 tsp. sugar
½ tsp. basil
¼ tsp. thyme
6 peppercorns

1 garlic clove, sliced
1 bay leaf
1 carrot, sliced
½ zucchini, sliced
1½ lbs. mushrooms

Put all ingredients except carrot, zucchini, and mushrooms in a saucepan. Heat to boiling, then lower to simmer. Add sliced carrot and simmer for 8 minutes. Add zucchini and mushrooms. (If mushrooms are small, leave them whole; if large, slice them.) Simmer 3 more minutes. Transfer to storage container and chill.

NUTRITIONAL INFORMATION PER SERVING:				Serving Size: 7 oz. Total Servings: 6	
Calories	287	Sodium	10 mg	**PERCENT OF DAILY VALUE**	
Calories from fat	265	Carbohydrates	7 g	Vitamin A	43 %
Fat	29 g	Fiber	1 g	Vitamin C	5 %
Saturated Fat	3 g	Protein	4 g	Calcium	1 %
Cholesterol	0 mg			Iron	7 %

Carrot Cutlets

1 lb. carrots, peeled and
shredded
1 large onion
4 large or 3 extra-large eggs

1 tsp. salt
½ cup matzah meal
oil for frying

Put all ingredients except oil into food processor and use steel blade to blend. Shape into small cutlets and fry in oil.

NUTRITIONAL INFORMATION PER SERVING:			Serving Size: 2 oz. Total Servings: 15		
Calories	70	Sodium	170 mg	PERCENT OF DAILY VALUE	
Calories from fat	29	Carbohydrates	8 g	Vitamin A	109 %
Fat	3 g	Fiber	1 g	Vitamin C	5 %
Saturated Fat	1 g	Protein	3 g	Calcium	2 %
Cholesterol	57 mg			Iron	5 %

Potato Bilkies (Puffs)

2 onions, chopped
3 Tbs. oil
5 potatoes, peeled and
quartered
2 eggs

¼ cup water
salt and pepper, to taste
½ cup matzah meal
paprika

Sauté onions in oil until lightly browned. Set aside. Cook potatoes until soft, and mash. Add eggs, water, seasonings, and matzah meal until smooth. Add sautéed onions with the oil. If mixture is not thick enough to hold a shape, add more matzah meal. Shape into mounds, using about 2 heaping tablespoonfuls for each one. Place on a greased cookie sheet. Sprinkle with paprika and bake at 350° for 1 hour or until crisp and brown.

NUTRITIONAL INFORMATION PER SERVING:			Serving Size: 3½ oz. Total Servings: 12		
Calories	117	Sodium	103 mg	PERCENT OF DAILY VALUE	
Calories from fat	40	Carbohydrates	16 g	Vitamin C	20 %
Fat	4 g	Fiber	1 g	Calcium	1 %
Saturated Fat	1 g	Protein	3 g	Iron	11 %
Cholesterol	36 mg				

Scalloped Potatoes

10 medium potatoes
1½–2 large onions
4 Tbs. margarine
1 cup potato water

1 cup mayonnaise
½ cup flour
½ cup bread crumbs
2 Tbs. parsley flakes

Slice potatoes, boil until soft, and reserve water. While potatoes are boiling, sauté onions in margarine. Add potato water, mayonnaise, and flour, and stir over a low flame. Layer sliced potatoes with sauce in a 9x13-inch pan. Sprinkle with bread crumbs and parsley flakes. Bake at 350° for 30 minutes, covered, then uncover and bake an additional 30 minutes, until brown and sizzling.

NUTRITIONAL INFORMATION PER SERVING:				Serving Size: 8 oz. Total Servings: 8	
Calories	420	Sodium	278 mg	**PERCENT OF DAILY VALUE**	
Calories from fat	255	Carbohydrates	37 g	Vitamin A	12 %
Fat	28 g	Fiber	3 g	Vitamin C	47 %
Saturated Fat	4 g	Protein	6 g	Calcium	5 %
Cholesterol	16 mg			Iron	23 %

Potato Latkes

6 potatoes
1 onion
2 eggs, slightly beaten
3 Tbs. flour

¼ tsp. pepper
1 tsp. salt
½ tsp. baking powder
¼ cup oil for frying

Peel and grate potatoes and onion. Stir in eggs. Add remaining ingredients. Into a well-greased frying pan, drop batter by spoonfuls. Brown on both sides.

NUTRITIONAL INFORMATION PER SERVING:				Serving Size: 3 oz. Total Servings: 15	
Calories	96	Sodium	154 mg	**PERCENT OF DAILY VALUE**	
Calories from fat	40	Carbohydrates	12 g	Vitamin A	1 %
Fat	4 g	Fiber	1 g	Vitamin C	19 %
Saturated Fat	1 g	Protein	3 g	Calcium	1 %
Cholesterol	28 mg			Iron	6 %

French Fries

8 potatoes (approx. 3 lbs.)   2 cups (approx.) oil

Heat oil in a large frying pan. The oil should be ½-inch deep, no less. Slice potatoes the long way, French-fry size. When the oil is hot, slip potatoes into frying pan. The flame should be medium-low. Once the potatoes are brown on one side, turn them over. Fry until brown. Place paper towels on plates. Remove potatoes from pan with a slotted spoon onto plates. They won't last long!

NUTRITIONAL INFORMATION PER SERVING:		Serving Size: 4½ oz. Total Servings: 12		
Calories	390	Sodium	3 mg	**PERCENT OF DAILY VALUE**
Calories from fat	328	Carbohydrates	15 g	Vitamin C	28 %
Fat	36 g	Fiber	2 g	Calcium	1 %
Saturated Fat	5 g	Protein	2 g	Iron	5 %
Cholesterol	0 mg			

Brown Rice with Tofu and Almonds

1 cup brown rice   **1 16-oz. pkg. soft tofu,**
2½ cups boiling water   **diced**
1 onion, diced   **½ cup slivered almonds**
2 Tbs. oil for sautéing   **1½ Tbs. tamari soy sauce**

Cook brown rice in boiling water, covered, on a low flame for 40 minutes or until water is absorbed. Meanwhile, sauté onion in oil until transparent. Add tofu and sauté an additional 10 minutes. Add almonds and soy sauce, cover, and simmer for 15 minutes more. Mix into cooked rice.

NUTRITIONAL INFORMATION PER SERVING:		Serving Size: 4 oz. Total Servings: 12		
Calories	156	Sodium	145 mg	**PERCENT OF DAILY VALUE**
Calories from fat	73	Carbohydrates	16 g	Vitamin C	1 %
Fat	8 g	Fiber	2 g	Calcium	5 %
Saturated Fat	1 g	Protein	6 g	Iron	9 %
Cholesterol	0 mg			

Tofu Noodle Kugel
Compliments of Monsey Glatt, Monsey, NY

½ cup raisins
boiling water
½ cup tofu, drained well
¾ cup rice syrup
2 Tbs. techina
¾ tsp. salt

2 tsp. vanilla
1½ tsp. lemon juice
8 oz. thin whole-wheat
    noodles, cooked and
    drained

Preheat oven to 350°. Put raisins in a bowl, cover with boiling water, and allow to stand for several minutes; drain well. In a food processor or blender, combine tofu, rice syrup, techina, salt, vanilla, and lemon juice, and process until smooth. Stir together tofu mixture and raisins with noodles. Pour into a well-greased, 9x9-inch baking pan. Bake for 20 minutes or until top turns brown.

NUTRITIONAL INFORMATION PER SERVING:				Serving Size: 3 oz. Total Servings: 9	
Calories	234	Sodium	187 mg	**PERCENT OF DAILY VALUE**	
Calories from fat	31	Carbohydrates	45 g	Vitamin C	1 %
Fat	3 g	Fiber	1 g	Calcium	5 %
Saturated Fat	0 g	Protein	6 g	Iron	20 %
Cholesterol	0 mg				

Baked Tofu
Compliments of Monsey Glatt, Monsey, NY

1 lb. firm tofu
¼ cup water
½ medium onion, grated
¼ cup tamari soy sauce

1 tsp. grated fresh ginger
1 Tbs. lemon juice
1 Tbs. sesame seeds
    (optional)

Cut tofu into eight equal slices and lay out on paper towels to drain. After they are drained well, lay them flat in a 9x13-inch baking dish. Mix together the rest of the ingredients, except the sesame seeds, pour them over the sliced tofu and marinate for several hours or overnight. Preheat oven to 350°. Sprinkle tofu with sesame seeds and bake for 30 minutes or longer, until lightly browned. Tofu slices can be served in a sandwich, or sliced and added to a stir fry with vegetables.

Note: Tofu slices can also be breaded and fried like cutlets instead of baked.

NUTRITIONAL INFORMATION PER SERVING:				Serving Size: 6 oz. Total Servings: 4	
Calories	116	Sodium	1048 mg	PERCENT OF DAILY VALUE	
Calories from fat	42	Carbohydrates	9 g	Vitamin C	5 %
Fat	5 g	Fiber	1 g	Calcium	6 %
Saturated Fat	1 g	Protein	11 g	Iron	20 %
Cholesterol	0 mg				

Sautéed Tofu and Veggies

6 Tbs. dark sesame oil
1 cup onions, sliced into thin wedges
1 cup fresh sweet corn, removed from the cob
1 cup cabbage, sliced into 1-inch chunks

1 lb. firm tofu, crumbled
1–2 pinches sea salt or 2 tsp. soy sauce (optional)
1 Tbs. sliced scallion (for garnish)

Heat oil in a skillet. Add onions and sauté 1 to 2 minutes. Stir in corn and cabbage. Sprinkle tofu over vegies. Sprinkle sea salt or soy sauce on top, and cover. Cook on a low flame until veggies are done and tofu is fluffy. The veggies are best if they are slightly crisp. Remove from heat and place in a serving bowl. Garnish with scallion slices.

NUTRITIONAL INFORMATION PER SERVING:				Serving Size: 6 oz. Total Servings: 6	
Calories	262	Sodium	73 mg	PERCENT OF DAILY VALUE	
Calories from fat	150	Carbohydrates	23 g	Vitamin A	1 %
Fat	17 g	Fiber	1 g	Vitamin C	23 %
Saturated Fat	2 g	Protein	6 g	Calcium	7 %
Cholesterol	0 mg			Iron	25 %

Tofu "Egg" Salad

Compliments of Monsey Glatt, Monsey, NY

1 lb. tofu, drained well
3 Tbs. olives, chopped
3 scallions, finely chopped
3 Tbs. NAYONAISE (tofu-based
   mayonnaise)

2 Tbs. prepared mustard
½ green pepper, chopped
salt, garlic powder, pepper,
   and thyme, to taste

Mash tofu very well with a fork. Combine with remaining ingredients, mixing well. Chill. Serve on lettuce leaves with Israeli-style salad on the side.

Note: To make this salad more closely resemble egg salad, you may add a pinch of turmeric or curry powder for yellow coloring. You can also cut the tofu into chunks and boil them for several minutes first in order to give tofu a slightly firmer consistency. Drain well before continuing with above recipe.

NUTRITIONAL INFORMATION PER SERVING:				Serving Size: 4½ oz. Total Servings: 5	
Calories	101	Sodium	583 mg	**PERCENT OF DAILY VALUE**	
Calories from fat	56	Carbohydrates	5 g	Vitamin A	3 %
Fat	6 g	Fiber	1 g	Vitamin C	19 %
Saturated Fat	1 g	Protein	7 g	Calcium	6 %
Cholesterol	0 mg			Iron	8 %

Nutty Rice Casserole

1 cup short-grain brown rice
2 cups boiling water with 1
   tsp. salt
1 cup chopped onions
1 cup chopped green pepper
1 cup chopped celery

1½ Tbs. margarine
⅓ cup toasted, slivered
   almonds
1 apple, cut up (or ½ cup
   raisins)

Pour rice into boiling water. Simmer uncovered for 45 to 60 minutes. Preheat oven to 375°. Grease a loaf pan. Sauté vegetables in margarine until tender. Add almonds, apple (or raisins), and cooked rice; mix well. Pour mixture into the loaf pan. Bake covered for about 30 minutes.

NUTRITIONAL INFORMATION PER SERVING:				Serving Size: 8 oz. Total Servings: 12	
Calories	147	Sodium	35 mg	PERCENT OF DAILY VALUE	
Calories from fat	35	Carbohydrates	27 g	Vitamin A	14 %
Fat	4 g	Fiber	5 g	Vitamin C	229 %
Saturated Fat	1 g	Protein	4 g	Calcium	4 %
Cholesterol	0 mg			Iron	13 %

Sunflower Rice Salad

1 cup raw rice
3 cups boiling water
10 green beans, cut into
    1-inch pieces
½ cup carrots, diced small

1 small onion, diced
3 Tbs. sunflower seeds
1½ cups cabbage, shredded

Cook rice according to directions on its package. In the boiling water, cook green beans, carrots, and onion together for 2 to 3 minutes. Lift out with a slotted spoon, drain, and cool. (Save the cooking broth for a soup.) Mix vegetables together with the cooked rice, sunflower seeds, and cabbage. Toss with Lemon Vinaigrette Dressing (see recipe on p. 48).

NUTRITIONAL INFORMATION PER SERVING:				Serving Size: 4 oz. Total Servings: 10	
Calories	140	Sodium	15 mg	PERCENT OF DAILY VALUE	
Calories from fat	15	Carbohydrates	28 g	Vitamin A	26 %
Fat	2 g	Fiber	2 g	Vitamin C	50 %
Saturated Fat	0 g	Protein	4 g	Calcium	4 %
Cholesterol	0 mg			Iron	13 %

Tomato Rice

1½ Tbs. olive oil	1 tsp. dried basil
2 scallions	1 tsp. tamari soy sauce
1 cup chopped tomatoes	1 garlic clove
2 Tbs. minced fresh parsley	2 cups cooked brown rice

Heat oil in pan. Chop scallions and add to oil. Stir 1 to 2 minutes. Add tomatoes, parsley, basil, and tamari. Push garlic through garlic press and add. Simmer over low heat until the liquid from the tomatoes has nearly evaporated and the vegetables are soft. Add rice and stir.

NUTRITIONAL INFORMATION PER SERVING:				Serving Size: 3 oz. Total Servings: 8	
Calories	85	Sodium	93 mg	**PERCENT OF DAILY VALUE**	
Calories from fat	27	Carbohydrates	13 g	Vitamin A	6 %
Fat	3 g	Fiber	1 g	Vitamin C	15 %
Saturated Fat	0 g	Protein	2 g	Calcium	1 %
Cholesterol	0 mg			Iron	4 %

Spanish Rice

½ cup chopped green pepper	1 cup rice
½ cup chopped celery	3 cups boiling water
½ cup chopped onion	1 fresh tomato, diced
2 Tbs. oil	salt to taste

In a 2-quart pot, sauté pepper, celery, and onion in oil until browned. Add rice and water. Cover and cook for 20 minutes on a low flame. Add tomato and salt, and cook for an additional 2 minutes.

NUTRITIONAL INFORMATION PER SERVING:				Serving Size: 5 oz. Total Servings: 8	
Calories	137	Sodium	324 mg	**PERCENT OF DAILY VALUE**	
Calories from fat	33	Carbohydrates	24 g	Vitamin A	3 %
Fat	4 g	Fiber	1 g	Vitamin C	31 %
Saturated Fat	0 g	Protein	2 g	Calcium	2 %
Cholesterol	0 mg			Iron	13 %

Fried Rice

2 eggs
1 Tbs. + 2 Tbs. olive oil
3 onions, diced

3 cups cooked brown rice
1 Tbs. soy sauce
¼ tsp. sugar

In a small skillet, scramble eggs in 1 Tbs. oil and set aside. In a larger skillet, sauté onions in 2 Tbs. oil until light brown. Add rice and mix. Stir in soy sauce and sugar. Stir in eggs. Mix well.

NUTRITIONAL INFORMATION PER SERVING:			Serving Size: 6 oz. Total Servings: 6		
Calories	215	Sodium	187 mg	**PERCENT OF DAILY VALUE**	
Calories from fat	84	Carbohydrates	27 g	Vitamin A	3 %
Fat	9 g	Fiber	2 g	Vitamin C	5 %
Saturated Fat	2 g	Protein	5 g	Calcium	3 %
Cholesterol	71 mg			Iron	6 %

Mom's Rice with Zucchini

1 small zucchini
2 Tbs. + 1 Tbs. margarine
⅓ cup finely chopped onion
1 cup rice

1½ cups chicken broth
1 tsp. salt, or to taste
freshly ground pepper, to
    taste

Trim ends from zucchini and cut into half-inch cubes. In a saucepan, heat 2 Tbs. of margarine and add onion. Cook, stirring until soft. Add zucchini and stir. Add rice, chicken broth, salt, and pepper. Bring to a boil, cover, and simmer for 17 minutes. Gently stir in remaining margarine and serve.

NUTRITIONAL INFORMATION PER SERVING:			Serving Size: 5 oz. Total Servings: 6		
Calories	272	Sodium	710 mg	**PERCENT OF DAILY VALUE**	
Calories from fat	94	Carbohydrates	28 g	Vitamin A	14 %
Fat	10 g	Fiber	1 g	Vitamin C	7 %
Saturated Fat	2 g	Protein	15 g	Calcium	3 %
Cholesterol	31 mg			Iron	20 %

Pasta Salad
Compliments of Sabel's Catering, Monsey, NY

1 lb. multicolor pasta	2 carrots
1 red pepper	broccoli stems from ½–¾ of
1 green pepper	a bunch
1 yellow pepper	1 15-oz. can corn
1 small can pitted black	1 8-oz. bottle Italian salad
olives	dressing

Cook pasta, following directions on package. Drain well and set aside. Cut peppers into thin strips. Slice olives into rounds. Cut carrots into julienne strips. Clean broccoli stems and cut into pieces. Drain can of corn. Add all ingredients to pasta and mix. Add dressing and chill, covered, in refrigerator for at least 1 hour or overnight.

NUTRITIONAL INFORMATION PER SERVING:				Serving Size: 5 oz. Total Servings: 15	
Calories	221	Sodium	267 mg	**PERCENT OF DAILY VALUE**	
Calories from fat	80	Carbohydrates	31 g	Vitamin A	36 %
Fat	9 g	Fiber	1 g	Vitamin C	45 %
Saturated Fat	1 g	Protein	5 g	Calcium	2 %
Cholesterol	0 mg			Iron	12 %

Sneak-Vegetables-to-the-Kids Tomato Sauce

2 zucchini (medium–small),	1 1 lb. 2-oz. can tomato
sliced	paste
1 onion, sliced	1 tsp. garlic powder
1½ lb. carrots (or 3 big	½ tsp. oregano
ones), sliced	2 tsp. salt
½ medium winter squash	1 8-oz. can mushrooms
(butternut), peeled and	(optional)
cubed, or 1 sweet potato	
in big chunks	

Put vegetables in a 6-quart pot and cover with water. If using canned mushrooms, add mushroom water to vegetables at beginning of cooking and save drained mushrooms to add to sauce after puréeing. Simmer until very soft. Purée in blender or food processor, adding tomato paste and spices at end of blending. This makes enough sauce for 2 spaghetti/noodle suppers and it freezes well.

NUTRITIONAL INFORMATION PER SERVING:		Serving Size: 3½ oz. Total Servings: 20			
Calories	46	Sodium	431 mg	**PERCENT OF DAILY VALUE**	
Calories from fat	3	Carbohydrates	11 g	Vitamin A	140 %
Fat	0 g	Fiber	3 g	Vitamin C	26 %
Saturated Fat	0 g	Protein	2 g	Calcium	3 %
Cholesterol	0 mg			Iron	8 %

Festive Pasta Salad

1 12-oz. pkg. tricolor twists
1 red pepper
1 green pepper
1 yellow pepper (optional)
1 sour pickle
1 15-oz. can baby corn, drained
½ red onion or 2 Tbs. finely diced onion

Dressing:
½ cup vinegar
⅓ cup sugar (optional)
⅓ cup oil
1 tsp. salt
1 tsp. pepper

Cook noodles 10 minutes and drain. Slice peppers and sour pickle thin. Mix corn and onion with peppers. Mix ingredients for dressing. While noodles are still hot, toss with vegetables and dressing. Chill in tightly covered container before serving.

NUTRITIONAL INFORMATION PER SERVING:		Serving Size: 5 oz. Total Servings: 12			
Calories	216	Sodium	383 mg	**PERCENT OF DAILY VALUE**	
Calories from fat	62	Carbohydrates	35 g	Vitamin A	2 %
Fat	7 g	Fiber	1 g	Vitamin C	48 %
Saturated Fat	1 g	Protein	5 g	Calcium	1 %
Cholesterol	0 mg			Iron	12 %

Noodle Salad

1 12-oz. pkg. buckwheat
   noodles
2 radishes, sliced

1 green onion, thinly sliced
1 cucumber, diced

Boil noodles until tender. Before draining, add radishes and green onion. Strain and run briefly under cool water. Add cucumber. Toss with Lemon Vinaigrette Dressing (see recipe on p. 48).
Variation: Use 1½ cups corn or wheat elbows in place of buckwheat noodles.

NUTRITIONAL INFORMATION PER SERVING:*				Serving Size: 4 oz. Total Servings: 8	
Calories	147	Sodium	339 mg	**PERCENT OF DAILY VALUE**	
Calories from fat	5	Carbohydrates	33 g	Vitamin A	1 %
Fat	1 g	Fiber	1 g	Vitamin C	4 %
Saturated Fat	0 g	Protein	6 g	Calcium	2 %
Cholesterol	0 mg			Iron	8 %

* Analysis does *not* include vinaigrette dressing.

Lo Mein

½ cup rice
1 cup water
1 stick margarine

2½ cups boiling water
1 pkg. onion soup mix
¾ lb. fine noodles

Cook rice in 1 cup water. Meanwhile, in another pot, melt margarine. Add boiling water and soup mix. Mix well and add noodles. Cook until water is absorbed. Combine the cooked rice with the noodles.
Variation: Sautéed mushrooms can also be added.

NUTRITIONAL INFORMATION PER SERVING:				Serving Size: 6½ oz. Total Servings: 6	
Calories	406	Cholesterol	0 mg	**PERCENT OF DAILY VALUE**	
Calories from fat	147	Sodium	238 mg	Vitamin A	23 %
Fat	16 g	Carbohydrates	56 g	Calcium	2 %
Saturated Fat	3 g	Protein	8 g	Iron	19 %

Fettuccine Florentine

1 12-oz. box fettuccine
　Florentine (spinach and
　egg noodles)
6 Tbs. olive oil

6 garlic cloves, minced
1 cup chopped parsley
1 tsp. salt
½ tsp. pepper

Cook noodles as directed on package. In a small saucepan, heat olive oil. Sauté garlic, parsley, salt, and pepper, and toss with noodles. Goes well with fish dishes.

NUTRITIONAL INFORMATION PER SERVING:		Serving Size: 4 oz. Total Servings: 8			
Calories	208	Sodium	281 mg	**PERCENT OF DAILY VALUE**	
Calories from fat	104	Carbohydrates	22 g	Vitamin A	6 %
Fat	12 g	Fiber	1 g	Vitamin C	13 %
Saturated Fat	2 g	Protein	5 g	Calcium	4 %
Cholesterol	28 mg			Iron	10 %

Four-Pepper Pasta

1 green pepper
1 red pepper
1 yellow pepper
1 orange pepper
1 large onion
3 Tbs. olive oil
¼ tsp. black pepper

¼ cup brown sugar
¼ tsp. basil
1 tsp. salt
1 Tbs. vinegar
1 box (16 oz.) penne pasta
　or ziti noodles, cooked
　and drained

Dice peppers and onion and sauté in oil. When browned, add all remaining ingredients, except pasta, and simmer for an additional 15 minutes. Toss with cooked pasta. Serve immediately.

NUTRITIONAL INFORMATION PER SERVING:		Serving Size: 4 oz. Total Servings: 15			
Calories	159	Sodium	147 mg	**PERCENT OF DAILY VALUE**	
Calories from fat	29	Carbohydrates	28 g	Vitamin A	2 %
Fat	3 g	Fiber	1 g	Vitamin C	46 %
Saturated Fat	0 g	Protein	4 g	Calcium	1 %
Cholesterol	0 mg			Iron	13 %

Savory Orzo

1 1-lb. box orzo (RONZONI #47)
1 20-oz. bag frozen vegetables (broccoli, cauliflower, and carrots)

1 pkg. onion soup mix
3 Tbs. soy sauce
¾ stick margarine

Boil orzo as per package directions. Drain and pour into a 9x13-inch pan. Microwave, or conventionally cook, frozen vegetables. Drain, and pour them over the orzo. Sprinkle soup mix on top. Add soy sauce. Dot with margarine. Cover with aluminum foil. Bake for 30 minutes at 350°, then uncover and stir with a spoon. Cover again and bake 15 minutes more. A yummy side dish that's easy to make.

NUTRITIONAL INFORMATION PER SERVING:				Serving Size: 5 oz. Total Servings: 12	
Calories	207	Sodium	369 mg	**PERCENT OF DAILY VALUE**	
Calories from fat	58	Carbohydrates	31 g	Vitamin A	44 %
Fat	6 g	Fiber	2 g	Vitamin C	20 %
Saturated Fat	1 g	Protein	6 g	Calcium	3 %
Cholesterol	0 mg			Iron	14 %

Sesame Lo Mein

16 oz. linguine
6 Tbs. sliced scallions
6 Tbs. sesame oil

2 oz. sesame seeds
6 Tbs. soy sauce

Boil linguine as directed on box, drain and set aside. Sauté scallions in oil. Add sesame seeds. Stir in soy sauce and toss mixture with cooked linguine.

NUTRITIONAL INFORMATION PER SERVING:				Serving Size: 4 oz. Total Servings: 10	
Calories	278	Sodium	621 mg	**PERCENT OF DAILY VALUE**	
Calories from fat	104	Carbohydrates	36 g	Calcium	8 %
Fat	12 g	Fiber	2 g	Iron	21 %
Saturated Fat	2 g	Protein	7 g		
Cholesterol	0 mg				

Vegetable Linguine

¾ lb. linguine
3 medium onions
4 Tbs. oil

1 10-oz. pkg. frozen
   broccoli
1 8-oz. can mushrooms,
   drained

Cook linguine according to package directions. Rinse and drain. Dice onions and sauté in oil on low flame. Cook broccoli for 5 to 10 minutes — **not longer**. Mix broccoli and mushrooms into onions and cook for 5 minutes. Mix into linguine. Serve hot.

NUTRITIONAL INFORMATION PER SERVING:			Serving Size: 6½ oz. Total Servings: 8		
Calories	251	Sodium	136 mg	**PERCENT OF DAILY VALUE**	
Calories from fat	68	Carbohydrates	39 g	Vitamin A	8 %
Fat	8 g	Fiber	3 g	Vitamin C	28 %
Saturated Fat	1 g	Protein	7 g	Calcium	5 %
Cholesterol	0 mg			Iron	26 %

Mushroom Orzo

½ stick margarine or 4 Tbs.
   oil
1 red pepper, cut in ½-inch
   chunks
1 green pepper, cut in ½-
   inch chunks
1 medium squash, diced

1 6-oz. can water chestnuts
1 large onion, diced
1 8-oz. can mushrooms,
   drained
1 pkg. onion soup mix
1 1-lb. box orzo, cooked

Put margarine or oil into a frying pan, and add all vegetables except mushrooms. Simmer for 5 minutes, then add mushrooms and soup mix. Mix in cooked orzo and bake for 25 minutes at 350°. This is a good side dish and it freezes well.

NUTRITIONAL INFORMATION PER SERVING:			Serving Size: 4½ oz. Total Servings: 12		
Calories	204	Sodium	93 mg	**PERCENT OF DAILY VALUE**	
Calories from fat	47	Carbohydrates	34 g	Vitamin A	2 %
Fat	5 g	Fiber	2 g	Vitamin C	33 %
Saturated Fat	1 g	Protein	6 g	Calcium	2 %
Cholesterol	0 mg			Iron	18 %

Kasha Varnishkes

1 egg
1 cup kasha
1 large or 2 small onions
3 Tbs. + 1 Tbs. oil

2 cups boiling water
1 tsp. salt, or to taste
1 8-oz. box bow tie noodles

Beat egg in a deep dish. Add kasha and stir until kasha is wet. In a 2-quart saucepan, sauté onions in 3 Tbs. oil. Meanwhile, put 1 Tbs. oil in a frying pan. Then put in kasha and make the flame a little higher. With a fork, keep stirring and flattening the kasha, separating the grains. Continue until kasha is dry and not lumpy. Put kasha into pot with onions, pour in boiling water, and add salt. Cover and cook over low flame for 15 minutes. Cook bow tie noodles as directed on box and mix with kasha.

NUTRITIONAL INFORMATION PER SERVING:				Serving Size: 3½ oz. Total Servings: 8	
Calories	256	Sodium	285 mg	**PERCENT OF DAILY VALUE**	
Calories from fat	83	Carbohydrates	37 g	Vitamin A	2 %
Fat	9 g	Fiber	2 g	Vitamin C	1 %
Saturated Fat	1 g	Protein	7 g	Calcium	2 %
Cholesterol	53 mg			Iron	16 %

Noodles with Poppy Seeds

1 12-oz. bag wide noodles
2 Tbs. butter

2 Tbs. poppy seeds
1½ tsp. + 1 tsp. sugar

Cook noodles for 5 minutes and drain. Add butter and toss to melt. Add poppy seeds and 1½ tsp. sugar (and salt if desired) to noodles and toss again. Sprinkle with remaining 1 tsp. sugar.

NUTRITIONAL INFORMATION PER SERVING:				Serving Size: 6½ oz. Total Servings: 4	
Calories	407	Sodium	80 mg	**PERCENT OF DAILY VALUE**	
Calories from fat	101	Carbohydrates	64 g	Vitamin A	8 %
Fat	11 g	Fiber	0 g	Calcium	11 %
Saturated Fat	5 g	Protein	13 g	Iron	28 %
Cholesterol	96 mg				

Kugels and Quiches

Kugels and Quiches

"Emesdike" Yerushalmi Kugel

⅔ cup + 4 Tbs. oil
¾ cup sugar
12 oz. thin noodles, cooked
    and drained (do not
    rinse)

4 eggs
¾ tsp. salt
¼ tsp. pepper (more if
    desired)
dash of paprika (optional)

This is the real thing.

Pour ⅔ cup oil into a small pan. Add sugar and heat over a low flame to caramelize. When sugar has mostly melted and mixture begins to turn dark and bubbly, pour over noodles. Careful — the mixture is very hot and will splatter. Stir quickly before caramelized sugar hardens. Add eggs, salt, and pepper, and optional paprika. Put 4 Tbs. oil into a round aluminum pan with high sides, or an aluminum pot. Heat in oven for 5 minutes. Pour in noodle mixture and bake at 350° for 45 minutes to 1 hour. Before Shabbos, pour ¾ cup boiling water over kugel and cover well. Leave on blech overnight. Accompany each serving with sour pickle.

NUTRITIONAL INFORMATION PER SERVING:		Serving Size: 2 oz. Total Servings: 15		
Calories	260	Sodium	128 mg	**PERCENT OF DAILY VALUE**
Calories from fat	140	Carbohydrates	26 g	Vitamin A 3 %
Fat	16 g	Fiber	0 g	Calcium 1 %
Saturated Fat	2 g	Protein	5 g	Iron 8 %
Cholesterol	78 mg			

Easy Yerushalmi Kugel

1 lb. thin noodles
3 eggs
2 cups brown sugar
⅓ cup oil

2 tsp. salt
¾ tsp. pepper
2 oz. honey

Cook noodles as directed on package and drain. Add eggs, sugar, oil, salt, and pepper to noodles. Mix well. Pour into a 9x13-inch pan. Drizzle honey on top. Bake at 350° for 1 hour.

NUTRITIONAL INFORMATION PER SERVING:				Serving Size: 3½ oz. Total Servings: 15	
Calories	274	Sodium	312 mg	**PERCENT OF DAILY VALUE**	
Calories from fat	64	Carbohydrates	48 g	Vitamin A	3 %
Fat	7 g	Protein	6 g	Calcium	4 %
Saturated Fat	1 g			Iron	14 %
Cholesterol	71 mg				

Yerushalmi Kugel I

4¼ cups water
1 cup sugar
2 tsp. salt
¼ tsp. pepper
¾ stick margarine

1 12-oz. pkg. thin noodles, uncooked
2 eggs
2 Tbs. oil
3 Tbs. brown sugar

Mix first 5 ingredients together in a pot and bring to a boil. Add remaining ingredients. Pour entire mixture into a tube pan. Do not drain water. Bake at 350° for 20 to 25 minutes, until done.

NUTRITIONAL INFORMATION PER SERVING:				Serving Size: 4 oz. Total Servings: 10	
Calories	303	Sodium	526 mg	**PERCENT OF DAILY VALUE**	
Calories from fat	99	Carbohydrates	47 g	Vitamin A	11 %
Fat	11 g	Fiber	0 g	Calcium	2 %
Saturated Fat	2 g	Protein	5 g	Iron	10 %
Cholesterol	32 mg				

Yerushalmi Kugel II

6 tsp. honey
½ cup oil
1 cup sugar
⅔ cup brown sugar

12 oz. thin noodles, cooked
   and drained
4 eggs
1 tsp. salt
1 tsp. pepper

Mix together honey, oil, and both sugars, and cook on a low flame about 20 minutes, until liquid browns. Pour in noodles. Let cool a few minutes, then add final three ingredients. Bake in a 9x13-inch pan for 1 hour at 350°.

NUTRITIONAL INFORMATION PER SERVING:		Serving Size: 3 oz. Total Servings: 15			
Calories	254	Sodium	166 mg	**PERCENT OF DAILY VALUE**	
Calories from fat	86	Carbohydrates	38 g	Vitamin A	3 %
Fat	10 g	Fiber	0 g	Calcium	2 %
Saturated Fat	2 g	Protein	5 g	Iron	9 %
Cholesterol	78 mg				

Mom's Potato Kugel

8 large potatoes
3 onions
4 eggs, well beaten
⅓ cup oil

2 tsp. salt
1 tsp. pepper
1 cup matzah meal

Grate potatoes and onions in food processor. Add eggs, oil, salt, and pepper, and mix together. Slowly add matzah meal. Turn mixture into a greased 9x13-inch pan and bake at 350° for 1 to 1¼ hours.

NUTRITIONAL INFORMATION PER SERVING:		Serving Size: 4 oz. Total Servings: 15			
Calories	161	Sodium	305 mg	**PERCENT OF DAILY VALUE**	
Calories from fat	57	Carbohydrates	21 g	Vitamin A	3 %
Fat	6 g	Fiber	2 g	Vitamin C	25 %
Saturated Fat	2 g	Protein	5 g	Calcium	3 %
Cholesterol	57 mg			Iron	12 %

Apple Kugel

12 apples, peeled and sliced as for pie	*Batter:*
½ cup sugar	3 eggs
1 tsp. cinnamon	1 tsp. baking powder
	1 cup flour
	1 cup sugar
	½ cup oil

Prepare 2 round or square tins (approx. 9 inches). Place thin layer of apple slices in both pans. Then sprinkle sugar and cinnamon on top of the apples. Repeat this layering process until both pans are full, almost to the top. Combine batter ingredients in a bowl and mix well with a wooden spoon. Spread batter on top of apples in both pans. Bake at 350° for at least 1 hour.

NUTRITIONAL INFORMATION PER SERVING:		Serving Size: 4 oz. Total Servings: 18			
Calories	201	Sodium	12 mg	**PERCENT OF DAILY VALUE**	
Calories from fat	65	Carbohydrates	34 g	Vitamin A	2 %
Fat	7 g	Fiber	2 g	Vitamin C	5 %
Saturated Fat	1 g	Protein	2 g	Calcium	1 %
Cholesterol	36 mg			Iron	3 %

Shabbos Apple Kugel Crisp

8 eggs	1 tsp. cinnamon
1½ cups sugar	1 tsp. sugar
2 pkgs. vanilla sugar	
1 cup oil	*Topping:*
3¾ cups flour	¼ cup flour
2 tsp. baking powder	¼ cup sugar
1 Tbs. lemon juice	½ stick margarine, softened
8 large apples	

Beat eggs, sugar, and vanilla for 10 minutes. Add oil and beat 1 or 2 more minutes. Slowly add flour, baking powder, and lemon juice. Peel and slice apples. Mix apple slices with cinnamon and sugar. Combine with flour mixture and pour into two 9x13-inch greased pans. For topping, cut margarine into flour and sugar with a knife. Sprinkle topping onto batter in pans. Bake at 350° for 1 hour. (Recipe can be cut in half.)

NUTRITIONAL INFORMATION PER SERVING:				Serving Size: 5 oz. Total Servings: 20	
Calories	348	Sodium	54 mg	**PERCENT OF DAILY VALUE**	
Calories from fat	141	Carbohydrates	47 g	Vitamin A	8 %
Fat	16 g	Fiber	2 g	Vitamin C	4 %
Saturated Fat	2 g	Protein	5 g	Calcium	2 %
Cholesterol	85 mg			Iron	10 %

Tricolor Vegetable Kugel

20 oz. frozen broccoli cuts
20 oz. frozen cauliflower
   florets
20 oz. frozen carrots
4½ Tbs. flour

4½ Tbs. margarine
1½ cup parve milk
1 cup mayonnaise
9 eggs
3 Tbs. onion soup mix

Steam vegetables separately. In a separate pot, bring to a boil flour, margarine, and parve milk. Remove from heat. In a bowl, mix mayonnaise, eggs, and soup mix, and combine with flour mixture. Mix broccoli with ⅓ of the mixture. Pour into a 9x13-inch casserole dish and bake for about 10 minutes at 350°, until solid. Repeat the above procedure with cauliflower — i.e., combine cauliflower with ⅓ of flour mixture, layer on top of broccoli, and bake for 10 minutes.
Next, do the same with carrots in the same dish.

NUTRITIONAL INFORMATION PER SERVING:				Serving Size: 5 oz. Total Servings: 15	
Calories	103	Sodium	98 mg	**PERCENT OF DAILY VALUE**	
Calories from fat	61	Carbohydrates	8 g	Vitamin A	97 %
Fat	7 g	Fiber	4 g	Vitamin C	46 %
Saturated Fat	1 g	Protein	4 g	Calcium	5 %
Cholesterol	45 mg			Iron	5 %

Delicious Lukshen Kugel

1 16-oz. pkg. medium
   noodles
1 16-oz. pkg. fine noodles
10 eggs
1¼ sticks margarine,
   softened
2½ cups sugar
½ cup coffee whitener

Topping:
crushed cornflake crumbs
   (approx. ½ cup)
½ tsp. cinnamon
½ tsp. sugar

Cook and drain noodles. Combine with remaining ingredients. Pour into a greased, 10x16-inch aluminum pan or two 9x13-inch pans. Mix ingredients for topping and sprinkle on top of noodle mixture. Bake at 350° for 1 hour.

NUTRITIONAL INFORMATION PER SERVING:				Serving Size: 4½ oz. Total Servings: 24	
Calories	308	Cholesterol	125 mg	**PERCENT OF DAILY VALUE**	
Calories from fat	79	Sodium	119 mg	Vitamin A	17 %
Fat	9 g	Carbohydrates	50 g	Calcium	3 %
Saturated Fat	2 g	Protein	8 g	Iron	13 %

Broccoli-Spinach Kugel

1 onion, chopped
3 Tbs. oil for frying
1 20-oz. bag frozen
   chopped broccoli
1 20-oz. bag frozen
   chopped spinach
6 eggs, beaten
Original Blend MRS. DASH, to
   taste

garlic powder, to taste
onion powder, to taste
4 Tbs. mayonnaise
2 Tbs. flour
1 cup cornflakes or WHEATIES
½ cup cornflake crumbs
paprika

Fry onion in oil at the bottom of an 8-quart pot.. Add broccoli and spinach to the onions for 15 to 20 minutes. In a separate bowl, beat the eggs. Add spices and pour in vegetables. Add mayonnaise and flour. Mix well. Grease a 9x13-inch pan. Spread crushed cornflakes or WHEATIES on bottom of pan. Pour in mixture and put cornflake crumbs on top. Sprinkle with paprika. Bake at 350° for 40-45 minutes.

NUTRITIONAL INFORMATION PER SERVING:				Serving Size: 4 oz. Total Servings: 15	
Calories	132	Sodium	126 mg	**PERCENT OF DAILY VALUE**	
Calories from fat	78	Carbohydrates	10 g	Vitamin A	50 %
Fat	9 g	Fiber	2 g	Vitamin C	34 %
Saturated Fat	2 g	Protein	5 g	Calcium	11 %
Cholesterol	87 mg			Iron	13 %

Sweet Noodle Kugel

1 12-oz. pkg. fine egg
   noodles
4 eggs
1 cup sugar
¼ cup oil
¾ cup applesauce
1 tsp. cinnamon

1 tsp. vanilla sugar
1 Tbs. instant vanilla
   pudding powder

Topping:
½ tsp. cinnamon
⅛ cup sugar

Cook noodles, rinse in cold water, and let drain. Return noodles to pot. Meanwhile, in a large mixing bowl, mix eggs, sugar, oil, applesauce, cinnamon, and vanilla sugar. Add to noodles and mix well. Add pudding powder and mix very well (mixture will be watery). Put into a 9x13-inch pan (do not oil pan). Sprinkle top with cinnamon and sugar mixture. Bake at 375° for about 1 to 1½ hours, until center is firm. Delicious hot or cold.

NUTRITIONAL INFORMATION PER SERVING:				Serving Size: 3 oz. Total Servings: 15	
Calories	208	Sodium	36 mg	**PERCENT OF DAILY VALUE**	
Calories from fat	54	Carbohydrates	34 g	Vitamin A	3 %
Fat	6 g	Protein	5 g	Calcium	2 %
Saturated Fat	1 g			Iron	9 %
Cholesterol	78 mg				

Bubby's Challah Kugel

2 large onions, coarsely
    diced
2 Tbs. oil
3 stalks celery, coarsely
    diced
3 carrots, coarsely diced

8 slices of leftover challah
1 tsp. salt, or to taste
garlic powder, to taste
pepper, to taste
4 eggs
¼ cup oil

Sauté onions in 2 Tbs. oil until soft. Add celery and carrots, and sauté all vegetables until lightly browned. Break challah into small pieces. Season to taste. Add eggs, challah, and ¼ cup oil to vegetables. Bake in a 2-quart baking dish at 350° for approximately 45 minutes or until golden.

NUTRITIONAL INFORMATION PER SERVING:				Serving Size: 4 oz. Total Servings: 10	
Calories	246	Sodium	433 mg	**PERCENT OF DAILY VALUE**	
Calories from fat	135	Carbohydrates	22 g	Vitamin A	81 %
Fat	15 g	Fiber	2 g	Vitamin C	8 %
Saturated Fat	2 g	Protein	6 g	Calcium	4 %
Cholesterol	97 mg			Iron	15 %

Sweet Potato Pie
Compliments of The Natural Place, Monsey, NY

1 unbaked pie crust (see
    recipe on p. 268)
3 lbs. sweet potatoes, baked
2 eggs
¼ cup honey
½ cup oil

½ cup orange juice
1 tsp. cinnamon
1 cup whole pecans
3 Tbs. SUCANAT[*] (natural
    evaporated sugar cane)

Press pie crust into an oiled pan. With mixer, blend flesh of sweet potato. Beat in all ingredients, except pecans and SUCANAT, using half

* This and all other ingredients available at The Natural Place.

of the oil. Smooth out over crust. Top with pecans. Sprinkle SUCANAT and remaining oil on top. Bake at 375° for 30 minutes.

NUTRITIONAL INFORMATION PER SERVING:[*]		Serving Size: 4½ oz. Total Servings: 15		
Calories	239	Sodium	18 mg	**PERCENT OF DAILY VALUE**
Calories from fat	119	Carbohydrates	29 g	Vitamin A 249 %
Fat	13 g	Fiber	3 g	Vitamin C 42 %
Saturated Fat	2 g	Protein	3 g	Calcium 4 %
Cholesterol	28 mg			Iron 5 %

* Analysis does not include pie crust.

Spinach-Lukshen Kugel

1 8-oz. pkg. thin noodles
½ cup oil
1 10-oz. pkg. frozen
    chopped spinach
3 eggs

1 cup COFFEE RICH
1 pkg. onion soup mix
½ cup seasoned bread
    crumbs or cornflake
    crumbs

Cook noodles and drain. Transfer noodles to a bowl and add oil. Cook spinach and drain. In a separate bowl, beat eggs with a fork. Add COFFEE RICH and soup mix to eggs. Add spinach. Pour spinach mixture into noodles and mix well. Pour into an 8x8-inch baking dish. Top with bread crumbs or cornflake crumbs. Bake at 350° for 45 minutes uncovered, and 15 minutes covered.

NUTRITIONAL INFORMATION PER SERVING:		Serving Size: 4 oz. Total Servings: 12		
Calories	216	Sodium	102 mg	**PERCENT OF DAILY VALUE**
Calories from fat	115	Carbohydrates	21 g	Vitamin A 26 %
Fat	13 g	Fiber	1 g	Vitamin C 4 %
Saturated Fat	2 g	Protein	6 g	Calcium 6 %
Cholesterol	71 mg			Iron 10 %

Challah Kugel
Compliments of Sabel's Catering, Monsey, NY

1 large challah (approx. 1½ lb.)	3 pkgs. vanilla sugar
5 eggs	1 cup sugar, or to taste
⅓ cup oil	1 tsp. lemon juice

Soak challah briefly in water and then squeeze out all water. Beat together eggs, oil, sugars, and lemon juice in a bowl. Mix thoroughly by hand until well blended. Oil a 9x13-inch pan and pat mixture in evenly. Bake at 350° for 45 minutes until golden.

Note: Check at 45 minutes; if not done, keep checking every 10 minutes.

NUTRITIONAL INFORMATION PER SERVING:				Serving Size: 2½ oz. Total Servings: 15	
Calories	277	Sodium	268 mg	**PERCENT OF DAILY VALUE**	
Calories from fat	101	Carbohydrates	38 g	Vitamin A	4 %
Fat	11 g	Fiber	1 g	Calcium	2 %
Saturated Fat	2 g	Protein	5 g	Iron	9 %
Cholesterol	87 mg				

Salt and Pepper Noodle Kugel

1 lb. medium egg noodles	2 tsp. salt
6 eggs	½ tsp. pepper
½ cup oil	

Cook noodles as directed on package. Beat eggs and add oil, salt, and pepper. Mix with noodles. Bake in a greased, 9x13-inch pan at 350° for 1 hour.

Variation: Add raw broccoli, cauliflower and/or zucchini.

NUTRITIONAL INFORMATION PER SERVING:				Serving Size: 3 oz. Total Servings: 15	
Calories	210	Sodium	316 mg	**PERCENT OF DAILY VALUE**	
Calories from fat	95	Carbohydrates	22 g	Vitamin A	5 %
Fat	11 g	Protein	7 g	Calcium	1 %
Saturated Fat	2 g			Iron	9 %
Cholesterol	114 mg				

Garlic Potato Kugel

2 eggs
5 cloves fresh garlic
3 cups potatoes, grated and
    drained
½ cup flour

½ tsp. baking powder
1½ tsp. salt
4 Tbs. oil
1 tsp. pepper

Beat eggs well. Grate garlic into potatoes. Add eggs and all remaining ingredients. Mix well. Bake in an 8x8-inch pan at 350° for 1 hour.

NUTRITIONAL INFORMATION PER SERVING:		Serving Size: 4 oz. Total Servings: 9		
Calories	162	Sodium	375 mg	**PERCENT OF DAILY VALUE**
Calories from fat	66	Carbohydrates	20 g	Vitamin A 2 %
Fat	7 g	Fiber	1 g	Vitamin C 26 %
Saturated Fat	1 g	Protein	4 g	Calcium 2 %
Cholesterol	47 mg			Iron 7 %

Carrot Kugel

2 sticks margarine
1 cup brown sugar
4 eggs
juice of 1 lemon, or 3 Tbs.
    lemon juice
4 large carrots, grated

1 cup flour
½ tsp. salt
2 tsp. baking powder
½ tsp. baking soda
2 tsp. vanilla

Cream margarine with brown sugar. Add eggs one at a time. Add lemon juice and grated carrots. Add flour, salt, baking powder, baking soda, and vanilla. Turn into a greased 9x13-inch pan. Bake at 350° for 40 minutes or until lightly browned.

NUTRITIONAL INFORMATION PER SERVING:		Serving Size: 2½ oz. Total Servings: 15		
Calories	215	Sodium	271 mg	**PERCENT OF DAILY VALUE**
Calories from fat	123	Carbohydrates	21 g	Vitamin A 89 %
Fat	14 g	Fiber	1 g	Vitamin C 4 %
Saturated Fat	2 g	Protein	3 g	Calcium 4 %
Cholesterol	57 mg			Iron 6 %

Apple Challah Kugel

2 challahs
8 eggs
2 sticks margarine, softened
12 oz. apricot jam
2 tsp. vanilla
8 apples, sliced

dash of cinnamon
dash of sugar
1 16-oz. container parve
   milk
chopped walnuts (optional)

Soak challah in water. Meanwhile, beat eggs with a fork. In a large bowl, cream margarine and add eggs. Add all remaining ingredients, except challah, and mix well. Squeeze out water from the soaking challah and add challah to mixture. Bake in a 9x13-inch pan at 350° for 1 hour.

NUTRITIONAL INFORMATION PER SERVING:		Serving Size: 5½ oz. Total Servings: 20			
Calories	355	Sodium	356 mg	**PERCENT OF DAILY VALUE**	
Calories from fat	155	Carbohydrates	45 g	Vitamin A	20 %
Fat	17 g	Fiber	2 g	Vitamin C	4 %
Saturated Fat	3 g	Protein	6 g	Calcium	3 %
Cholesterol	99 mg			Iron	10 %

Easy Carrot Kugel

2 16-oz. cans sliced carrots
½ stick margarine, softened
1 cup brown sugar
4 eggs

½ tsp. salt (optional)
2 tsp. baking powder
1 cup flour

Drain and mash carrots. Add remaining ingredients to carrots. Bake in a tube pan at 350° for 20 to 25 minutes.

NUTRITIONAL INFORMATION PER SERVING:		Serving Size: 4 oz. Total Servings: 12			
Calories	169	Sodium	321 mg	**PERCENT OF DAILY VALUE**	
Calories from fat	51	Carbohydrates	26 g	Vitamin A	123 %
Fat	6 g	Fiber	1 g	Vitamin C	2 %
Saturated Fat	1 g	Protein	4 g	Calcium	5 %
Cholesterol	71 mg			Iron	9 %

Squash Kugel

4 lbs. yellow or zucchini
   squash
2 eggs, beaten
4 Tbs. softened margarine
1 small onion, diced

2 Tbs. sugar
4 Tbs. flour
2 Tbs. onion soup mix
salt to taste

Peel and slice squash. Cook in boiling water until tender. Drain squash and mash. Add remaining ingredients, and mix well. Grease a square baking pan (8x8-inch) and pour mixture into pan. Bake at 350° for 45 to 60 minutes until set, and bottom is slightly browned.

NUTRITIONAL INFORMATION PER SERVING:				Serving Size: 6 oz. Total Servings: 12	
Calories	88	Sodium	247 mg	**PERCENT OF DAILY VALUE**	
Calories from fat	44	Carbohydrates	9 g	Vitamin A	14 %
Fat	5 g	Fiber	2 g	Vitamin C	23 %
Saturated Fat	1 g	Protein	3 g	Calcium	4 %
Cholesterol	36 mg			Iron	8 %

Apple Lukshen Kugel

1 16-oz. pkg. medium
   noodles
½ cup oil
7 Cortland apples, peeled
   and grated

1½ cups sugar
5 eggs
1 pkg. vanilla sugar
1 heaping tsp. cinnamon
¼ cup farina

Cook noodles and drain. Heat oil and add, together with remaining ingredients, to noodles. Bake at 350° for 1 hour and 15 minutes in a 9x13-inch pan.

NUTRITIONAL INFORMATION PER SERVING:				Serving Size: 5 oz. Total Servings: 15	
Calories	333	Sodium	28 mg	**PERCENT OF DAILY VALUE**	
Calories from fat	94	Carbohydrates	54 g	Vitamin A	5 %
Fat	10 g	Fiber	1 g	Vitamin C	4 %
Saturated Fat	2 g	Protein	7 g	Calcium	2 %
Cholesterol	100 mg			Iron	12 %

Dietetic Broccoli and Spinach Kugel

1 10-oz. box chopped
broccoli
1 10-oz. box chopped
spinach

2 tsp. low-calorie
mayonnaise
2 eggs
½ pkg. onion soup mix

Cook broccoli and spinach for 15 minutes. Drain. Combine all ingredients. Pour into a 2-quart baking dish. Bake at 325°–350° for 45 minutes.

NUTRITIONAL INFORMATION PER SERVING:				Serving Size: 3 oz. Total Servings: 9	
Calories	38	Sodium	66 mg	**PERCENT OF DAILY VALUE**	
Calories from fat	14	Carbohydrates	4 g	Vitamin A	40 %
Fat	2 g	Fiber	2 g	Vitamin C	27 %
Saturated Fat	0 g	Protein	3 g	Calcium	8 %
Cholesterol	48 mg			Iron	5 %

Zucchini Quiche Kugel

5 cups zucchini, peeled (2
large or 4 small)
4 eggs
8 Tbs. mayonnaise

8 Tbs. flour
2 Tbs. onion soup mix
2 pie crusts, unbaked

Grate zucchini by hand or in food processor. Drain liquid. Mix in other ingredients and pour into pie crusts. Bake at 350° for 45 minutes. Freezes well. Reheat open or partially covered.

Variation: Instead of 5 cups zucchini, use 4 cups zucchini plus 1 small can mushrooms.

NUTRITIONAL INFORMATION PER SERVING:[*]				Serving Size: 2 oz. Total Servings: 16	
Calories	86	Sodium	62 mg	**PERCENT OF DAILY VALUE**	
Calories from fat	61	Carbohydrates	4 g	Vitamin A	4 %
Fat	7 g	Protein	2 g	Vitamin C	3 %
Saturated Fat	1 g			Calcium	1 %
Cholesterol	57 mg			Iron	3 %

* Analysis does not include pie crust.

Pineapple Quiche

1 20-oz. can crushed
   pineapple, drained
4 eggs
½ cup oil
½ cup sugar

½ cup flour
1 pkg. vanilla sugar
1 tsp. baking powder
1 unbaked pie shell

Mix all ingredients together and pour into pie shell. Bake at 350° until golden (approximately 30 minutes). Serve hot or cold.

NUTRITIONAL INFORMATION PER SERVING:*		Serving Size: 4 oz. Total Servings: 9		
Calories	235	Sodium	54 mg	**PERCENT OF DAILY VALUE**
Calories from fat	150	Carbohydrates	17 g	Vitamin A 5 %
Fat	17 g	Fiber	1 g	Vitamin C 7 %
Saturated Fat	2 g	Protein	4 g	Calcium 3 %
Cholesterol	96 mg			Iron 5 %

* Analysis does not include pie shell.

Cranberry Apple Kugel

1 stick margarine, melted
1 tsp. cinnamon
½ cup brown sugar
1 cup flour

1 cup oatmeal
1 16-oz. can whole-berry
   cranberry sauce
3 apples, sliced

Mix first five ingredients into a crumbly mixture. Press half of mixture into an 8x8-inch pan. Spread cranberry sauce over pressed crumbs. Pour in sliced apples. Top with remaining crumb mixture. Bake at 350° until golden brown (approximately 45 minutes). This is a great accompaniment to chicken!

NUTRITIONAL INFORMATION PER SERVING:		Serving Size: 5½ oz. Total Servings: 12		
Calories	266	Sodium	103 mg	**PERCENT OF DAILY VALUE**
Calories from fat	76	Carbohydrates	47 g	Vitamin A 12 %
Fat	8 g	Fiber	3 g	Vitamin C 8 %
Saturated Fat	1 g	Protein	2 g	Calcium 2 %
Cholesterol	0 mg			Iron 7 %

Pineapple Bread Kugel

1 20-oz. can crushed
  pineapple
1 cup margarine
1 cup sugar
2 tsp. vanilla

1½ tsp. cinnamon
8 eggs
12 slices of leftover bread or
  challah, soaked

Drain pineapple and reserve ¾ cup liquid. Cream margarine, sugar, vanilla, and cinnamon. Beat in eggs. Fold in pineapple and juice. Stir in bread. Bake in a greased 9x13-inch pan at 350° for 1 hour.

NUTRITIONAL INFORMATION PER SERVING:				Serving Size: 5 oz. Total Servings: 15	
Calories	291	Sodium	280 mg	PERCENT OF DAILY VALUE	
Calories from fat	141	Carbohydrates	33 g	Vitamin A	25 %
Fat	16 g	Fiber	1 g	Vitamin C	9 %
Saturated Fat	3 g	Protein	5 g	Calcium	7 %
Cholesterol	114 mg			Iron	8 %

Broccoli Casserole

1⅓ cup minute rice,
  uncooked
1 20-oz. pkg. frozen
  chopped broccoli (don't
  defrost)

2 Tbs. margarine
1 pkg. onion soup mix
1 Tbs. lemon juice
2 cups boiling water

Combine all ingredients except boiling water and turn into a 2-quart baking dish. Pour boiling water over mixture. Bake, uncovered, at 350° for 35 to 40 minutes.

NUTRITIONAL INFORMATION PER SERVING:				Serving Size: 6 oz. Total Servings: 7	
Calories	184	Sodium	103 mg	PERCENT OF DAILY VALUE	
Calories from fat	32	Carbohydrates	33 g	Vitamin A	24 %
Fat	4 g	Fiber	4 g	Vitamin C	55 %
Saturated Fat	1 g	Protein	5 g	Calcium	8 %
Cholesterol	0 mg			Iron	11 %

Vegetable Pie

2 16-oz. bags any BODEK
    frozen vegetables
3 eggs
1 Tbs. flour
½ cup COFFEE RICH

½ cup mayonnaise
½ pkg. onion soup mix (or
    to taste)
1 frozen pie shell, thawed

Boil vegetables until soft. Drain and mash well. Add remaining ingredients and mix by hand. Spoon into pie shell. Bake at 350° for 20 to 25 minutes.

NUTRITIONAL INFORMATION PER SERVING:				Serving Size: 6 oz. Total Servings: 8	
Calories	204	Sodium	182 mg	**PERCENT OF DAILY VALUE**	
Calories from fat	144	Carbohydrates	12 g	Vitamin A	19 %
Fat	16 g	Fiber	3 g	Vitamin C	67 %
Saturated Fat	2 g	Protein	6 g	Calcium	6 %
Cholesterol	90 mg			Iron	6 %

Sweet Potato Kugel

5–6 medium-sized sweet
    potatoes
1 20-oz. can crushed
    pineapple
1 egg

⅓ cup bread crumbs
⅓ cup brown sugar
2 Tbs. lemon juice
1 tsp. cinnamon
1 tsp. nutmeg (optional)

Cook sweet potatoes. When done, peel and mash them and then add remaining ingredients. Pour into a round pan and bake at 350° for 1 hour.

NUTRITIONAL INFORMATION PER SERVING:				Serving Size: 6 oz. Total Servings: 12	
Calories	192	Sodium	62 mg	**PERCENT OF DAILY VALUE**	
Calories from fat	10	Carbohydrates	43 g	Vitamin A	1 %
Fat	1 g	Fiber	1 g	Vitamin C	44 %
Saturated Fat	1 g	Protein	3 g	Calcium	4 %
Cholesterol	18 mg			Iron	7 %

Potato Kugel

Compliments of Sabel's Catering, Monsey, NY

4 eggs	½ cup oil
5 large potatoes	2 tsp. salt, or to taste
1 medium onion	¼ tsp. pepper, or to taste

Beat eggs. Peel and grate potatoes and onion directly into beaten eggs. (This prevents potatoes from turning black.) Add oil, salt, and pepper to mixture. Turn into two greased, 8-inch round pans and bake at 375° for approximately 1 hour.

NUTRITIONAL INFORMATION PER SERVING:			Serving Size: 3½ oz. Total Servings: 16	
Calories	136	Sodium	286 mg	**PERCENT OF DAILY VALUE**
Calories from fat	74	Carbohydrates	12 g	Vitamin A 2 %
Fat	8 g	Fiber	1 g	Vitamin C 22 %
Saturated Fat	1 g	Protein	3 g	Calcium 2 %
Cholesterol	53 mg			Iron 8 %

Mom's Noodle Kugel

12-oz. pkg. medium egg noodles	½ tsp. salt, or to taste
1 onion, grated	pepper, to taste
1 egg	¼ cup cornflake crumbs
	¼ cup oil for frying

Cook noodles 8 to 10 minutes and drain. Add onion, egg, salt, and pepper to the noodles, then mix in cornflake crumbs. Meanwhile, heat oil in a large frying pan. Pour in noodle mixture and fry on a medium flame until brown (about 10 to 15 minutes). Then slip kugel onto a plate, add more oil to pan if necessary, and slide kugel back into the pan to fry on the other side. Fry another 10 to 15 minutes.

NUTRITIONAL INFORMATION PER SERVING:			Serving Size: 4 oz. Total Servings: 8	
Calories	246	Cholesterol	67 g	**PERCENT OF DAILY VALUE**
Calories from fat	83	Sodium	170 mg	Vitamin A 2 %
Fat	9 g	Carbohydrates	34 g	Vitamin C 2 %
Saturated Fat	1 g	Protein	7 g	Calcium 3 %
				Iron 19 %

Apple Crumb Kugel

1 cup oil
1 cup sugar (or less)
1 tsp. vanilla
3 eggs
1 cup flour
2 tsp. baking powder

¼ tsp. salt
2 tsp. cinnamon
¼ cup cold water
6 apples, shredded
½ cup cornflake crumbs

Mix oil and sugar. Add vanilla, then eggs. Combine flour, baking powder, salt, and cinnamon. Add to mixture alternately with water. Pour batter into a 9x13-inch greased pan, reserving some for later. Spread on shredded apples. Spoon remaining batter on top of apples. Top with cornflake crumbs. Bake at 350° for 1 hour.

NUTRITIONAL INFORMATION PER SERVING:			Serving Size: 3½ oz. Total Servings: 15	
Calories	260	Sodium	69 mg	**PERCENT OF DAILY VALUE**
Calories from fat	142	Carbohydrates	29 g	Vitamin A 5 %
Fat	16 g	Fiber	1 g	Vitamin C 4 %
Saturated Fat	2 g	Protein	2 g	Calcium 2 %
Cholesterol	43 mg			Iron 5 %

Tofu-Spinach Quiche

1 unbaked 9-inch pie shell
1 Tbs. olive oil
1½ cups chopped onion
1 10-oz. package frozen
   chopped spinach

1 lb. tofu, mashed
1 Tbs. lemon juice
1 tsp. salt
½ tsp. garlic powder

Bake pie shell at 350° for 5 minutes. Add olive oil to saucepan and sauté onion over low heat. Add spinach and sauté for 2 minutes. Mix together with tofu, lemon juice, salt, and garlic powder. Pour into pie shell. Bake at 400° for 30 minutes, or until crust is a golden color.

NUTRITIONAL INFORMATION PER SERVING:			Serving Size: 5¼ oz. Total Servings: 8	
Calories	180	Sodium	439 mg	**PERCENT OF DAILY VALUE**
Calories from fat	98	Carbohydrates	16 g	Vitamin A 34 %
Fat	11 g	Fiber	2 g	Vitamin C 11 %
Saturated Fat	2 g	Protein	6 g	Calcium 9 %
Cholesterol	0 mg			Iron 9 %

Rebbetzin's Quick Blender Potato Kugel

4 eggs
½ cup oil
5 potatoes, cubed

1 tsp. salt
½ tsp. pepper

Fill up blender with eggs, oil, and potatoes. Add salt and pepper. Blend until smooth. Pour into a deep 9 x 7 rectangular pan. Bake at 400° for 1½ hours or until nicely browned.

NUTRITIONAL INFORMATION PER SERVING:				Serving Size: 4¾ oz. Total Servings: 8	
Calories	257	Sodium	353 mg	PERCENT OF DAILY VALUE	
Calories from fat	168	Carbohydrates	15 g	Vitamin A	11 %
Fat	19 g	Fiber	1 g	Vitamin C	21 %
Saturated Fat	3 g	Protein	7 g	Calcium	5 %
Cholesterol	213 mg			Iron	11 %

Dried Fruit Kugel (dairy)

8 oz. medium noodles
8-oz. container low-fat
  cottage cheese
11-oz. bag mixed dried fruit,
  pitted and chopped
8-oz. pkg. low-fat cream
  cheese, cut into chunks

2 cups low-fat milk
¼ cup sugar
1 tsp. cinnamon
½ tsp. salt
2 large eggs, slightly beaten

Preheat oven to 350°. Cook noodles as directed on package (do not add salt) and drain. In a food processor (using the knife blade attachment), blend cottage cheese until smooth. In a large bowl, mix cottage cheese with dried fruit and remaining ingredients. Stir in noodles. Pour into ungreased 2½-quart baking dish and bake uncovered for 50 minutes. Kugel might look wet in center, but will set after standing about 10 minutes.

NUTRITIONAL INFORMATION PER SERVING:				Serving Size: 8 oz. Total Servings: 8	
Calories	364	Sodium	465 mg	PERCENT OF DAILY VALUE	
Calories from fat	77	Carbohydrates	61 g	Vitamin A	37 %
Fat	9 g	Fiber	1 g	Vitamin C	3 %
Saturated Fat	7 g	Protein	15 g	Calcium	21 %
Cholesterol	94 mg			Iron	19 %

Sandwich Suggestions and Spreads

Techina	Date Butter
Vegetable Liver	Natural Homemade Mayonnaise
Garlic Techina	Felafel
Veggie-Rice Burgers	Babaghanoush
Wheat Germ Spread	Peanut Butter Tofu Spread
Sesame-Honey Spread	Hummus
Peanut Butter and Honey Spread	Crunchy Tofu Spread
Israeli Olive Spread	Tofu Spread
Tofu, Fruit, and Seed Spread	Apple-Butter Spread

Sandwich Suggestions and Spreads

Techina

3 Tbs. techina
3 Tbs. water

1 tsp. lemon juice
1 Tbs. garlic powder

Mix all ingredients together until smooth. Add more water if necessary.

NUTRITIONAL INFORMATION PER SERVING:			Serving Size: 1 Tbs. Total Servings: 10		
Calories	28	Cholesterol	0 mg	Protein	1 g
Calories from fat	20	Sodium	2 mg	**PERCENT OF DAILY VALUE**	
Fat	2 g	Carbohydrates	2 g	Iron	1 %
Saturated Fat	0 g	Fiber	0 g		

Vegetable Liver

4 large onions, chopped
2 Tbs. oil
4 hard-boiled eggs
½ cup chopped walnuts

1 cup canned green beans
1 cup canned green peas
½ tsp. salt, or to taste
pepper, to taste

Sauté onions in oil. Mix all ingredients in a food processor. Serve chilled.

NUTRITIONAL INFORMATION PER SERVING:			Serving Size: 4 oz. Total Servings: 10		
Calories	208	Sodium	175 mg	**PERCENT OF DAILY VALUE**	
Calories from fat	150	Carbohydrates	10 g	Vitamin A	8 %
Fat	17 g	Fiber	2 g	Vitamin C	17 %
Saturated Fat	2 g	Protein	6 g	Calcium	6 %
Cholesterol	85 mg			Iron	19 %

Garlic Techina

1 17-oz. can of techina
17 oz. water
4 cloves of garlic

2–3 Tbs. vinegar or lemon
    juice
dash of salt
pepper, to taste

Mix techina and water in a food processor. Add garlic, vinegar or lemon juice, salt, and pepper. Blend until smooth. If too thick, add more water. More spices can be added according to taste. It should have a tart garlic taste. Good with salads, fish on Shabbos, or as a spread. Can be used in sandwiches with slices of tomato, pickles, or olives. Can be frozen in small plastic containers and used as needed.

NUTRITIONAL INFORMATION PER SERVING:		Serving Size: 1 Tbs. Total Servings: 75		
Calories	38	Sodium	33 mg	**PERCENT OF DAILY VALUE**
Calories from fat	31	Carbohydrates	1 g	Calcium 1 %
Fat	3 g	Fiber	0 g	Iron 1 %
Saturated Fat	0 g	Protein	1 g	
Cholesterol	0 mg			

Veggie-Rice Burgers

1 onion, diced
2 Tbs. + 4 Tbs. oil for
    sautéing
1 8-oz. can mushrooms,
    drained, or 5 oz. fresh
2 carrots, grated
⅔ cup frozen peas
4 cups cooked brown rice

4 eggs, beaten
2 Tbs. tamari soy sauce, or
    ½ tsp. salt, to taste
dash of cayenne red pepper
½ tsp. garlic powder or dill
    or curry
¾ cup bread crumbs

Sauté onion in 2 Tbs. oil for 3 to 5 minutes. Add mushrooms (if using fresh) and carrots. Sauté 3 to 5 minutes more, stirring occasionally. Drain mushrooms (if using canned) and add mushrooms and peas to carrots. Stir and remove from heat. Put cooked rice in a large bowl. Add vegetable mixture and blend well. Add eggs and blend. Add seasonings and spices. Add bread crumbs and mix together well.

Form into patties. Fry in 4 Tbs. oil on low heat, covered for first side.

Variation: Add 1 cup cooked chickpeas, or pinto or navy beans, for full protein.

NUTRITIONAL INFORMATION PER SERVING:			Serving Size: 5 oz. Total Servings: 12		
Calories	207	Sodium	258 mg	**PERCENT OF DAILY VALUE**	
Calories from fat	87	Carbohydrates	24 g	Vitamin A	47 %
Fat	10 g	Fiber	2 g	Vitamin C	5 %
Saturated Fat	2 g	Protein	6 g	Calcium	4 %
Cholesterol	71 mg			Iron	10 %

Wheat Germ Spread

½ cup wheat germ
½ cup natural peanut butter

¼ cup honey

Mix all ingredients together.

NUTRITIONAL INFORMATION PER SERVING:			Serving Size: 1 Tbs. Total Servings: 20		
Calories	82	Cholesterol	0 mg	Protein	2 g
Calories from fat	60	Sodium	33 mg		
Fat	7 g	Carbohydrates	4 g	**PERCENT OF DAILY VALUE**	
Saturated Fat	1 g	Fiber	1 g	Iron	15 %

Sesame-Honey Spread

¼ cup honey

1 cup sesame techina

Mix honey with techina. For a sweeter taste, add more honey. For a tasty dip, add water to make the mixture into a paste.

NUTRITIONAL INFORMATION PER SERVING:			Serving Size: 1 Tbs. Total Servings: 20		
Calories	76	Sodium	4 mg	**PERCENT OF DAILY VALUE**	
Calories from fat	54	Carbohydrates	5 g	Calcium	2 %
Fat	6 g	Fiber	1 g	Iron	3 %
Saturated Fat	1 g	Protein	2 g		
Cholesterol	0 mg				

Peanut Butter and Honey Spread

½ cup peanut butter   **½ cup honey**

Mix well with a wooden spoon or fork. Spread on whole-wheat bread and enjoy.

Variations:
1. Add 2 Tbs. ground sunflower seeds.
2. Add chopped dates.
3. Use techina instead of peanut butter, or use half techina and half peanut butter.

NUTRITIONAL INFORMATION PER SERVING:				Serving Size: 1 Tbs. Total Servings: 20	
Calories	55	Saturated Fat	1 g	Carbohydrates	6 g
Calories from fat	29	Cholesterol	0 mg	Fiber	0 g
Fat	3 g	Sodium	31 mg	Protein	2 g

Israeli Olive Spread

1 cup chopped olives
½ cup finely ground roasted nuts
¼ cup finely ground almonds

¼ cup finely ground sesame or sunflower seeds
¼ cup finely chopped celery
1 cup mayonnaise

Mix all ingredients with enough mayonnaise to make an easy-to-spread consistency.

NUTRITIONAL INFORMATION PER SERVING:				Serving Size: 1 Tbs. Total Servings: 35	
Calories	55	Sodium	65 mg	**PERCENT OF DAILY VALUE**	
Calories from fat	46	Carbohydrates	2 g	Calcium	2 %
Fat	5 g	Fiber	1 g	Iron	3 %
Saturated Fat	1 g	Protein	2 g		
Cholesterol	1 mg				

Tofu, Fruit, and Seed Spread

1 medium Golden Delicious
   apple
1 Tbs. lemon juice
3 Tbs. soft tofu
1 tsp. honey

½ cup toasted sunflower
   seeds
½ cup toasted sesame
   seeds
1 Tbs. grated orange rind
pinch of nutmeg

Cut apple into thin slices. Put apple slices and remaining ingredients into a food processor or blender. Mix until well blended and smooth.

NUTRITIONAL INFORMATION PER SERVING:				Serving Size: 1 Tbs. Total Servings: 25	
Calories	46	Sodium	1 mg	**PERCENT OF DAILY VALUE**	
Calories from fat	33	Carbohydrates	3 g	Vitamin C	1 %
Fat	4 g	Fiber	1 g	Calcium	6 %
Saturated Fat	0 g	Protein	2 g	Iron	5 %
Cholesterol	0 mg				

Date Butter

5 cups chopped dates
3 cups hot water

2 tsp. orange or lemon rind

Soak dates in hot water until soft. Peel and remove pits. Blend with orange or lemon rind in a blender until smooth.

Variations: Instead of 5 cups of dates, use 2½ cups chopped dates with 2½ cups finely ground nuts, or use 2½ cups chopped dates with 2½ cups fresh apricots.

NUTRITIONAL INFORMATION PER SERVING:				Serving Size: 1 Tbs. Total Servings: 100	
Calories	25	Saturated Fat	0 g	Carbohydrates	7 g
Calories from fat	0	Cholesterol	0 mg	Fiber	1 g
Fat	0 g	Sodium	0 mg		

Natural Homemade Mayonnaise
Compliments of The Natural Place, Monsey, NY

1 organic egg
2 tsp. apple cider vinegar
1 Tbs. raw white honey
1½ tsp. LIMA Sea Salt

pinch of dry mustard
(optional)
1 cup safflower oil

Mix all ingredients, except for oil, in a food processor or blender until well blended. While machine is running, pour in oil slowly, in a fine stream. Let blend until mixture thickens. Refrigerate.

NUTRITIONAL INFORMATION PER SERVING:			Serving Size: 1 tsp. Total Servings: 40		
Calories	51	Fat	6 g	Cholesterol	5 mg
Calories from fat	50	Saturated Fat	0 g	Sodium	82 mg

Falafel
Compliments of Supreme Health Food Center, Monsey, NY

2 cups cooked chickpeas
(garbanzo beans)
(approx. 1 cup dried)
⅓ cup cooking water
(necessary only if using
blender)
crumbs from 1 slice whole-
wheat bread
1 Tbs. soy flour
2 cloves garlic, finely minced
1 egg, lightly beaten
2 Tbs. chopped fresh parsley

¾ tsp. salt
¼ tsp. ground cumin
¼ tsp. basil
¼ tsp. marjoram
¼ tsp. cayenne pepper, or
less, to taste
white pepper, to taste
1 Tbs. techina (sesame
paste)
whole-wheat or soy flour for
coating
5 Tbs. vegetable oil

Mash or grind chickpeas, or put them through a blender with the cooking water. Combine the chickpeas and all the remaining ingredients, except flour for coating and oil. The mixture will be soft. Form it into 1-inch balls, coat with the flour, and sauté in oil, turning the balls and sautéing until crisp on all sides.

NUTRITIONAL INFORMATION PER SERVING:				Serving Size: 3 oz. Total Servings: 5	
Calories	307	Sodium	542 mg	**PERCENT OF DAILY VALUE**	
Calories from fat	187	Carbohydrates	24 g	Vitamin A	3 %
Fat	21 g	Fiber	5 g	Vitamin C	4 %
Saturated Fat	4 g	Protein	8 g	Calcium	6 %
Cholesterol	46 g			Iron	13 %

Babaghanoush

1 medium eggplant
1 Tbs. salt, or to taste
¼ cup freshly squeezed
    lemon juice
3 Tbs. techina

⅓ cup chopped parsley
2 small cloves of garlic,
    finely chopped
tamari soy sauce, to taste
    (approx. 1 Tbs.)

Peel eggplant and cut into cubes, then salt it and set aside for 15 minutes. Rinse salt off well and steam eggplant until soft. Purée in blender or food processor. Blend in remaining ingredients.

NUTRITIONAL INFORMATION PER SERVING:				Serving Size: 3 oz. Total Servings: 4	
Calories	85	Sodium	537 mg	**PERCENT OF DAILY VALUE**	
Calories from fat	52	Carbohydrates	7 g	Vitamin A	4 %
Fat	6 g	Fiber	1 g	Vitamin C	28 %
Saturated Fat	1 g	Protein	3 g	Calcium	4 %
Cholesterol	0 mg			Iron	7 %

Peanut-Butter Tofu Spread

8 oz. tofu, drained
½ cup peanut butter
1 Tbs. honey
1 banana, mashed

¼ cup sunflower seeds,
chopped (optional)
¼ cup raisins (optional)

Mix tofu, peanut butter, honey, and banana in a food processor or blender. Add seeds and raisins and blend thoroughly.

NUTRITIONAL INFORMATION PER SERVING:				Serving Size: 1 Tbs. Total Servings: 40	
Calories	36	Cholesterol	0 mg	Protein	1 g
Calories from fat	20	Sodium	18 mg	**PERCENT OF DAILY VALUE**	
Fat	2 g	Carbohydrates	3 g	Iron	1 %
Saturated Fat	0 g	Fiber	0 g		

Hummus

2 cups canned chickpeas
(garbanzo beans),
drained
⅔ cups techina

¾ cup lemon juice
2 cloves garlic
1 tsp. salt

Place ingredients in blender and blend until smooth.

NUTRITIONAL INFORMATION PER SERVING:				Serving Size: 2½ oz. Total Servings: 30	
Calories	72	Sodium	137 mg	**PERCENT OF DAILY VALUE**	
Calories from fat	36	Carbohydrates	8 g	Vitamin C	20 %
Fat	4 g	Fiber	1 g	Calcium	2 %
Saturated Fat	1 g	Protein	2 g	Iron	4 %
Cholesterol	0 mg				

Crunchy Tofu Spread

¼ cup oat bran
¼ cup soft tofu
1 tsp. lemon juice
½ banana, sliced

1 Tbs. maple syrup
½ tsp. vanilla
½ tsp. cinnamon
1 tsp. grated orange rind

Combine all ingredients in a food processor or blender until well mixed. (It will not be perfectly smooth.)

NUTRITIONAL INFORMATION PER SERVING:		Serving Size: 1 Tbs. Total Servings: 15			
Calories	15	Sodium	3 mg	**PERCENT OF DAILY VALUE**	
Calories from fat	2	Carbohydrates	3 g	Vitamin C	1 %
Fat	0 g	Fiber	0 g	Iron	1 %
Saturated Fat	0 g	Protein	0 g		
Cholesterol	0 mg				

Tofu Spread

2 cups soft tofu
1 Tbs. tamari soy sauce

1 tsp. dry mustard
¼ cup chopped onion

Combine all ingredients in a food processor or blender. Blend until smooth.

NUTRITIONAL INFORMATION PER SERVING:		Serving Size: 1 Tbs. Total Servings: 40			
Calories	11	Cholesterol	0 mg	**PERCENT OF DAILY VALUE**	
Calories from fat	6	Sodium	27 mg	Calcium	1 %
Fat	1 g	Protein	1 g	Iron	4 %
Saturated Fat	0 g				

Apple-Butter Spread

4 lbs. apples, peeled and
    sliced
⅓ cup apple juice (not from
    concentrate)
⅔ cup dark brown sugar

2 tsp. vanilla extract
1 Tbs. lemon juice
1 tsp. cinnamon
½ tsp. nutmeg
½ tsp. ground cloves

Place all ingredients on stove-top in a large stock pot with a tight-fitting lid. Bring to a boil and reduce heat. Simmer on medium-low heat until the apples are soft enough to mash (around 15 to 25 minutes). Remove from heat and put mixture in a food processor. Process in short spurts until smooth. If overdone, it will turn watery. Makes 2 cups.

NUTRITIONAL INFORMATION PER SERVING:		Serving Size: 1½ oz. Total Servings: 50		
Calories	33	Sodium	1 mg	**PERCENT OF DAILY VALUE**
Calories from fat	1	Carbohydrates	9 g	Vitamin C 2 %
Fat	0 g	Fiber	1 g	Iron 1 %
Saturated Fat	0 g	Protein	0 g	
Cholesterol	0 mg			

Satisfying That Sweet Tooth...

Nature's Sweets

Homemade Halva
Pineapple Coconut Bars
Yummy Maple Oatmeal Crisp
Peanut Butter Candies
Raisin Bars
Fruity Bars
Granola Fruit Bars
Sesame Wafers (Dairy)
Fruit and Nut Snack
Pineapple Chunk Ices
Fruit Leather
Carob and Peanut Butter
Fudge
Carob Bananas with Granola
Candy Apples
Fruit Chews
Crispy Cake
Granola Delight
Chocolate-Covered Banana Pops
Simple Chunky Applesauce
Frozen Grapes

Candy Bars
Pineapple-Glazed Bananas
Mama's Fruit Salad
Peach Cobbler with Strawberry Topping
No-Sugar Compote
Cranberry Crisp
Frulati Di Fruta (frothy banana drink)
Raspberry Pears
Punch
Baked Apples
Ambrosia Drink
Stuffed Peaches
Orange Julius Delight
Super Fruit Salad
Apple Betty
Fruit Salad
Blueberry Dessert
Apple Crisp
Apple-Cranberry Dessert
Fancy Fruit Cup

Nature's Sweets

Homemade Halva

2 cups sesame seeds   **½ cup techina**
½ cup honey, or to taste   **½ cup coconut**

Toast sesame seeds until they have been popping for about 2 minutes and are all puffed up.

To toast: Place seeds in a dry nonstick sauté pan and heat on high, stirring constantly until they are lightly browned. Once they get hot they'll pop. Let pop for about 2 minutes.

Or: Place seeds on an ungreased tray in oven at 350° for about 10 minutes. Seeds will start to pop. Let pop for about 2 minutes.

Let seeds cool a bit, then grind in a coffee grinder or blender. Mix well with other ingredients. Add the techina and honey only as needed to make a stiff paste; don't let it get too thin. Form into a roll and store in refrigerator or freezer. Cut into slices as needed.

NUTRITIONAL INFORMATION PER SERVING:		Serving Size: 1 oz. Total Servings: 24			
Calories	178	Sodium	15 mg	**PERCENT OF DAILY VALUE**	
Calories from fat	124	Carbohydrates	12 g	Calcium	24 %
Fat	14 g	Fiber	4 g	Iron	20 %
Saturated Fat	2 g	Protein	4 g		
Cholesterol	0 mg				

Pineapple Coconut Bars

1 20-oz. can crushed
  pineapple
1 egg, beaten
1¾ cups coconut flakes

¾ cup whole-wheat flour
¼ cup wheat germ
¼ tsp. salt

Drain pineapple and reserve juice. Measure, separately, ¾ cup pineapple juice and ¾ cup pineapple. Set both aside. In a large bowl, beat egg. Add the pineapple juice. Mix in the crushed pineapple and coconut flakes. Set aside. In another bowl, mix flour, wheat germ, and salt. Pour into the pineapple mixture and mix well. Pour into a greased 8-inch square pan. Pat down mixture evenly. Bake at 350° for 45 minutes or until brown. Cut into bars. Wrap individually and store in container in refrigerator.

NUTRITIONAL INFORMATION PER SERVING:		Serving Size: 1¾ oz. Total Servings: 20			
Calories	88	Sodium	32 mg	**PERCENT OF DAILY VALUE**	
Calories from fat	24	Carbohydrates	15 g	Vitamin C	3 %
Fat	3 g	Fiber	1 g	Calcium	1 %
Saturated Fat	2 g	Protein	2 g	Iron	6 %
Cholesterol	11 mg				

Yummy Maple Oatmeal Crisp

2½ cups rolled oats
1½ cups whole-wheat pastry
  flour
1 cup ground almonds

¾ cup maple syrup or ½
  cup honey
¾ cup oil
1 tsp. vanilla
½ tsp. almond extract
  (optional)

Mix together dry ingredients. In a separate bowl, blend the liquid ingredients and pour them into the dry ingredients. Blend well. Drop by teaspoonfuls onto a greased cookie sheet, flattening out dough if you like it crispy. Bake at 325° for 20 to 25 minutes, until golden brown.

Variation: Flatten out dough on 2 pans to make bar cookies. After baking, cut into squares while still warm.

NUTRITIONAL INFORMATION PER SERVING:		Serving Size: 1 oz. Total Servings: 48			
Calories	88	Sodium	1 mg	**PERCENT OF DAILY VALUE**	
Calories from fat	52	Carbohydrates	8 g	Calcium	2 %
Fat	6 g	Fiber	1 g	Iron	3 %
Saturated Fat	1 g	Protein	2 g		
Cholesterol	0 mg				

Peanut Butter Candies

½ cup sesame seeds
¼ cup wheat germ
4 Tbs. honey
½ cup peanut butter
1 tsp. lemon extract

¼ cup raisins
¼ cup shelled peanuts
¼ cup ground walnuts or
  almonds

Put sesame seeds and wheat germ in a small baking pan and bake at 350° for 10 to 15 minutes. In a large bowl, cream together honey and peanut butter until smooth. Add lemon extract and blend. Add sesame seeds, wheat germ, raisins, and peanuts. Mix thoroughly until all are coated with peanut butter. With hands, form candy mixture into 15 balls. Roll each ball in ground nuts, and wrap each candy in cellophane. Does not need refrigeration.

NUTRITIONAL INFORMATION PER SERVING:		Serving Size: 1 ball Total Servings: 15			
Calories	182	Sodium	48 mg	**PERCENT OF DAILY VALUE**	
Calories from fat	127	Carbohydrates	10 g	Calcium	10 %
Fat	14 g	Fiber	3 g	Iron	10 %
Saturated Fat	2 g	Protein	6 g		
Cholesterol	0 mg				

Raisin Bars

Compliments of Supreme Health Food Center, Monsey, NY

1 cup whole-wheat pastry
   flour
1 cup rolled oats
½ tsp. salt (preferably sea
   salt)

¼ cup oil (canola or
   sunflower)
1¼ cups finely chopped or
   ground raisins
1 cup chopped walnuts
⅓–½ cup water

Preheat oven to 325°. Blend flour, oats, salt, and oil with fingers until evenly mixed. Add raisins, nuts, and water, and mix them in, pressing together with fingers. (Use larger amount of water only if absolutely necessary to make it all hold together.) Press down very well into a greased, 8x8-inch pan and cut into bars with a spatula before baking. Bake for 30 minutes.

NUTRITIONAL INFORMATION PER SERVING:				Serving Size: 1 bar Total Servings: 16	
Calories	198	Sodium	70 mg	**PERCENT OF DAILY VALUE**	
Calories from fat	77	Carbohydrates	27 g	Calcium	3 %
Fat	9 g	Fiber	2 g	Iron	10 %
Saturated Fat	1 g	Protein	5 g		
Cholesterol	0 mg				

Fruity Bars

1 lb. (2¼ cups) pitted dates
2 cups ground almonds or
   walnuts

½ cup raisins
⅓ cup shredded coconut

Blend dates, nuts, and raisins together in a blender. Place this mixture on a large piece of waxed paper. Work the mixture into a firmly packed ball. Flatten the ball a bit and cover it with another sheet of waxed paper. With a rolling pin, roll over the waxed paper until mixture is ½-inch thick. Peel off the top sheet of waxed paper. Cut into small bars. Press coconut into each bar so that the bar is covered. Wrap each bar in cellophane and store in a container.

NUTRITIONAL INFORMATION PER SERVING:[*]		Serving Size: 1 bar Total Servings: 10		
Calories	263	Sodium	3 mg	PERCENT OF DAILY VALUE
Calories from fat	90	Carbohydrates	41 g	Vitamin A 1 %
Fat	10 g	Fiber	2 g	Vitamin C 1 %
Saturated Fat	1 g	Protein	5 g	Calcium 4 %
Cholesterol	0 mg			Iron 7 %

* Analysis done with walnuts.

Granola Fruit Bars

2 cups rolled oats
½ cup coarsely chopped
    walnuts or sunflower
    seeds
½ cup raisins
½ tsp. cinnamon

2 Tbs. margarine
¼ cup honey
2 Tbs. apple juice
1 banana, mashed
1 egg, beaten

Combine oats, nuts, raisins, and cinnamon, and set aside. In a saucepan, melt margarine and honey. Add apple juice and pour over dry ingredients. Mix in banana and egg. Line a 9-inch square pan with parchment paper and press the mixture into the pan. Bake at 350° for 20 to 25 minutes. Cut into bars.

NUTRITIONAL INFORMATION PER SERVING:		Serving Size: 1 bar Total Servings: 25		
Calories	75	Sodium	14 mg	PERCENT OF DAILY VALUE
Calories from fat	27	Carbohydrates	10 g	Vitamin A 2 %
Fat	3 g	Fiber	1 g	Vitamin C 2 %
Saturated Fat	0 g	Protein	2 g	Calcium 1 %
Cholesterol	9 mg			Iron 3 %

Sesame Wafers (Dairy)

½ cup whole-wheat flour
½ cup enriched white flour
2 Tbs. honey
2 Tbs. vegetable oil or
    sesame oil
1 tsp. vanilla

½ tsp. cinnamon
¼ tsp. ginger
⅛ tsp. nutmeg
2 Tbs. sesame seeds
¼–½ cup milk

Preheat oven to 400°. In a bowl, mix flours, honey, oil, vanilla, spices, and sesame seeds. Gradually add milk until a firm dough is formed. On a lightly floured surface, roll dough ¼-inch thick. Using cookie cutters, cut shapes and place on a greased baking sheet. Bake 10 to 12 minutes or until lightly browned. Remove from pan and cool.

NUTRITIONAL INFORMATION PER SERVING:		Serving Size: ½ oz. Total Servings: 24		
Calories	41	Sodium	2 mg	**PERCENT OF DAILY VALUE**
Calories from fat	16	Carbohydrates	5 g	Calcium 2 %
Fat	2 g	Fiber	1 g	Iron 2 %
Saturated Fat	0 g	Protein	1 g	
Cholesterol	0 mg			

Fruit and Nut Snack

⅓ cup raisins
⅓ cup sunflower seeds

⅓ cup chopped walnuts

Combine ingredients. Keep mixture in a sealed bag or jar. Refrigerate if uisng raw sunflower seeds.

NUTRITIONAL INFORMATION PER SERVING:		Serving Size: ¼ cup Total Servings: 4		
Calories	166	Sodium	2 mg	**PERCENT OF DAILY VALUE**
Calories from fat	106	Carbohydrates	13 g	Vitamin C 1 %
Fat	12 g	Fiber	2 g	Calcium 3 %
Saturated Fat	1 g	Protein	6 g	Iron 9 %
Cholesterol	0 mg			

Pineapple Chunk Ices

14 pineapple chunks
1 cup orange juice

1 cup cranberry juice
14 popsicle sticks

Place 1 pineapple chunk in each section of an ice cube tray. Mix orange juice with cranberry juice and pour over pineapple. Insert a popsicle stick into each pineapple chunk, and freeze. This is a good snack for small children.

NUTRITIONAL INFORMATION PER SERVING:		Serving Size: 1 cube Total Servings: 14			
Calories	16	Cholesterol	0 mg	Protein	0 g
Calories from fat	0	Sodium	1 mg	**PERCENT OF DAILY VALUE**	
Fat	0 g	Carbohydrates	6 g	Vitamin C	25 %
Saturated Fat	0 g	Fiber	0 g		

Fruit Leather

½ cup dried apricots
½ cup raisins

½ cup fruit juice (apple,
pineapple, or orange)

Soak dried fruits in juice overnight in a jar or bowl. Blend in blender until completely smooth. Spread parchment paper on a cookie sheet. Pour fruit mixture thinly over paper. Put in oven on the lowest setting, or for gas ovens, pilot alone is fine. Leave for 48 hours. When it is dried up enough to lift off, peel it off and roll up into a long roll. Makes one 12-inch roll.

Variation: Any other combination of dried fruits and juice may be used.

NUTRITIONAL INFORMATION PER SERVING:		Serving Size: 2 oz. Total Servings: 4			
Calories	112	Sodium	4 mg	**PERCENT OF DAILY VALUE**	
Calories from fat	2	Carbohydrates	29 g	Vitamin A	14 %
Fat	0 g	Fiber	3 g	Vitamin C	6 %
Saturated Fat	0 g	Protein	1 g	Calcium	2 %
Cholesterol	0 mg			Iron	8 %

Carob and Peanut Butter Fudge

½ cup honey
½ cup natural peanut butter
2 Tbs. hot water
½ cup chopped walnuts
½ cup carob powder
½ cup toasted sesame
    seeds

½ cup ground sunflower
    seeds
2 Tbs. lecithin granules
1 tsp. vanilla extract
⅓ cup coconut

Combine honey with peanut butter. Add remaining ingredients, excluding coconut. Roll into 1-inch balls, then roll in coconut. Refrigerate in an airtight container.

NUTRITIONAL INFORMATION PER SERVING:				Serving Size: 1 oz. Total Servings: 30	
Calories	131	Sodium	30 mg	**PERCENT OF DAILY VALUE**	
Calories from fat	89	Carbohydrates	10 g	Calcium	7 %
Fat	10 g	Fiber	2 g	Iron	8 %
Saturated Fat	1 g	Protein	4 g		
Cholesterol	0 mg				

Carob Bananas with Granola

1 cup carob powder
1 cup water

3 bananas
1 cup granola

In a small saucepan, combine carob powder and water. Bring to a boil over low heat, stirring constantly. Cook for 5 minutes until syrup is thickened, and cool. Cut bananas into thirds. Pour syrup into a shallow dish. Place granola on waxed paper. Roll bananas in syrup and then in granola. Place on a tray covered with waxed paper and freeze. After bananas are frozen, remove from tray and store in a plastic bag in the freezer. (Store unused portion of syrup in refrigerator — it will keep for weeks.)

NUTRITIONAL INFORMATION PER SERVING:		Serving Size: ⅓ banana Total Servings: 9			
Calories	159	Sodium	35 mg	**PERCENT OF DAILY VALUE**	
Calories from fat	25	Carbohydrates	40 g	Vitamin C	9 %
Fat	3 g	Fiber	4 g	Calcium	11 %
Saturated Fat	1 g	Protein	3 g	Iron	8 %
Cholesterol	0 mg				

Candy Apples

apples (as many as you think will be eaten)	1⅓ cups ground walnuts or pecans
1 oz. honey per apple	popsicle sticks, one per apple

Pour honey into a bowl. Pour the ground nuts into another bowl. Insert a stick into the center of each apple so that apples can be lifted by sticks. Dip each apple into honey, covering every part of the apple. Hold apple over bowl so excess honey can drip off. Roll apple in ground nuts to cover completely. Repeat with remaining apples. Refrigerate until ready to serve.

NUTRITIONAL INFORMATION PER SERVING:		Serving Size: 6 oz. Total Servings: 1			
Calories	248	Sodium	2 mg	**PERCENT OF DAILY VALUE**	
Calories from fat	76	Carbohydrates	43 g	Vitamin A	1 %
Fat	8 g	Fiber	3 g	Vitamin C	9 %
Saturated Fat	1 g	Protein	4 g	Calcium	2 %
Cholesterol	0 mg			Iron	4 %

Fruit Chews

¼ cup pitted dates
¼ cup raisins
¼ cup pitted prunes
¼ cup dried apricots

½ tsp. brewer's yeast
2 Tbs. ground walnuts
¼ cup wheat germ

Place all dried fruit in a blender along with brewer's yeast and walnuts. Blend on low speed. When fruits are chopped and combined, form into small balls. Roll in wheat germ. Chill before serving.

NUTRITIONAL INFORMATION PER SERVING:				Serving Size: 1 oz. Total Servings: 15	
Calories	74	Sodium	5 mg	PERCENT OF DAILY VALUE	
Calories from fat	29	Carbohydrates	11 g	Vitamin A	4 %
Fat	3 g	Fiber	1 g	Calcium	1 %
Saturated Fat	0 g	Protein	1 g	Iron	2 %
Cholesterol	0 mg				

Crispy Cake

1 cup honey
1 cup peanut butter

8 cups crisp rice cereal

Heat honey and peanut butter just to boiling point. Quickly add rice cereal and stir. Transfer mixture quickly to a 9x13-inch pan. Dip a potato masher into water and press gently all over mixture for a smooth surface. Cover and keep in freezer until needed. Defrost at least 10 minutes before slicing.

Variations: In place of 1 cup rice cereal: toss in 1 cup carob chips; toss in 1 cup roasted sesame or sunflower seeds, or coconut; or mix in 1 cup finely chopped dates or dried apricots.

NUTRITIONAL INFORMATION PER SERVING:				Serving Size: 1 oz. Total Servings: 25	
Calories	115	Cholesterol	0 mg	Protein	3 g
Calories from fat	41	Sodium	138 mg	PERCENT OF DAILY VALUE	
Fat	5 g	Carbohydrates	17 g	Iron	9 %
Saturated Fat	1 g	Fiber	1 g		

Granola Delight
Compliments of Supreme Health Food Center, Monsey, NY

8 cups rolled oats	¾ cup honey
1½ cups sesame seeds	1½ cups wheat germ
1½ cups sunflower seeds	¾ cup canola oil

Mix all ingredients well. Spread on a cookie sheet. Bake for 1 hour at 300°. Stir occasionally. When done, raisins, almonds, or walnuts can be added.

NUTRITIONAL INFORMATION PER SERVING:		Serving Size: ½ cup Total Servings: 35			
Calories	324	Sodium	4 mg	**PERCENT OF DAILY VALUE**	
Calories from fat	124	Carbohydrates	43 g	Calcium	4 %
Fat	14 g	Fiber	2 g	Iron	18 %
Saturated Fat	1 g	Protein	8 g		
Cholesterol	0 mg				

Chocolate-Covered Banana Pops

3 large ripe bananas	2 Tbs. shortening
9 popsicle sticks	1–2 cups coarsely chopped
2 cups chocolate chips	peanuts

Peel bananas and cut into thirds. Insert a popsicle stick into each banana piece and place on a tray covered with waxed paper. Cover and freeze. Melt chocolate chips and shortening in the top of a double boiler over hot water. Remove bananas from freezer and dip each piece into the melted chocolate. Roll immediately in chopped nuts. Place on tray, cover, and freeze. Serve frozen.

NUTRITIONAL INFORMATION PER SERVING:		Serving Size: ⅓ banana Total Servings: 9			
Calories	456	Sodium	36 mg	**PERCENT OF DAILY VALUE**	
Calories from fat	230	Carbohydrates	53 g	Vitamin C	9 %
Fat	26 g	Fiber	4 g	Calcium	12 %
Saturated Fat	2 g	Protein	9 g	Iron	10 %
Cholesterol	0 mg				

Simple Chunky Applesauce

1 dozen large apples
2 cups water

½ cup honey
2–3 tsp. cinnamon

Peel, core, and cut apples into large pieces. (Do not use Red Delicious apples — McIntosh or Cortland are better.) Put into a large pot and add water. Cover and bring to a boil. Reduce heat and simmer for 20 minutes. Add honey and cinnamon. Mash apples with a potato masher. Let cool, then refrigerate until chilled. You can also serve this warm with a scoop of ice cream on top.

NUTRITIONAL INFORMATION PER SERVING:		Serving Size: 5 oz. Total Servings: 12		
Calories	104	Sodium	1 mg	**PERCENT OF DAILY VALUE**
Calories from fat	4	Carbohydrates	27 g	Vitamin C 8 %
Fat	0 g	Fiber	2 g	Calcium 1 %
Saturated Fat	0 g	Protein	0 g	Iron 2 %
Cholesterol	0 mg			

Frozen Grapes

2 cups seedless grapes

Wash grapes and remove stems. Freeze grapes in a single layer on a cookie sheet. When frozen, store in covered plastic containers. Serve frozen or slightly defrosted. Eat plain or use them as a garnish for desserts.

NUTRITIONAL INFORMATION PER SERVING:		Serving Size: ½ cup Total Servings: 4		
Calories	42	Sodium	0 mg	**PERCENT OF DAILY VALUE**
Calories from fat	1	Carbohydrates	11 g	Vitamin C 71 %
Fat	0 g	Fiber	2 g	Calcium 1 %
Saturated Fat	0 g	Protein	1 g	
Cholesterol	0 mg			

Candy Bars

1 cup sugar
¾ cup all-purpose flour
1 tsp. baking powder
½ tsp. salt

1 cup dates, floured and
  chopped
1 cup peanuts, chopped
2 eggs, slightly beaten

Mix and sift dry ingredients twice. Stir in dates and peanuts. Add eggs. Mix thoroughly. Spread into a well-greased, 8-inch square pan. Bake at 350° for 25 to 30 minutes. Cool thoroughly. Cut into bars.

NUTRITIONAL INFORMATION PER SERVING:				Serving Size: 1 bar Total Servings: 16	
Calories	187	Sodium	79 mg	**PERCENT OF DAILY VALUE**	
Calories from fat	69	Carbohydrates	27 g	Vitamin A	1 %
Fat	8 g	Fiber	1 g	Calcium	2 %
Saturated Fat	1 g	Protein	5 g	Iron	7 %
Cholesterol	27 mg				

Pineapple-Glazed Bananas

½ cup crushed pineapple
  with juice
1 tsp. lemon juice
½ tsp. cornstarch

4 bananas, peeled
⅓ cup chopped walnuts
whipped cream (optional)

Combine pineapple, lemon juice, and cornstarch in a small saucepan. Cook and stir over low flame until slightly thickened and clear. Place bananas in individual dessert dishes. Spoon the warm sauce over bananas, and top with nuts and whipped cream.

NUTRITIONAL INFORMATION PER SERVING:				Serving Size: 1 banana Total Servings: 4	
Calories	233	Sodium	5 mg	**PERCENT OF DAILY VALUE**	
Calories from fat	41	Carbohydrates	45 g	Vitamin A	2 %
Fat	5 g	Fiber	6 g	Vitamin C	32 %
Saturated Fat	0 g	Protein	3 g	Calcium	2 %
Cholesterol	0 mg			Iron	4 %

Mama's Fruit Salad

1 cantaloupe and/or
   honeydew, in chunks
1 bunch grapes
1 banana
½ cup raisins
½ cup walnuts

1 20-oz. can pineapple
   (tidbits or chunks) in its
   own juice
1 orange
1 apple
¼ cup orange juice
¼ cup red wine

If possible, prepare one night before serving. In a large bowl, place pieces of cantaloupe and/or honeydew. Add grapes. The more colorful the fruits are, the better. Cut the banana lengthwise and slice into about 10 pieces (depending on size). Add to bowl. Put in raisins and walnuts. Add pineapple with its juice. Cut in small pieces of apples and oranges. Pour in orange juice and red wine and mix. Refrigerate overnight.

Jen's Peach Cobbler with Strawberry Topping

¾ cup cubed peaches
1½ Tbs. lemon juice
3 Tbs. sugar
½-1 Tbs. cinnamon
raisins (optional)
2 cups flour
2 cups sugar
2 tsp. baking powder
2 eggs, beaten
2 Tbs. margarine

Topping:
1 pint strawberries
¼ cup sugar
1 Tbs. vanilla extract or
   raspberry liqueur
1 Tbs. lemon juice
cinnamon, to taste

Cobbler: Sprinkle peaches with lemon juice, sugar, and cinnamon, to taste. Add raisins if desired. Mix together and put into an 8x8-inch pan. Then mix together flour, sugar, baking powder, and eggs. Stir

212

until crumbly. Pour on top of fruit in pan. Dot with margarine and drops of water. Bake at 350° for 45 minutes to 1 hour.

Topping: Slice strawberries. Put in a saucepan with sugar to taste. Cook over a low flame for 5 minutes, adding vanilla or liqueur, and lemon juice and cinnamon to taste.

Serve peach cobbler with hot topping over it.

Variation: Apples or berries may be substituted for peaches.

No-Sugar Compote

1 bag frozen strawberries (approx. 16 oz.)
1 20-oz. can unsweetened crushed pineapple, undrained

1 apple, sliced
½ cup raspberries (optional)

Blend all ingredients until smooth. Refrigerate.

Cranberry Crisp

1 cup rolled oats
1 stick margarine, softened
⅔ cup brown sugar
1 cup flour
1 tsp. cinnamon

1 16-oz. can whole-berry cranberry sauce
1 8-oz. can crushed pineapple, drained

Mix all ingredients except cranberries and pineapple. Coat a 9-inch round pan with half of the crumbs. Mix fruit and pour in. Cover with remaining crumbs. Bake at 350° for 45 minutes.

Frulati Di Fruta (Thick, frothy banana drink)

3 apples
3 bananas
1 cup milk

6 oz. frozen orange juice
   concentrate
12 ice cubes

Peel apples and cut in quarters. Combine all ingredients in a blender and blend until smooth.

NUTRITIONAL INFORMATION PER SERVING:			Serving Size: 5 oz. Total Servings: 10	
Calories	111	Sodium	13 mg	**PERCENT OF DAILY VALUE**
Calories from fat	6	Carbohydrates	25 g	Vitamin A 3 %
Fat	1 g	Fiber	3 g	Vitamin C 50 %
Saturated Fat	0 g	Protein	2 g	Calcium 4 %
Cholesterol	1 mg			Iron 1 %

Raspberry Pears

1 12-oz. pkg. frozen
   raspberries, thawed
½ cup dark brown sugar

2 tsp. lemon juice
½ tsp. cornstarch
4 large pears, peeled

Purée first 3 ingredients in blender. Mix in cornstarch. Pour mixture over whole peeled pears. Cook for ½ hour on low flame. Serve hot or cold.

Punch

16 oz. frozen orange juice
16 oz. frozen strawberries
½ gallon strawberry or
   raspberry sherbet

2 trays of ice cubes
1 large (750 ml.) bottle pink
   champagne
1 2-liter bottle ginger ale

Mix all ingredients together, putting champagne and ginger ale in last. Drink and enjoy!

Baked Apples

6 Rome apples
2 tsp. ground almonds

1 tsp. cinnamon
4 Tbs. honey

Core apples. Cut off a small part from the top of each apple to create a flat surface. Arrange apples in a pan, cut side up. Mix almonds, cinnamon, and honey in a small saucepan over a low flame. When mixture stirs easily, pour evenly over the top of the apples. Bake for 1½ hours at 350°.

Ambrosia Drink

1 10-oz. container dessert
   whip
1 12-oz. container frozen
   strawberries with liquid

1 20-oz. can pineapple
   chunks, undrained

Beat dessert whip in a blender. Add strawberries and pineapple and blend again. Pour each serving into a tall, elegant glass with a slice of kiwi on the edge of the glass, or garnish with strawberries.

Stuffed Peaches

½ cup ground almonds
⅓ 4½-oz. pkg. tea biscuits,
   crushed
2 Tbs. margarine
2 Tbs. + 2 Tbs. sugar

1 egg, separated
1 29-oz. can peach halves,
   drained, with juice
   reserved
½ cup red wine

Mix almonds and biscuits with margarine, 2 Tbs. of the sugar, and egg yolk. Mix well until its consistency is like dough. Fill each peach half with a spoonful of this mixture. Mix wine with reserved peach syrup and pour over peach halves. Bake for 25 minutes at 325°. Meanwhile, whip egg white with remaining 2 Tbs. of sugar until peaks form. Put some meringue on top of each baked peach half. Bake for 8 more minutes. Let cool and refrigerate.

Orange Julius Delight

⅓ cup frozen orange juice
    concentrate
½ cup milk
½ cup water

½ tsp. vanilla extract
6 ice cubes
¼ cup sugar (optional)

Combine all ingredients in a blender and blend until smooth.

NUTRITIONAL INFORMATION PER SERVING:			Serving Size: 4 oz. Total Servings: 4	
Calories	97	Sodium	17 mg	**PERCENT OF DAILY VALUE**
Calories from fat	3	Carbohydrates	23 g	Vitamin A 3 %
Fat	0 g	Fiber	0 g	Vitamin C 54 %
Saturated Fat	0 g	Protein	2 g	Calcium 5 %
Cholesterol	1 mg			

Super Fruit Salad

2 8-oz. cans mandarin
    oranges, drained
2 20-oz. cans crushed
    pineapple, drained

2 pts. frozen strawberries in
    juice
5 apples, cubed
handful of raisins (optional)
handful of chopped walnuts

Mix all ingredients together and enjoy. Serves 20 people. At a simcha, serve with a scoop of sherbet on top!

Apple Betty

5 large apples
½ pkg. frozen strawberries
½ cup brown sugar

¾ cup flour
½ stick margarine

Peel and thinly slice apples into a 9-inch round pan. Add well-drained strawberries. Combine brown sugar and flour. Cut margarine into this mixture to form crumbs. Sprinkle on top of fruit. Bake at least 2 hours at 300°. Spoon into cupcake holders. Serve warm. Makes a delicious accompaniment for a simcha meal or Friday night dinner.

Fruit Salad

1 16-oz. bag frozen cut rhubarb
1 16-oz. bag frozen unsweetened strawberries
1 pint frozen presweetened strawberries

1 20-oz. can crushed pineapple, undrained
1 20-oz. can pineapple chunks, undrained

Cook rhubarb and both types of strawberries on low flame for approximately 1 hour, until rhubarb dissolves. Add both cans of pineapple and cook another 15 minutes. Freeze and serve slightly frozen. Serves 15.

Blueberry Dessert

3 pints blueberries
½ cup sugar
½ cup flour
2 Tbs. lemon juice

Topping:
2 sticks margarine
3¼ cups flour
¼ cup brown sugar
1 tsp. vanilla extract
1 tsp. cinnamon
½ tsp. salt

Mix blueberries, sugar, flour, and lemon juice by hand until smooth. Put into an ungreased 9x13-inch baking pan. Mix together topping ingredients. Crumble topping over blueberry mixture. Bake at 375° for 45 minutes.

Apple Crisp

6 large or 8 medium apples
½ cup flour
¼ cup sugar

¼ cup brown sugar
4 Tbs. margarine
1 tsp. cinnamon

Peel and core apples, slice into rings, and place in an 8-inch square baking pan (rings may overlap). Combine remaining ingredients and sprinkle over apples. Cover with aluminum foil. Bake at 350°, covered for ½ hour, and uncovered for ½ hour.

Apple-Cranberry Dessert

5 baking apples
1 16-oz. can whole-berry
    cranberry sauce

Topping:
½ stick margarine
½ cup sugar
½ cup flour
dash of cinnamon

Slice apples by hand or in food processor. Mix with cranberry sauce. Put into a round baking dish. Mix topping ingredients by hand and crumble on top of apple-cranberry mixture. Bake, uncovered, at 350° for more than 1 hour, until top is golden brown.

Fancy Fruit Cup

2 29-oz. cans fruit cocktail
2 20-oz. cans pineapple
    chunks
3 8-oz. cans mandarin
    oranges
2 bananas, sliced (optional)

2 12-oz. containers frozen
    strawberries in syrup,
    defrosted
1 10-oz. container dessert
    whip (do not whip)

Drain canned fruits and mix together. Add bananas, if using. Add strawberries with their syrup. Then add dessert whip. Cover and refrigerate before serving.

Ice Cream, Puddings, and Mousses

Ice Cream, Puddings, and Mousses

Mom's Parve Ice Cream

3 eggs
¼ cup + ¼ cup sugar

1 tsp. vanilla or almond
   extract
1 10-oz. container dessert
   whip

Separate eggs. Mix yolks with ¼ cup sugar and almond or vanilla extract. Beat for 8 to 10 minutes. Whip egg whites at high speed until firm peaks form. Add remaining ¼ cup sugar. Beat dessert whip until stiff. Fold whites into yolks and add dessert whip until the mixture foams. Freeze.

Variation: To make chocolate ice cream, add about 4 Tbs. cocoa to the mixture.

Pistachio Ice Cream

4 eggs, separated
1 10-oz. container dessert
   whip
¾ cup corn syrup

1 tsp. vanilla
pistachio nuts (approx. 1
   cup)

Whip egg whites with dessert whip. Mix yolks with corn syrup and vanilla. Add nuts. Mix all together and freeze.

Variation: For almond ice cream, substitute approximately 1 cup toasted almonds for pistachio nuts.

Frozen Chocolate Mousse

Compliments of CYRK CAFE, Monsey, NY

¼ cup water
2¼ cups chocolate chips

6 eggs, separated
½ cup sugar

Bring water to a boil in a saucepan. Add chocolate and turn off flame. Mix thoroughly until chocolate is smooth. Add egg yolks while mixing and leave to cool. In a mixing bowl, beat egg whites until stiff, adding sugar slowly to make meringue. Add a large spoonful of meringue to chocolate mixture to lighten it. Add chocolate mixture back to rest of meringue and fold in with a large spoon until mixed. Fill container and freeze before serving.

Sugar-Free Chocolate Pudding

3¼ cups carob flavor RICE
    DREAM* (non-dairy
    beverage)
2 Tbs. carob powder

3 Tbs. cornstarch
1 tsp. instant coffee
    granules

Heat up 3 cups RICE DREAM in a pot. Meanwhile, make a paste with remaining RICE DREAM, carob powder, cornstarch, and coffee. Before liquid boils, add paste to pot and stir until thick. Remove from heat and refrigerate when cool.

* RICE DREAM is made from brown rice and comes in 32-oz. containers.

Ice Cream Crunch Topping

½ cup nuts (any kind)
¼ cup oats
1 cup flour

¼ cup brown sugar
½ cup margarine

Mix ingredients to form coarse crumbs. Pat into a 9x13-inch pan. Bake at 400° for 15 minutes. Stir, crumble, and cool. Use as a topping for ice cream.

Chocolate Mousse Supreme

7 oz. chocolate chips
1 stick margarine
7 eggs, separated

¼ cup + ½ cup sugar
1 10-oz. container dessert
   whip

Melt chocolate chips with margarine, in a microwave, double boiler, or saucepan, over a very low flame. Beat 7 egg whites with ¼ cup sugar. Set aside. Beat the egg yolks with remaining ½ cup sugar. Add melted chocolate and beat well. Fold in whites. Pour ¾ of mixture into a lightly greased springform pan or a 9x13-inch pan. Bake for 35 minutes at 350°. Let cool. Pour remaining chocolate mixture on top and freeze overnight. Next day, top with whipped cream and freeze. Serve frozen.

Ice Cream Cake

Cake:
5 eggs, separated
1 Tbs. sugar
2 Tbs. flour
4 Tbs. cocoa

Ice Cream:
2 10-oz. containers dessert
   whip

1 pkg. instant vanilla
   pudding
2 Tbs. sugar

Topping:
8 oz. bitter chocolate
7 Tbs. water

Cake: Whip egg whites and add sugar, flour, and cocoa. Add yolks and mix very well. Turn into a 9x13-inch pan and bake at 350° for 20 minutes. Let cool.

Ice cream: Whip dessert whip and add pudding and sugar. Pour over cold cake.

Topping: Melt chocolate with water over low flame. Cool a little. Pour over ice cream, slowly and carefully, and spread gently with a spoon. Freeze. Let defrost for 15 minutes before serving.

Creamsicle Roll

Orange mixture:
1 pkg. orange jello
1 cup boiling water
¼ cup sugar
¼ cup orange juice
1 egg yolk

White mixture:
1 10-oz. container dessert
   whip
¼ cup sugar
1 Tbs. vanilla

Orange mixture: Dissolve jello in boiling water. With a mixer, beat jello, sugar, and orange juice for 10 minutes. adding 1 egg yolk for the last 2 minutes. Line a 17x11-inch shallow pan (or any other size pan, depending on how thick you want the mixture to be) with aluminum foil and then waxed paper. Pour orange mixture into pan and freeze for 2 hours.

White mixture: Whip dessert whip and add sugar and vanilla. Pour white mixture over frozen orange mixture. Then, using the waxed paper, roll the two together and freeze.

Butterscotch Ice Cream

½ cup + 1 Tbs. firmly
   packed brown sugar
1 stick margarine
3 eggs, separated
2 tsp. vanilla
½ tsp. salt

2 10-oz. containers dessert
   whip
1 cup small chocolate chips
1 cup chopped walnuts,
   toasted

In a pot, combine sugar and margarine over low heat, boil 1 minute, and remove from heat. In a blender, blend egg yolks, vanilla, and salt for 30 seconds, then add the boiled mixture. Blend on high for 1 minute and set aside to cool. Beat egg whites until stiff. Whip dessert whip and fold in egg whites. Fold in chocolate chips and walnuts. Combine with sugar mixture and freeze.

Luscious Ice Cream

Ice cream:
2 10-oz. containers dessert
　whip
2 pkgs. vanilla sugar
4 eggs
1 cup sugar

Crunch:
10 oz. chocolate chips,
　melted
⅓ cup peanut butter
1½ cups crushed cornflakes

Mix ingredients for crunch and press into a 9x13-inch pan. Freeze for 15 to 30 minutes, then break into small pieces. Mix ingredients for ice cream with mixer on high speed until soft peaks form. Add crunch pieces to ice cream mixture. Pour into a 2-quart container and freeze.

Vanilla-Chocolate Trifle

6 oz. chocolate chips
⅛ cup water
2 eggs
1 tsp. + 1 tsp. vanilla
3 10-oz. containers dessert
　whip

¼ cup sugar
3 Tbs. confectioners' sugar
2 9-inch round chocolate
　cakes
chocolate chips, slivered
　nuts (optional)

Chocolate cream: Melt chocolate chips in water in top of a double boiler. Add eggs and 1 tsp. vanilla. Then whip together ½ container dessert whip and ¼ cup sugar. Add melted chocolate mixture to this cream mixture. Set aside.

White cream: Whip the rest of the dessert whip, confectioners' sugar, and remaining vanilla.

In a clear glass bowl, place one cake, then layer in the following order: chocolate cream, white cream, the second cake, chocolate cream, and white cream. Top with chocolate chips or slivered nuts. Chill.

Raspberry Sherbet

1 pkg. raspberry jello
1 cup hot water
⅓ cup sugar

1 cup orange juice
1 cup pineapple juice

Mix ingredients by hand. Freeze in a medium-size container for one day. Take out and let thaw. Blend in a blender and refreeze until ready to serve.

Strawberry Freeze Dessert

2 pints fresh strawberries
2 egg whites

1 cup sugar

Put ingredients in a food processor. Using the steel blade, blend until nice and fluffy. Pour into a storage container and freeze. Serve frozen.

Creamsicle

1 cup powdered orange
   drink
4 cups parve milk or COFFEE
   RICH
6 eggs, separated

1 cup sugar
3 10-oz. containers dessert
   whip
1 tsp. vanilla flavoring

Whip orange drink powder and parve milk or COFFEE RICH until bubbly. Set aside. Beat egg whites until stiff and add sugar. Set aside. Whip dessert whip, egg yolks, and vanilla. Fold whites into this mixture and mix well. Pour ⅓ of this mixture into a 9x13-inch foil pan and freeze. Then pour ½ of the orange mixture on top and freeze. Then pour ½ of remaining white mixture on top and freeze. Repeat with remaining orange mixture, freezing again, and then top with the last of the white mixture. Freeze.

Chocolate Trifle

4 eggs, separated
¼ cup + ¼ cup sugar
1½ sticks margarine
6 oz. chocolate chips, melted
1 10-oz. container dessert whip

1 9-inch chocolate sponge cake (bought or homemade)
grated chocolate curls (optional)

Mousse: Beat egg whites until stiff. Gradually add ¼ cup sugar and set aside. To the yolks, add remaining sugar and the margarine; beat well. Then add melted chocolate. Fold yolk mixture into white mixture.

Topping: Whip parve topping into a cream.

In a large, transparent bowl, layer cake, mousse, then cream. Top with grated chocolate curls.

Carob Tofu Pudding

1 16-oz. cake soft tofu
½ cup cold soy milk or apple juice

3 medium bananas, peeled and frozen
4 Tbs. carob powder
1 tsp. vanilla

Cube tofu into 1-inch sections. Blend all ingredients together. Refrigerate before serving. Good on a graham-cracker pie crust.

2 pkgs. regular chocolate pudding (not instant)
1 10-oz. container dessert whip

2½ cups water
¼ tsp. instant coffee granules
¼ cup sugar

Put all ingredients into a 3-quart pot and cook over medium heat, stirring constantly until thick. Put into a container, let cool, and then refrigerate.

Banana-Honey Pudding

1½ lbs. tofu (soft)
½ cup honey
¼ cup oil

1 Tbs. vanilla extract
¼ tsp. salt
3 medium ripe bananas

Blend ingredients in blender until smooth. Chill until set.

Carob-Tofu Pudding

2 cups soft tofu, cut into
   1-inch cubes
½ cup cold soy milk
3 medium ripe bananas, cut
   into 2-inch pieces

4 Tbs. carob powder
1 tsp. vanilla extract

Blend all ingredients in blender until smooth. Chill until set.

Parve Cakes, Dairy Cakes, and Frostings

Babka

Mocha Cake

Three-Layer Cake

Tofu Cheeseless "Cheesecake"

Carrot-Sweet Potato Cake

Banana-Coconut Cake

Kokosh Babka Supreme

Amaretto Cake

Chocolate Glazed Brownie

Delicious Carrot Cake

Chocolate Chip Pound Cake

Kokosh Cake

Carrot-Pineapple Cake

Pineapple Tofu Cake

Pound Cake

Whole-Wheat Carrot Cake

Fruit Cake

Walnut-Raisin Cake

Nana's Brownies

Coffee Cloud Sponge Cake

Easy Crumb Cake

ZC's Sponge Cake

Moist Chocolate Cake

Chocolate Sprinkle Cake

Cinnamon Coffee Cake

Parve "Cheese" Cake

No-Egg Chocolate Cake

"Cherries in a Pit" Cake

Nana's Delicious Apple Cake

Coffee Cake

Best Honey Cake

One-Bowl White Cake

Apple Cake

Marble Cake

Brownie Cake

Easy Marble Cake

Carrot Cake

Mom's Delicious Brownies

Toasted Coconut Cake

Mini Cheesecakes

Rich Chocolate Cheesecake

Cheesecake

Sour Cream Delight Cake

Scrumptious Dietetic Cheesecake

Richest Cheesecake in the World

Rich Chocolate Frosting

Chocolate Glaze

Butterscotch Frosting

Coffee Icing

Delicious Chocolate Cream Frosting

Chocolate-Nut Frosting

Coconut Icing

Lemon Frosting

Parve Cakes

Babka

Dough:
5 lbs. flour
5½ cups water
4 oz. yeast
4 sticks margarine
1½ tsp. salt
1½ cups sugar
2 pkgs. vanilla sugar
2 eggs
6 egg yolks

Filling:
2 sticks margarine

6 egg whites
6 cups sugar
⅓ cup water
1 cup cocoa plus a handful
   of chocolate bits
4 tsp. cinnamon + 1 7-oz.
   bag ground nuts

Crumb Topping:
½ cup sugar
1½ cups flour
1 pkg. vanilla sugar
1 stick margarine

Mix all ingredients for dough and let rise until double in size. Divide dough into 16 balls. Roll out balls into round flat pieces, about ¼ to ⅛-inch thick. For filling, combine margarine, egg whites, sugar, and water. Divide mixture in half. Into one half, add cocoa and chocolate bits. Into the other half, add cinnamon and nuts.

Fill 8 pieces of dough with cocoa mixture and roll up jelly-roll fashion. Fill the remaining 8 pieces with cinnamon mixture and roll also. Twist one cocoa roll together with one cinnamon roll. Repeat for all the rolls, making 4 pairs of rolls twisted together. Put each twist into a greased 8x4-inch loaf pan.

To make crumb topping, stir together dry ingredients. Cut in margarine. Mix until crumbly texture is attained.

Brush egg white on top of each twist and then sprinkle on crumb topping. Bake at 350° for 45 minutes.

Mocha Cake

2 cups sugar
1 cup oil
4 eggs
2 tsp. vanilla
2 cups flour
¼ cup cocoa
2 tsp. baking powder
¾ tsp. instant coffee,
    dissolved in ¾ cup
    boiling water

Glaze:
2 tsp. coffee dissolved in 3
    Tbs. hot water
1½ cups confectioners'
    sugar

Put sugar and oil into blender. Beat hard for 5 minutes. Add eggs and vanilla. Beat well. In a separate bowl, combine flour, cocoa, and baking powder. Add to egg mixture, alternating with coffee, until blended. Pour into a greased 9x13-inch pan. Bake at 350° for 1 hour. Cool. Mix together ingredients for glaze and drizzle over cooled cake.

Three-Layer Cake

White:
10 eggs, separated
1 cup + 1 cup sugar
2 cups flour
1 tsp. vanilla sugar
1 tsp. baking powder
¼ cup juice
¼ cup oil

Chocolate:
5 eggs, separated
½ cup + ½ cup sugar
1 cup flour

1 tsp. vanilla sugar
¼ cup juice
¼ cup oil
1–2 tsp. cocoa
½ tsp. coffee

Icing:
¾ lb. margarine
¾ lb. confectioners' sugar
3 eggs
3 tsp. vanilla sugar
4 tsp. lemon juice
sprinkles (optional)

White: Whip a snow with egg whites and 1 cup sugar; set aside. Add remaining 1 cup sugar to other ingredients and mix. Combine with egg whites. Pour onto two 11x16-inch cookie sheets and bake at 350° for 20 to 25 minutes.

Chocolate: Whip a snow with egg whites and ½ cup sugar. Add remaining ½ cup sugar to other ingredients and mix. Combine with egg whites. Pour onto cookie sheet and bake for 20 to 25 minutes.

Icing: Mix all ingredients. Ice one white layer. On top, put the chocolate layer and ice it. On top of that, put the other white layer and ice it. Cover with sprinkles.

Tofu Cheeseless "Cheesecake"

Compliments of Supreme Health Food Center, Monsey, NY

Filling:	Crust:
1 cup raisins	½ cup ground sunflower
½ cup apple juice	seeds
2 tsp. grated lemon rind	½ cup wheat germ
3 Tbs. techina (sesame	2 tsp. honey
paste)	3 Tbs. oil
1 Tbs. vanilla extract	½ tsp. cinnamon
4 lbs. tofu	¼ tsp. allspice
3 Tbs. lemon juice	
½ cup light honey	

Preheat oven to 350°.

Filling: Soak raisins in apple juice until soft, about 2 hours. In a blender, purée raisins with apple juice and lemon rind. Remove this mixture from blender and blend remaining ingredients to make a tofu purée. Combine raisin mixture with tofu purée and stir thoroughly. Set aside while preparing cheesecake crust.

Crust: Combine all ingredients and mix well until mixture feels crumbly. Put mixture into a 9-inch pan, covering the bottom and about 1½ inches up the sides. Put in filling and spread evenly. Bake for 25 to 30 minutes, until top begins to brown delicately. Allow to cool. Chill in refrigerator. Serves 10.

Carrot-Sweet Potato Cake

1 lb. carrots, grated
2 medium-size sweet
    potatoes, grated
1 cup EDEN SOY parve soy
    milk beverage
4 eggs
2½–3 cups sugar

1 cup oil (preferably
    safflower)
2 tsp. vanilla extract
1½ cups whole-wheat flour
1½ cups regular flour
2 tsp. baking soda
2 tsp. cinnamon

Blend carrots and sweet potatoes with EDEN SOY. In a large bowl, beat eggs and sugar until fluffy. Add carrot mixture to eggs. Add oil and vanilla, and mix. Add remaining ingredients, mixing well. Pour into a 9x13-inch pan. Bake at 350° for 1 hour and 15 minutes.

Banana-Coconut Cake

¾ cup margarine, softened
1½ cups sugar
2 eggs
1 cup mashed bananas (2
    bananas)
1 tsp. baking soda
1 tsp. baking powder
1 tsp. vanilla extract
2 cups flour

½ cup apple or orange juice
½ cup chopped pecans
1 cup shredded coconut

Frosting:
1 egg yolk
1½ sticks margarine
½ tsp. vanilla extract
2 cups confectioners' sugar

Preheat oven to 350°. Grease and flour one 9x13-inch pan. In a mixing bowl, cream margarine and sugar. Add eggs, one at a time, beating after each addition until light and fluffy. Add mashed bananas and beat for 2 minutes. Then add baking soda, baking powder, and vanilla. Add flour alternately with juice, beginning and ending with flour. Fold in pecans and coconut and mix well. Pour into pan and bake for about 45 minutes to 1 hour.

Frosting: Combine all ingredients in a mixing bowl and beat until light and fluffy. Frost when cake has cooled.

Kokosh Babka Supreme

Dough:
1 cup water
10 cups flour
1 cup sugar
2 eggs
4 egg yolks
3 sticks margarine
2½ oz. yeast
¼ cup oil
1 cup applesauce
1 tsp. salt

Filling:
6 eggs
3 sticks margarine
3 cups sugar
3 cups confectioners' sugar
2 cups cocoa
4 Tbs. coffee
4 pkgs. vanilla sugar
½ tsp. salt

Mix together all ingredients for dough. Place in a well-greased bowl. Cover well and allow to rise 1 hour or until double in bulk. Meanwhile, prepare filling mixture by mixing ingredients well. Divide dough into 4 balls and roll out each one into a ⅛ to ¼-inch thick rectangle, approximately 10 x 14 inches in size. Spread ¼ of filling mixture on each rectangle. Roll up jelly-roll fashion, and place seam-side down on a waxed paper-lined cookie sheet. Allow to rise again for 30 minutes. Before placing the rolls in the oven, prick them with a fork and then spread a beaten egg all over the dough. Bake at 350° for 1 hour or until a very rich, deep brown color. If baking as a babka, after cake is rolled, slice it, line a tube pan with the slices, and bake, as above.

Amaretto Cake

1 box instant vanilla
    pudding
1 box yellow cake mix
¼ cup amaretto

¼ cup vodka
4 eggs
1 cup oil
¾ cup orange juice

Preheat oven to 350°. Mix all ingredients together with mixer. Pour into an ungreased tube pan. Bake for 45 minutes to 1 hour. Cake is done when top springs back when lightly touched.

Chocolate Glazed Brownie

Cake:
1½ sticks margarine
1 cup sugar
3 eggs
4 Tbs. cocoa
2 cups flour
1 tsp. baking powder
¾ cup water
1 tsp. coffee, dissolved in ½
    cup boiling water

Glaze:
4 oz. baking chocolate
1 Tbs. cocoa
3 Tbs. sugar
4 Tbs. water
1 pkg. vanilla sugar
½ stick margarine

Cake: Cream margarine, sugar, and eggs. Add cocoa. Sift flour and baking powder and add them, along with water, to flour mixture, and blend. Bake in a lightly oiled 8-inch square pan at 350° for 30 minutes. Remove from oven, and immediately sprinkle on the coffee dissolved in boiling water.

Glaze: Melt first 5 ingredients, then add margarine. Spread glaze on cooled brownie.

Delicious Carrot Cake

2 cups sugar
1 cup oil
4 eggs
3 cups grated carrots
1½ cup almonds, chopped

1 cup regular flour
1 cup whole-wheat flour
1 tsp. salt
2 tsp. cinnamon
1½ tsp. seltzer

Combine sugar, oil, and eggs. Add carrots and almonds. Slowly add dry ingredients and mix well. Add seltzer. Bake in a greased tube pan at 350° for about 45 minutes, or until a toothpick inserted into center of cake comes out clean and dry.

Variation: 2 cups regular flour can be substituted for 1 cup regular flour and 1 cup whole-wheat flour.

Chocolate Chip Pound Cake

½ lb. margarine, softened
1½ cups sugar
1 tsp. vanilla
3 eggs
3 cups flour

1½ tsp. baking powder
⅛ tsp. salt
½ cup orange juice
12 oz. chocolate chips

Preheat oven to 350°. Cream margarine, sugar, and vanilla. Beat until smooth. Add eggs. In a separate bowl, combine flour, baking powder, and salt. Add this mixture alternately with orange juice to the egg mixture. Add chocolate chips. Mix well and pour into a well-greased, 10-inch tube pan. Bake for 1 hour.

Kokosh Cake

2 oz. yeast
2 cups seltzer
6 cups flour
1 tsp. salt
5 Tbs. sugar
2 sticks margarine
1 egg
3 egg yolks

2 pkgs. vanilla sugar

Filling:
1 cup cocoa
2 cups sugar
1 pkg. vanilla sugar
4 Tbs. oil

Combine yeast and seltzer in a bowl. Place rest of ingredients in a separate mixing bowl. Mix for 1 minute, then add the yeast and seltzer mixture. Mix for another 10 minutes. Combine the filling ingredients. Divide dough in half. Roll out each half on a floured board into a 9x5-inch rectangle. Brush dough with oil and spread cocoa filling smoothly on dough. Roll up each rectangle jelly-roll style. Place on a greased baking sheet, seam-side down, and brush the top with a little beaten egg. Bake at 325–350° for approximately 1 hour. The cakes are done when they turn light brown and form a slight crust.

Carrot-Pineapple Cake

3 cups flour
1 tsp. baking soda
2 tsp. cinnamon
½ tsp. salt
½ cup oil
2 cups sugar
1 tsp. + 1 tsp. vanilla
   extract

2 cups grated carrots
1 cup crushed pineapple,
   drained
1½ cups chopped walnuts
3 eggs

Preheat oven to 350°. Grease and flour a 10-inch tube pan. In a small bowl, sift together flour, baking soda, cinnamon, and salt. In a separate large mixing bowl, beat together oil, sugar, and 1 tsp. vanilla. Add half the flour mixture and mix well. Beat in carrots, pineapple, remaining teaspoon of vanilla, and nuts. Add remaining flour mixture and beat well. Beat in eggs, one at a time. Pour batter into the prepared pan, bake 70 minutes, and cool.

Pineapple Tofu Cake

cornmeal
1 16-oz. pkg. tofu
1 20-oz. can crushed
   pineapple

⅓ cup honey
3½ tsp. vanilla
1 Tbs. arrowroot flour

Use a stainless steel springform pan. Cover bottom of pan with cornmeal. Rinse tofu and squeeze out excess water. Drain crushed pineapple and reserve juice. Blend tofu, honey, 2 Tbs. of the pineapple, 5 Tbs. of the juice, and vanilla. Pour into pan on top of cornmeal. Bake at 350° for 1 hour.

Icing: Cook remaining drained pineapple with arrowroot flour for 1 minute. Spread on when cake is cool.

Pound Cake

4 eggs
pinch of salt
1½ cups sugar
1½ tsp. vanilla
⅔ cup oil
2¾ cups flour
3½ tsp. baking powder
¾ cup orange juice
1 box instant vanilla
    pudding

¼ cup amaretto (optional)
¼ cup vodka (optional)

Glaze:
1 cup confectioners' sugar
1 tsp. vodka
1 tsp. amaretto
1 tsp. water or orange juice
a little boiled water

Mix together all cake ingredients and put into a greased bundt pan. Bake at 350° for 1 hour. Meanwhile, mix together ingredients for glaze. When cake is cool, drizzle glaze on top.

Whole-Wheat Carrot Cake

2½ cups unsifted whole-
    wheat flour
1 tsp. baking powder
1 tsp. baking soda
1½ tsp. cinnamon
1 tsp. nutmeg (optional)
4 eggs
1 cup honey

1 cup oil
2½ cups shredded carrots
    (4–6 carrots)
1 cup raisins
1 cup chopped nuts or
    sunflower seeds
    (optional)

Combine first five ingredients and set aside. Beat eggs with honey until light. Slowly add oil until thoroughly combined. Add flour mixture, then stir in carrots, raisins, and nuts. Bake in a tube pan or 2 loaf pans for 65 minutes at 350°. Cool on a wire rack. This recipe can also be made into muffins — bake ½ hour. This cake contains fruit, vegetables, protein, and carbohydrates. Eaten together with a glass of milk, it's a meal!

Fruit Cake
Compliments of Sabel's Catering, Monsey, NY

¾ cup margarine
1 cup sugar
1 tsp. vanilla
2 eggs, beaten
2 cups flour

1 tsp. baking powder
pinch of salt
¾ cup orange juice
1 21-oz. can pie filling
1 tsp. lemon juice

Cream together margarine and sugar until light and fluffy. Add vanilla. Add beaten eggs, one at a time. Alternately add dry ingredients and orange juice to mixture. Grease and flour a 9x13-inch baking pan, and pour in ¾ of the batter. Spread pie filling evenly over batter. Sprinkle lemon juice over pie filling. Add remaining ¼ of batter by large spoonfuls over top. (It will not cover fully, but in baking it will spread.) Bake at 350° for 1 hour or until a toothpick inserted in center comes out clean.

Walnut-Raisin Cake

1 cup raisins
1 cup walnuts
1 tsp. baking soda
1 cup boiling water
1½ cups flour
1 tsp. cinnamon
¼ tsp. salt

1 stick margarine
1 cup sugar
1 egg
2 yolks
1 tsp. lemon juice
1 pkg. vanilla sugar

Combine raisins, nuts, and baking soda with boiling water and set aside. Sift together flour, cinnamon, and salt onto waxed paper. Set aside. Mix together remaining ingredients with a mixer. Mix well and set aside. Combine all three mixtures alternately, and mix well. Bake in a loaf pan at 350° for approximately 1 hour. Goes well with butterscotch frosting (see recipe on p. 253).

Nana's Brownies

4 eggs
2 cups sugar
½ lb. margarine
4 squares bittersweet
   chocolate
1½ cups flour

1 tsp. baking powder
½ tsp. salt
2 tsp. vanilla
4 Tbs. corn syrup
2 cups chopped nuts

Beat eggs and sugar a little at a time. Melt margarine and chocolate over a low flame. When cool, combine egg mixture with chocolate. In a separate bowl, mix together flour, baking powder, salt, vanilla, and corn syrup. Add chocolate mixture. Mix well. Fold in nuts. Pour into a shallow, greased 9x13-inch pan. Bake at 350° for 25 minutes.

Variation: Substitute 3 Tbs. cocoa plus 1 Tbs. oil for 1 square of bittersweet chocolate.

Coffee Cloud Sponge Cake

6 eggs, separated
½ tsp. baking soda
½ cup + 1½ cups sugar
1 tsp. vanilla
2 cups flour
3 tsp. baking powder
1 cup strong coffee, cooled
   (1 Tbs. coffee to 1 cup
   water)

1 cup ground nuts (optional)

Icing:
2 Tbs. margarine
2 cups confectioners' sugar
1½ tsp. coffee
2 Tbs. water
1 tsp. vanilla

Beat egg whites with baking soda until soft mounds form. Add ½ cup sugar and beat until stiff. Set aside. Beat yolks until light, and add remaining sugar. Beat well. Add vanilla. Add flour and baking powder alternately with coffee. Fold in egg whites. Fold in ground nuts, if using. Bake in a tube pan at 350° for 50 to 60 minutes. (Check after 50 minutes.) Mix ingredients for icing, and ice the cake when cooled.

Easy Crumb Cake

3 cups flour
3 tsp. baking powder
1 pkg. vanilla sugar
1 stick margarine, softened
1¼ cups sugar

½ cup oil
1 10-oz. container parve
   whip
3 eggs

Mix together all ingredients, except for whip and eggs; mixture will be crumbly. Remove 1 cup of mixture and set aside. Add whip and eggs to batter, and mix. Pour into a 9x13-inch pan and sprinkle with reserved crumb mixture. Bake at 350° for 1 hour.

ZC's Sponge Cake

7 eggs
2 cups sugar
1½ cups flour

½ cup oil
½ cup orange juice
2 tsp. baking powder

Separate eggs. Beat whites together with sugar. In a separate bowl, mix together remaining ingredients and fold into egg white mixture. Bake in a springform pan at 350° for 1 hour or until top is golden. Invert cake and cool.

Moist Chocolate Cake

1 cup oil
2 cups sugar
2 cups flour
3 eggs
⅔ cup cocoa

2 tsp. baking soda
2 tsp. coffee
1½ cups cold water
1 tsp. vanilla

Mix first 5 ingredients with a mixer. Add remaining ingredients and mix well. Pour into a tube pan or 9x13-inch pan. Bake at 350° for 45 minutes to 1 hour.

Chocolate Sprinkle Cake

7 eggs, separated
1 cup + ½ cup sugar
½ cup oil
2 cups flour
1 tsp. baking powder

¾ cup water
1 tsp. vanilla
3 oz. baking chocolate,
   grated

In a large mixing bowl, beat egg yolks together with 1 cup of sugar. Slowly add oil, beating until eggs are yellow and frothy (about 3 minutes). In a small bowl, sift together flour and baking powder. Add it slowly to the yolk mixture, alternating with water. Add vanilla. In a second large mixing bowl, whip egg whites into a snow. Add ½ cup sugar and whip until firm. Fold the yolk mixture into the beaten egg whites by hand. Add grated baking chocolate (or substitute chocolate sprinkles as a shortcut). Bake in a lightly greased 9x13-inch pan for 45 minutes at 350°, until cake is lightly browned and firm to the touch.

Cinnamon Coffee Cake

½ lb. margarine
1½ cups sugar
5 eggs
1 pkg. vanilla sugar
3 tsp. baking powder

3½ cups flour
1 container dessert whip
2 Tbs. sugar
1 Tbs. cinnamon

Cream margarine and sugar well. Add eggs one at a time. Add vanilla sugar. Mix baking powder into flour, then alternately mix flour and dessert whip into egg mixture. Place half of batter in tube pan. Sprinkle some sugar and cinnamon over it, leaving a bit for the top. Add remaining batter, then remaining cinnamon and sugar on top and dig it into the cake with a fork. Bake at 350° for 1 hour. Delicious cake to enjoy with coffee!

Parve "Cheese" Cake

2 containers BETTER THAN
    CREAM CHEESE (tofu
    product)
2 eggs
½ cup sugar

1 tsp. vanilla
1 9-inch graham-cracker pie
  crust
1 21-oz. can cherry pie
  filling

Combine "cheese," eggs, sugar, and vanilla by hand with a large fork. Put into pie crust. Top with cherry pie filling. Bake at 350° until it looks done — approximately 25 minutes. Make a few at a time, because they go fast!

No-Egg Chocolate Cake

3 cups flour
2 cups sugar
2 tsp. baking soda
½ cup cocoa

2 Tbs. vinegar
2 cups water
¾ cup oil

Mix all dry ingredients together. Make a well and add liquid ingredients. Combine in a mixer until thoroughly blended. Use a 9x13-inch pan or a tube pan. Bake for 35 to 40 minutes at 350°.

"Cherries in a Pit" Cake

1 lb. margarine
2 cups sugar
8 eggs
3½ cups flour
1 tsp. baking powder

2 tsp. vanilla
2 Tbs. lemon juice
1 21-oz. can cherry pie
  filling

Cream margarine, sugar, and eggs. Add flour, baking powder, vanilla, and lemon juice. Beat until smooth. Lightly grease a disposable cookie sheet and spread the mix out evenly on it. With a knife, lightly mark 30 rectangles in the batter. Fill the center of each one with 1 teaspoonful of pie filling (approximately 3 cherries per rectangle). Bake at 350° until lightly browned. When cooled, cut into 30 pieces.

Nana's Delicious Apple Cake

4 eggs
2 cups sugar
3 cups flour
1 cup oil
⅔ cup orange juice

2½ tsp. baking powder
5 large apples
cinnamon
sugar

Beat eggs well. Gradually add sugar. Sift flour and add to egg mixture alternately with oil and juice. Mix. Add baking powder and mix again. Pour half of the batter into a greased 9x13-inch pan. Cut apples into wedges and put half on top of the batter. Sprinkle cinnamon and sugar on top. Spread remaining batter on top, add remaining apples, and sprinkle more cinnamon and sugar on top. Bake at 350° for 1 hour.

Coffee Cake

1 cup oil
2 cups sugar
4 eggs
3 cups flour
1 tsp. vanilla
3 tsp. baking powder
½ tsp. salt

1 cup apricot nectar

Topping:
1 cup brown sugar
½ cup chopped nuts
2 tsp. cinnamon

Mix together all ingredients for batter and pour into a 9x13-inch pan. Mix topping ingredients together. Pour over cake batter, and with a spatula, swirl topping into cake. Bake at 350° for 45 minutes to 1 hour.

Best Honey Cake

¼ cup oil
1¼ cups sugar
3 eggs
1 tsp. vanilla
1 cup honey

1 tsp. cinnamon
2 tsp. baking soda
3 cups flour
1 Tbs. coffee dissolved in
    1¼ cups boiling water

Cream oil and sugar. Add eggs and then add vanilla, honey, cinnamon, and baking soda. Add flour alternately with coffee. Bake in tube pan at 350° for 45 minutes to 1 hour.

One-Bowl White Cake

2¼ cups flour
1¼ cups sugar
3 tsp. baking powder
1 cup orange juice

1 cup oil
2 eggs
1 tsp. vanilla

Combine dry ingredients and make a well. Add orange juice, oil, eggs, and vanilla. Mix 50 strokes by hand. Pour into a 9x13-inch pan. Bake at 350° for 30 minutes. Chocolate chips or fresh blueberries can be sprinkled on top before baking.

Apple Cake

2 tsp. baking powder
3 cups flour
2 sticks margarine, softened
½ cup sugar
4 egg yolks
½ cup seltzer
dash of lemon juice

apples (approx. 5)
½ cup sugar
dash of cinnamon
nuts and raisins (optional)
4 egg whites
1 cup sugar

Combine first seven ingredients and mix. Spread in two 9-inch round baking pans. Peel and slice apples. Mix sugar and cinnamon with apples. Add nuts and raisins, if desired. Spread over dough and bake at 350° for 1 hour. Meanwhile, beat egg whites and sugar until stiff. Spoon over cake, and bake for an additional 15 minutes.

Marble Cake

4 eggs	2 tsp. vanilla extract
2 cups sugar	grated zest of 1 lemon
1 cup oil	2 Tbs. cocoa
3 cups flour	4 oz. chocolate chips,
3 tsp. baking powder	melted
1 cup orange juice	1 tsp. rum or almond extract

Mix first eight ingredients together. Put ¾ of mixture into a 9x13-inch pan. Into the remaining ¼ mixture, add cocoa, melted chocolate chips, and extract. Mix well. Pour into pan and swirl with a knife to marbleize. Bake at 350° for 1 hour.

Brownie Cake
Compliments of Sabel's Catering, Monsey, NY

⅔ cup cocoa	1½ tsp. instant coffee
2¼ cups flour	powder
2 cups sugar	3 eggs
1½ tsp. baking powder	1½ cups orange juice
1½ tsp. baking soda	1 cup oil
½ tsp. salt	

This cake is best made using a food processor. Mix all dry ingredients in a food processor for 10 seconds. Add eggs, juice, and oil slowly and process for 45 seconds. Grease and flour with cocoa a 9x13-inch baking pan and pour in mixture. Bake at 350° for 50 to 60 minutes.

Easy Marble Cake

6 eggs
1¾ cups sugar
2 cups flour
1 tsp. baking powder
1 pkg. vanilla sugar

1 cup oil
1 tsp. almond extract
(optional)
⅔ cup chocolate syrup

Mix all ingredients, except chocolate syrup, in one bowl. Pour half the batter into a tube pan. Put chocolate syrup into the other half of the batter and mix well. Pour chocolate batter into tube pan and marbleize by swirling knife through both batters. Bake for 1 hour at 350°.

Carrot Cake

2 cups grated carrots (4
large carrots)
1 cup chopped walnuts
1 cup raisins
2 cups flour
1 tsp. baking soda

1 tsp. baking powder
pinch of salt
1 tsp. vanilla
4 eggs
1 cup oil
2 cups sugar

Mix all ingredients in a large bowl, by hand or with a mixer. Bake in a greased 9x13-inch pan at 350° for approximately 45 minutes.

Mom's Delicious Brownies

4 eggs
2 sticks margarine
½ cup cocoa
1 tsp. baking powder
2 cups sugar

2 tsp. vanilla
pinch of salt
1 cup flour
1 cup chopped walnuts

Beat eggs for 10 minutes. Add remaining ingredients, except walnuts, and mix until well blended. Stir in walnuts. Bake at 350° for about 45 minutes in a 9x13-inch pan.

Dairy Cakes

Toasted Coconut Cake

1 Tbs. margarine or butter
2 eggs
1 cup sugar
1 tsp. vanilla
⅓ cup milk or orange juice
1 cup flour
1½ tsp. baking powder
¼ tsp. salt

Topping:
3 Tbs. margarine or butter
½ tsp. vanilla
⅓ cup brown sugar
¾ cup grated coconut
2 Tbs. light cream

Melt margarine. Beat eggs and sugar very well. Add remaining ingredients and beat well. Bake in a greased, 8-inch square brownie pan for 30 minutes at 350°. Do not remove from pan. Cool cake for 5 minutes. Combine ingredients for topping. Spread topping on cake and broil until light brown, watching closely that it doesn't burn.

Mini Cheesecakes

16 oz. cream cheese
¾ cup sugar
2 eggs
1 Tbs. lemon juice

1 tsp. vanilla
vanilla wafers (round)
1 21-oz. can pie filling

With electric mixer, combine first 5 ingredients until fluffy and creamy. Mixture may be lumpy. Place small cupcake papers on a cookie sheet. Place 1 vanilla wafer on the bottom of each paper and fill with mixture. Bake at 375° for 15 minutes. Let cool. Top with pie filling. Serve chilled.

Rich Chocolate Cheesecake

Crust:
6 Tbs. margarine, melted
2 cups graham cracker
   crumbs
⅓ cup packed brown sugar

Filling:
2 eggs, separated

1 10-oz. container dessert
   whip, divided
8 oz. cream cheese,
   softened
½ cup sugar
6 oz. semisweet chocolate,
   melted
maraschino cherries,
   chocolate leaves, etc.

Crust: Combine all crust ingredients. Press into a 9-inch pie pan or springform pan. Refrigerate until firmly set.

Filling: **Work fast!!** Beat egg whites. Refrigerate. Beat whip. Refrigerate. Beat cream cheese, sugar, and yolks. Stir in chocolate. Fold in about one-third of the whipped cream. Fold in whites. Pour into crust. Garnish with remaining whipped cream, cherries, and chocolate leaves. Refrigerate until set.

Cheesecake

Base:
¾ stick margarine
1 cup flour
1 tsp. baking powder
1 egg
½ cup sugar

Filling:
1 lb. farmer cheese

½ cup sugar
12 oz. sour cream
½ pkg. OSEM instant vanilla
   pudding
3 eggs
1 pkg. vanilla sugar
graham cracker crumbs

Mix together ingredients for base and spread on bottom of a 9x13-inch pan. Mix together ingredients for filling and pour onto base. Sprinkle some graham cracker crumbs on top. Bake about 1 hour at 350°. Freezes well.

Sour Cream Delight Cake

Crust:
3 cups flour
3 tsp. baking powder
¾ cup sugar
2 eggs
⅓ cup milk or juice
1 Tbs. vanilla
2 sticks margarine

Filling:
1⅓ sticks margarine or
   butter
¾ cup sugar
2 eggs
1 Tbs. vanilla
2½ cups sour cream

Crust: Mix ingredients together. Put ⅔ of batter in a greased 9x13-inch pan. Put remaining ⅓ in a greased 8-inch round pan or 8-inch pie plate. Bake both pans at 425° for approximately 10 minutes until light golden. Remove from oven.

Filling: Beat first 4 ingredients until creamy. Add sour cream and mix well. Pour filling onto larger baked crust. Crumble cake from small pan over large cake. Cover and refrigerate overnight before serving.

Scrumptious Dietetic Cheese Cake

6 eggs, separated
16 oz. plain yogurt
16 oz. low-fat cottage
   cheese

6 tsp. vanilla
20 pkgs. sweetener
½ cup flour
2 Tbs. cocoa

Blend egg yolks, yogurt, cottage cheese, vanilla, 10 packages of sweetener, and flour. Divide this mixture in half and add cocoa to one half. Set aside. In another bowl, beat egg whites well and add the other 10 packages of sweetener. Fold this into the other half of the mixture, and divide this batter among 8 small (4x2½-inch) baking pans. Then take the cocoa mixture and divide that batter among the 8 small pans, pouring a little into each pan until the batter is used up. Swirl each with a knife to marbelize. Bake at 350° for 30 minutes. Turn off oven but let cakes remain for another 30 minutes.

Richest Cheesecake in the World

1 13-oz. bag lemon
   cookies, crushed
½ stick butter
6 eggs, separated
2 pkgs. vanilla sugar
1 cup sugar

1 16-oz. container sour
   cream
8 oz. cream cheese
8 heaping Tbs. flour
10 oz. farmer cheese

Brown cookie crumbs in butter over low flame. With an electric mixer, beat egg whites very well. In a separate bowl, combine vanilla sugar and regular sugar with egg yolks and beat with a mixer. Add remaining ingredients and mix well. Fold in beaten whites by hand. Lightly grease a 9-inch springform pan with some butter and pat down browned cookie crumbs, reserving some crumbs. Pour in cheese mixture and sprinkle reserved crumbs on top. Bake, uncovered, at 300° for 1 hour. Insert a toothpick in center to test if cake is done. When toothpick comes out dry, shut off oven immediately and leave cake in oven for an additional hour. Refrigerate and cover well with foil. Freezes well and defrosts in refrigerator.

Frostings

Rich Chocolate Frosting

3 cups unsifted
   confectioners' sugar
½ cup unsweetened cocoa
   powder

½ cup margarine or butter,
   cut up
⅓ cup boiling water
1 tsp. vanilla

In a large mixing bowl, stir together sugar and cocoa. Add margarine or butter, boiling water, and vanilla. Beat with an electric mixer on low speed until combined. Then beat for 1 minute on medium speed. Cool for 20 to 30 minutes or until frosting is spreadable. Frosts top and sides of 2 8- or 9-inch cake layers.

Chocolate Glaze

3 Tbs. cocoa
1 cup confectioners' sugar

2 Tbs. hot water
1 Tbs. oil

Mix together dry ingredients. Add water and oil. Mix, and spread over cooled cake.

¼ cup margarine
½ cup brown sugar
2 Tbs. boiling water or milk

pinch of salt
¾ cup confectioners' sugar
¾ tsp. vanilla extract

Beat margarine and sugar with mixer. Add boiling water and salt. Cool for 30 minutes. Add confectioners' sugar and vanilla. Beat until thick. Spoon over cake.

Coffee Icing

16 oz. confectioners' sugar
2 Tbs. oil

1½ Tbs. instant coffee mixed with ⅓ cup boiling water

Mix ingredients together and pour quickly over cake.

1 lb. unsweetened chocolate
½ cup water
½ cup sugar

2 Tbs. instant coffee
1 lb. margarine
4 eggs

Melt first four ingredients over a low flame. Cool slightly. Blend margarine and eggs well with a mixer. Add chocolate mixture to egg mixture and blend well. While cake is still warm, pour over to form a beautiful, glossy frosting.

Variation: Rum, almond extract, or mint flavor may be added.

Chocolate-Nut Frosting

½ cup margarine
1 egg
2 squares (2 oz.) chocolate
  (any kind)
1⅓ cups confectioners'
  sugar

⅛ tsp. salt
1 tsp. vanilla
1 cup chopped nuts

Cream margarine until soft. Beat in egg. Melt chocolate and add to margarine-egg mixture. Add in sugar, salt, and vanilla. Beat until smooth and creamy. Stir in chopped nuts.

Coconut Icing

2¼ cups confectioners'
  sugar
1 tsp. vanilla
¼ cup oil

¼ cup hot water
¾ cup cocoa
1½ cups shredded coconut

Mix sugar, vanilla, oil, water, and cocoa together. Spread on cake. Sprinkle with coconut.

Lemon Frosting

1 egg yolk
1½ Tbs. lemon juice
1 Tbs. grated orange rind

⅛ tsp. salt
2 cups confectioners' sugar

Combine egg yolk, lemon juice, orange rind, and salt. Beat until smooth. Gradually mix in sugar and beat until consistency is good for spreading.

Pies, Cookies, Pastries, and Candies

Lemon Meringue Pie
Marzipan
Doughnuts
Nutty Marshmallow Fudge
Peanut Butter Balls
Yummy Bars
Choco-Nut Dainties
Pinwheel Cookies
Peanut Chews
Chocolate Mousse Pie
Cookie-Gun Cookies
Honey Peanut Butter Cookies
Chocolate Rugelach
Favorite Chocolate Chip Cookies
Fortune Cookies
Lemon Pie
Caramel Popcorn
Chocolate Chip Mandelbrodt

Viennese Cookies (Crescents)
Peanut Butter Pie
Peanut Butter Cookies
Snowballs
Lacy Cookies
Easy Fruit Pie
Simple Pie Crust
Healthy Oatmeal Cookies
Crunchy Jumbo Cookies
Lemon Pie Freeze
Apple Pie
Marbleized Chinese Cookies
White Chocolate-Covered Pretzels
Devil Dogs
Oatmeal Rounds
Hamantaschen
Chocolate Chip Cookies

Pies, Cookies, Pastries, and Candies

Lemon Meringue Pie

Filling:
1½ cups sugar
⅛ tsp. salt
½ cup cornstarch
2 cups boiling water
1 Tbs. lemon rind
3 egg yolks
⅓ cup lemon juice
2 tsp. margarine

1 9-inch pie shell, baked
   and cooled

Meringue:
¼ tsp. salt
3 egg whites
¼ tsp. baking powder
   (optional)
6 Tbs. sugar
½ tsp. vanilla

Filling: In a saucepan, combine first 5 ingredients for filling and stir to blend well. Cook over very low flame for about 7 minutes, stirring constantly. Slightly beat egg yolks and add 2 tablespoons of warm filling ingredients. Slowly blend yolks into rest of filling. Add lemon juice and margarine and continue cooking for 5 minutes. Remove from heat, cool slightly, and pour into pie shell.

Meringue: Add salt to egg whites and beat until foamy. Add baking powder and beat until stiff. Add sugar and vanilla and continue beating until sugar is well beaten and meringue is fluffy. Spread on pie, bringing meringue out to edges of dough. (Unless it has something to cling to, it will shrink.) Spread in uneven strokes. Bake at 350° for 12 to 15 minutes or until brown.

Marzipan

2 egg whites
1 cup almond paste*
½ tsp. lemon or vanilla
    extract

1 cup confectioners' sugar
food coloring (optional)

Beat egg whites. Mix with almond paste. Add flavoring and sugar mixture. Should be stiff enough to handle. Let stand overnight. Tint with food coloring if desired, and shape as you like.

*To make 1 cup almond paste: Blanch and pound 2⅔ shelled almonds into a fine consistency.

Marzipan apples: Tint marzipan pale green. Divide into small pieces and shape into balls. A little red food coloring can be added to one side of each apple. Use a clove for a stalk.

Marzipan bananas: Tint marzipan yellow. Divide into small pieces and shape like bananas. Cocoa powder can be brushed on for shading. Put a clove on one end for a stalk.

Marzipan oranges: Tint marzipan orange. Divide into small pieces and roll into balls. Press a clove into the top for a stalk.

Marzipan strawberries: Tint marzipan red. Divide into small pieces and shape like strawberries. Roll each one lightly over a grater for an authentic appearance. Shape a leaf from green marzipan for the top.

Doughnuts

2 oz. fresh yeast
2 cups warm water
⅔ cup sugar
⅓ cup oil

3 eggs
pinch of salt
9 cups flour (approx.)

Place yeast in water with sugar for about 5 minutes. Yeast should bubble. Mix this with all the other ingredients. Let rise in bowl for 30 minutes.

Pinch off dough to form 2-inch balls, and flatten slightly, or roll out dough and use doughnut cutter. Reroll extra pieces to use all the dough.

Let the dough rest for 20 minutes. Then fry in hot oil, 2 to 3 inches deep, on both sides until golden. Watch carefully, because they cook quickly. Doughnuts with holes may be dusted with powdered sugar or dipped in melted chocolate. Doughnuts without holes may be filled with custard or your favorite jam. Then top with chocolate or powdered sugar. Mini-doughnuts may be rolled in powdered sugar. Best if eaten the same day. Dough may be frozen before frying.

Nutty Marshmallow Fudge

½ cup margarine
⅔ cup cocoa
½ cup light corn syrup
1 Tbs. water

1 tsp. vanilla
1 lb. confectioners' sugar
1 cup mini-marshmallows
½ cup chopped nuts

Grease an 8x8x2-inch baking pan. Melt margarine over low heat. Stir in cocoa, corn syrup, water, and vanilla. Blend well. Remove from heat. Slowly stir in confectioners' sugar until smooth. Stir in marshmallows and nuts. Turn into prepared baking pan. Cover and refrigerate until firm. Cut into squares.

Peanut Butter Balls

1 cup peanut butter
½ stick margarine
3 cups confectioners' sugar

1 tsp. vanilla
10–12 oz. baking chocolate

Mix together first four ingredients (easier with a mixer) and form balls. If mixture is too crumbly, add up to ¼ stick margarine plus ¼ cup peanut butter. Put in freezer for 30 minutes. Melt chocolate. To melt in oven, heat oven first for 15 minutes, then turn it off and put chocolate in until melted. To melt in microwave, put chocolate in a microwaveable bowl and cover. Set microwave to high for 1½ minutes and stir. Roll the balls individually in melted chocolate, using 2 forks. Freeze. Either remove from freezer 20 minutes before serving or store in refrigerator after balls harden.

Yummy Bars

Dough:
¾ cup solid shortening
2 cups flour
⅓ cup brown sugar
1 egg plus 1 egg yolk

Topping:
2 eggs plus 1 egg white
pinch of salt
2¼ cups brown sugar
1½ cups flaked coconut
¾ cup chopped nuts
6 oz. chocolate chips
1 tsp. vanilla extract

Preheat oven to 350°. Grease a 9x13-inch pan.

Dough: In a bowl, cut shortening into flour. Add brown sugar, egg, and egg yolk. Mix by hand or with mixer until crumbly. Press into prepared pan.

Topping: In a mixing bowl, combine all ingredients. Spread evenly over dough in pan. Bake for 45 minutes. Cool in pan and cut into bars or squares.

Choco-Nut Dainties

2¼ cups sifted flour
½ tsp. salt
¾ cup (1½ sticks)
    margarine, softened
¾ cup sugar
1 egg
1½ tsp. vanilla

6 oz. chocolate chips

Chocolate Coating:
12 oz. chocolate chips
¼ cup margarine
2 cups chopped walnuts

Preheat oven to 350°. Sift flour and salt onto waxed paper. Beat together margarine, sugar, egg, and vanilla in a large bowl until well mixed. Blend in flour mixture. Stir in chocolate chips. On a lightly floured surface, shape dough into logs (2x½-inch). Place on an ungreased cookie sheet. Bake for 12 to 15 minutes or until set. Cool on wire racks.

Chocolate Coating: Melt together chocolate chips and margarine in top of a double boiler over hot water, or in microwave. If mixture is too thick, add more margarine, 1 Tbs. at a time. Dip ends of logs into chocolate coating and roll ends in chopped walnuts. Place on waxed paper until set.

Pinwheel Cookies

4 eggs
2 sticks margarine
1 pkg. vanilla sugar
1 Tbs. baking powder
pinch of salt

2 cups confectioners' sugar
4 cups flour (or more)
cocoa or red or green food
    coloring for color

Mix first 7 ingredients together until smooth. Divide dough in half. Add cocoa or coloring to one half. Roll out white dough to ⅛-inch thickness. Do the same for the colored dough, on a piece of wax paper. Place colored dough on top of white dough. Roll up, jelly-roll fashion. Refrigerate for a few hours or overnight. Slice ¼-inch thick. Bake at 350° for 10 to 15 minutes on ungreased cookie sheets. Makes approximately 4½ dozen cookies.

Peanut Chews

1 cup sugar
1 cup corn syrup
1 cup peanut butter

5 cups crisp rice cereal
8 oz. sweetened baking
  chocolate, melted

Boil sugar and corn syrup until blended. Combine peanut butter with sugar and corn syrup mixture. Then add rice cereal and mix well by hand. Pour onto an ungreased cookie sheet and spread melted baking chocolate on top. Let stand 5 minutes and then cut into squares.

Chocolate Mousse Pie

8 oz. semi-sweet chocolate
8 eggs, separated
⅔ cup sugar

½ of a 10-oz. container
  dessert whip

Melt chocolate; add egg yolks. In a separate bowl, beat egg whites until firm. Add sugar, and mix into chocolate mixture. Pour ¼ of mixture into a 9-inch pie pan. Bake at 350° for 15 minutes, cool for 1 hour, then add remaining chocolate mixture. Beat dessert whip and spoon on top of mousse. Chill.

Cookie-Gun Cookies

1 stick margarine
1 cup sugar
2 cups flour

1 egg
½ tsp. baking powder
½ tsp. vanilla

Cream margarine and sugar. Slowly add remaining ingredients. Mix well. With cookie gun, "shoot" cookies onto ungreased, chilled cookie sheets. Bake at 350° for 15 minutes or until light brown. Makes approximately 40 cookies. (Dough can also be rolled out and cut with cookie cutters.)

Honey Peanut Butter Cookies

Compliments of Supreme Health Food Center, Monsey, NY

1 cup natural peanut butter (crunchy)
1 cup honey (buckwheat honey is great for honey taste)
1 egg, beaten

1½ tsp. vanilla
½ tsp. salt (sea salt is preferable)
½ tsp. baking soda
2 cups whole-wheat pastry flour

Preheat oven to 350°. Cream peanut butter and honey. Stir in egg and vanilla. Sift together salt, baking soda, and flour and stir into peanut butter mixture. Drop by teaspoonfuls onto an oiled cookie sheet. Flatten each cookie slightly with the back of a fork, wetting the fork frequently to prevent sticking. Bake for 10 to 12 minutes until cookies begin to turn golden brown on the edges. Keep a close eye on them, as cookies made with honey pass quickly from golden brown to black. Makes 3 to 4 dozen.

Chocolate Rugelach

2 oz. fresh yeast
½ cup + ½ cup seltzer (room temperature)
9 cups flour, divided
3 sticks margarine
3 whole eggs
2 egg yolks

1 tsp. salt
½ cup sugar

Chocolate Filling:
3 cups sugar
1 cup cocoa
1½ tsp. cinnamon

Dissolve yeast in ½ cup seltzer. Combine half the flour and the remaining ingredients in a large mixing bowl. After everything is mixed together, gradually add dissolved yeast mixture and remaining flour until a light, soft dough is formed. Let rise for 1 hour. Meanwhile, mix sugar, cocoa, and cinnamon for filling. Divide dough into 5 even balls. Roll out ¼-inch thick. Brush a thin layer of oil on dough, then spoon on chocolate mixture. Cut into wedges and roll up to form rugelach. Brush some beaten egg on top. Bake on ungreased cookie sheets at 350° for approximately 35 minutes. Yields about 100 rugelach.

Everybody's Favorite Chocolate Chip Cookies

¾ cup brown sugar
½ cup sugar
¼–½ cup oil
1 whole egg
2 egg whites
1 tsp. vanilla

1 tsp. baking soda
¼ tsp. salt
½ tsp. cinnamon
2½ cups flour
1 12-oz. bag chocolate
    chips

Beat sugars, oil, and eggs until well blended. Add remaining ingredients. Drop by teaspoonfuls onto ungreased cookie sheets. Bake 10 to 12 minutes at 350°. Do not let the cookies get too brown. Cookies will be soft and chewy. Yields approximately 5 dozen cookies. With their low fat and cholesterol content, these cookies really are everybody's favorites!

Fortune Cookies

1 egg
⅓ cup sugar
⅓ cup flour
3 Tbs. oil
2 Tbs. water

½ tsp. vanilla extract
¼ tsp. cinnamon (optional)
berachos written on small
    strips of paper

Generously grease a griddle or frying pan and heat over medium flame. Beat egg until foamy. Add sugar and beat until fluffy. Add remaining ingredients (including the 3 Tbs. oil, but not paper!). Mix until smooth. Drop batter onto hot griddle by tablespoonfuls. Spread into circles of about 3½ inches, using the back of the spoon. The cookies will be very thin. Fry until light brown (3 minutes). Flip and fry the other side, also for about 3 minutes. Lift cookies one at a time onto a plate. Place a paper *berachah* in the center of each cookie, then fold the cookie in half. Holding the edges, gently fold in half again. Place in a muffin pan to cool. This will help them hold their shape. Be very careful when folding cookies; they break easily.

Lemon Pie

Crust:
1 stick margarine
1 cup flour
2 Tbs. sugar
pinch of salt

Filling:
3 egg whites
¾ cup sugar
1 tsp. lemon juice
1 10-oz. container dessert
  whip

Crust: Mix together all ingredients. Press ¾ of dough onto bottom and sides of a 9-inch pie pan. Put the remaining dough on silver foil (dough should resemble crumbs). Bake both doughs for 20 minutes at 350°.

Filling: Beat egg whites until stiff. Add sugar and lemon juice. Set aside. Beat dessert whip and fold into egg mixture. Spoon into pan and sprinkle remaining dough on top. Serve frozen.

Caramel Popcorn

10 cups popped corn
½ cup margarine
1 cup packed brown sugar
¼ cup light corn syrup

½ tsp. salt
red or green food coloring
  (optional)
½ tsp. baking soda

Preheat oven to 225°. Place popped corn in a very large bowl. In a medium saucepan, melt margarine. Add sugar, corn syrup, and salt. Over a low-medium flame, stir constantly until bubbly around edges. Continue to cook for no less than 5 minutes. Remove from heat. Add food coloring, if desired, then add baking soda. Stir well until all foamy. **At this point, do not stir any more!** Pour over corn and toss to coat all kernels. Pour onto foil-lined, well-greased jelly-roll pan. Bake for 1 hour, removing from oven every 15 minutes to toss in bowl again.
Caution: Hot caramel burns skin **very** quickly. Be careful! Also, it's very hard to stop eating this.

Chocolate Chip Mandelbrodt

3 eggs
1 cup sugar
1 cup oil
3 Tbs. orange juice
1 tsp. vanilla

4 cups flour
4 tsp. baking powder
1 cup semi-sweet chocolate
   morsels

Preheat oven to 350°. Grease a cookie sheet. Beat eggs until thick and lemon colored. Gradually add sugar. Add oil, orange juice, and vanilla and blend well. Mix dry ingredients with chocolate morsels and add to mixture, blending to make a soft dough. Oil hands, scoop up dough, divide it into 3 parts, place them on a 12x17-inch cookie sheet, and form them into long straight bars the length of the cookie sheet. Three bars should fit on one cookie sheet. Bake for 35 to 40 minutes, until bars are lightly browned on top. Remove from oven and cut into slices. Can be frozen.

Viennese Cookies (Crescents)

2 cups flour
1 cup margarine, softened
1 cup ground almonds
½ cup confectioners' sugar
⅛ tsp. salt

1 tsp. vanilla extract
¼ tsp. almond extract
confectioners' sugar (for
   rolling cookies)

In a bowl, combine flour, margarine, nuts, sugar, salt, and flavorings. With hands, mix until thoroughly blended. Shape into a ball and refrigerate, covered, for 1 hour. Preheat oven to 375°. Form the dough into 1-inch balls. Roll each ball into 3-inch long rolls and curve the rolls to make crescent shapes. Place 2 inches apart on an ungreased cookie sheet. Bake 10 to 12 minutes or until set, but not brown. Let stand for 1 minute. Remove from pan and roll in confectioners' sugar. When cool, roll once more in confectioners' sugar. Makes 3½ dozen.

Peanut Butter Pie

½ cup peanut butter
1 cup confectioners' sugar
1 9-inch graham-cracker pie
    crust
½ cup coffee whitener

1 pkg. instant vanilla
    pudding
1 10-oz. container dessert
    whip

Mix peanut butter and confectioners' sugar until crumbly. Put ¾ of this in pie shell. Then mix coffee whitener and vanilla pudding and pour over peanut butter mixture. Freeze until firm. Whip up dessert whip and spoon on top. Pour remaining crumb mixture over whipped topping, and serve frozen.

Peanut Butter Cookies

1 cup margarine
1 cup sugar
1 cup brown sugar
1 cup peanut butter

¾ tsp. baking powder
3 cups flour
1 tsp. vanilla

Cream margarine and sugars. Add remaining ingredients. Roll into balls and place on ungreased cookie sheets. Flatten with tines of fork. Bake at 350° for 8 to 12 minutes.

Snowballs

1 cup margarine
½ cup confectioners' sugar
1 tsp. vanilla
2¼ cups flour

¼ tsp. salt
¾ cup finely chopped nuts
extra confectioners' sugar

Preheat oven to 400°. Mix margarine, sugar, and vanilla. Stir in flour, salt, and nuts. Shape dough into 1-inch balls. Place on ungreased cookie sheets. Bake until set, but not brown (8 to 9 minutes). While warm, roll in confectioners' sugar. Cool and roll in sugar again.

Lacy Cookies

½ cup flour
¼ tsp. baking soda
dash of salt
¼ cup margarine
⅓ cup firmly packed brown
    sugar

2 Tbs. light corn syrup
1 egg, well beaten
½ tsp. vanilla
2 squares semi-sweet
    chocolate
1 Tbs. margarine

Mix flour, baking soda, and salt, and set aside. In a large bowl, cream margarine. Gradually add sugar and beat until light and fluffy. Add corn syrup and egg. Blend well. Stir in flour mixture and vanilla. Drop by ½ teaspoonfuls onto greased cookie sheets, leaving 2 inches of space between each cookie. Bake at 350° for 10 minutes. Cool for 1 minute, remove quickly, and finish cooling on racks. Melt chocolate and margarine in a saucepan over a low flame. Stir until smooth. Drizzle over cookies.

Easy Fruit Pie

1 10-oz. container dessert
    whip
1 pkg. instant vanilla
    pudding

1 can fruit filling (cherry or
    blueberry)
1 ready-made graham
    cracker pie crust

Whip up dessert whip with pudding. Mix until creamy. Put into pie shell. Spoon fruit filling on top. Chill.

Simple Pie Crust

1¼ cups flour, sifted
½ tsp. salt

½ cup shortening or
    margarine
¼ cup cold water

Combine flour and salt. Cut in shortening and add water a little at a time. Shape dough into a firm ball. Press dough into a greased 10-inch pie pan and bake at 450° for 10 minutes.

Healthy Oatmeal Cookies

1½ cups oat flour (blended oatmeal)
1½ cups nuts, blended
½ tsp. salt
1 tsp. cinnamon

¾ cup rice syrup
½ cup canola oil
2 Tbs. apple juice
1 tsp. vanilla

First mix dry ingredients, then add liquid ingredients and mix together. Drop by rounded teaspoonfuls onto lightly greased cookie sheets. Bake at 350° for 15 minutes.

Crunchy Jumbo Cookies

1 stick margarine
1 cup sugar
1 egg
1 tsp. vanilla
1¼ cups flour

½ tsp. baking soda
¼ tsp. salt
2 cups crisp rice cereal
6 oz. chocolate chips
1 cup raisins

Preheat oven to 350°. Cream margarine and sugar. Add egg and vanilla. Then add flour and baking soda. Add remaining ingredients and mix well. Drop by tablespoonfuls onto an ungreased cookie sheet. Bake for 12 minutes. Do not overbake. Cookies should be chewy.

Lemon Pie Freeze

2 9-inch pie shells
4 eggs, separated
¾ cup + ¼ cup sugar
½ cup lemon juice

1½ Tbs. grated lemon rind
1 10-oz. container dessert whip, whipped

Bake empty pie shells as directed on package. Beat egg yolks with ¾ cup sugar until light and foamy. Add lemon juice. Beat egg whites with ¼ cup sugar until soft peaks (not dry ones) form. Fold in lemon rind and dessert whip. Fold white mixture into yellow mixture and freeze in baked pie shells. Thaw slightly before serving.

Apple Pie

1 9-inch pie shell	3 tsp. honey
5 apples	1 stick margarine
1 tsp. lemon juice	2 cups sugar
1 tsp. cinnamon	2 cups flour
1 tsp. sugar	3 tsp. cinnamon

Peel and slice apples. Combine lemon juice, cinnamon, sugar, and honey. Add to apples and mix. Place mixture in pie shell and bake for 20 minutes at 350°. In a separate bowl, cream margarine and add sugar, flour, and cinnamon. Mixture will be crumbly. Take pie out of oven and top with this mixture. Bake an additional 20 minutes or until golden brown.

Marbleized Chinese Cookies

3 cups cake flour	1½ tsp. baking soda
1½ cups sugar	1 egg
1½ cups solid vegetable	1 square melted chocolate,
shortening	any kind

Mix first 4 ingredients well. Add egg. Add melted chocolate and mix just enough to marbleize. Roll into 2 logs. For small cookies, logs should be 1¼ inches in diameter. For larger cookies, logs should be 2½ to 3 inches in diameter. Wrap in foil and refrigerate overnight. Slice rolls ½-inch thick. Bake on an ungreased cookie sheet at 350° for 15 to 20 minutes. If desired, when cooled, melt some more chocolate and place a dot in the center of each cookie.

White-Chocolate Covered Pretzels

2 3-oz. bars white chocolate	multicolored sprinkles
66 salted mini-pretzels	
(about 3 oz.)	

Line 2 cookie sheets with waxed paper. Break chocolate into pieces and place in a small saucepan. Stir constantly over very low heat until melted. Holding pretzels with small tongs, dip one at a time into melted chocolate. Place pretzels on lined cookie sheets and sprinkle immediately with nonpareils. Refrigerate for 30 minutes or until completely set. Store covered in a cool place with waxed paper between layers.

Devil Dogs

Batter:
1 cup shortening
2 cups sugar
2 eggs
2 cups water
4 cups flour
1½ tsp. baking soda

1 cup cocoa
½ tsp. salt

Filling:
1 cup shortening
2 tsp. vanilla extract
2 cups confectioners' sugar
2 cups marshmallow cream

Combine all ingredients for batter. Drop by tablespoonfuls onto an ungreased cookie sheet. Bake at 400° for 10 minutes. Cool. Combine ingredients for filling. Join pairs of cookies by spreading filling between them. Freeze or refrigerate.

Oatmeal Rounds

1½ cups uncooked oatmeal
¾ cup ground, blanched
    almonds
⅓ cup brown sugar
2 egg whites

2 Tbs. vegetable oil or
    melted margarine
1 Tbs. vanilla
1 tsp. cinnamon

Preheat oven to 400°. Grease cookie sheets. Combine all ingredients. Form mixture into small balls and place on cookie sheets. Bake for 20 to 30 minutes or until lightly browned.

Note: To blanch almonds, pour boiling water over them to loosen their skins. Skins then slide off easily and can be discarded.

Hamantaschen

2 cups flour
2 tsp. baking powder
½ tsp. salt
½ cup margarine

½ cup sugar
1 egg
2 Tbs. orange juice
1 tsp. vanilla extract

Mix flour, baking powder, and salt and set aside. Cream together margarine and sugar. Add egg. Add dry ingredients alternately with juice. Add vanilla. Roll out to ¼-inch thickness. Cut into 2-inch rounds. Spoon on your choice of filling. Shape into hamantaschen by pinching dough together to form triangles. Bake on ungreased cookie sheets at 375° until lightly browned, about 10 minutes.

Chocolate Chip Cookies

2⅓ cups flour
1 tsp. baking soda
1 cup softened margarine
¾ cup brown sugar, firmly
   packed

¼ cup white sugar
1 tsp. vanilla
2 eggs
1 12-oz. package semi-
   sweet chocolate morsels

Mix flour and baking soda and set aside. Combine margarine, sugars, and vanilla, and mix well. Beat in eggs. Add flour mixture and mix well. Stir in chocolate morsels. Line a cookie sheet with aluminum foil and do not grease. Drop teaspoonfuls of cookie mixture onto cookie sheet. Bake at 375° for 10 to 12 minutes.

Children's
Simcha Section

Children's Simcha Section

Pekelach for an *Upshirin*:

1. On a small white paper bag, draw two thick black stripes about ½-inch apart, as shown. With a hole puncher, make a hole in each bottom corner of the bag. Draw white string through each hole, and tie knots to resemble *tzitzis*. Fill the bag with candy, pretzels, popcorn, and small toys.

2. Decorate a lollipop to look like a face. Stick on wiggly eyes, draw a mouth, and a black semicircle for a *yarmulke*. Staple the lollipop to the *tzitzis* bag to resemble a little boy. Fill with goodies.

3. Cover a small box of raisins with white paper and draw two black stripes near the bottom, as shown. Tape winkies (cellophane-wrapped rolls of multicolored small candies) onto the bottom of the box for legs and wrapped candies onto the sides for arms. Make a cute face on a lollipop, as described in #2, and attach to box. This may also be used for a *vach nacht pekele*.

4. Tape assorted candies and toys to a small bag of potato chips or pretzels. With a hole puncher, make a hole in the bottom corners of the bag and pull a white string through each. Knot the strings like *tzitzis*.

"Tefillin" for a Bar Mitzvah:

Put one chocolate-covered graham cracker on top of another and "glue" them together with honey. Then place a chocolate-covered marshmallow on top to resemble *tefillin*.

Tu B'Shevat Man:

Using an assortment of dried fruits and nuts, assemble a *Tu b'Shevat* man, as shown, holding pieces together with toothpicks.

Mishlo'ach Manos Ideas for Purim:

1. Fill a round paper plate with all kinds of nosh. Bring the edges of the plate together to form a triangle and staple it together to look like a *hamentasch*.

2. Remove the outer wrapping from a large fruit roll-up, but leave the inner clear plastic intact. Shape the roll-up into an ice cream cone shape and tape closed. Fill the cone with sealed plastic bags of popcorn, using transparent tape to hold the bags to the cone.

3. To make a delicious "hot-air" balloon, inflate a balloon and tie it closed. With tape, attach a straw from the bottom of the balloon to the inside of a plastic cup. This secures the balloon in the "air." Decorate the balloon and the cup with colorful markers and ribbons. Fill the cup with goodies, cover the top with clear cellophane, and tape closed.

4. Fill an empty balloon with small wrapped candies. Blow up the balloon, being careful not to overinflate it. Tie it closed and decorate it as desired.

CHILDREN'S SIMCHA SECTION

5. Make a "barbell balloon" by starting with an empty cardboard tube from toilet paper or paper towels. Fill the tube with assorted treats, cover each end with cellophane, and tape  closed, as shown. Cover the tube with wrapping paper or contact paper and add a message or greeting. Inflate two balloons, decorate as desired, and attach one to each end of the tube to resemble barbells.

 6. To make a "picnic in a basket," fill an inexpensive "wicker" basket with a deli sandwich, potato chips, and a box of juice. Attach a cord or pipe cleaner to form a handle and decorate the basket with ribbons, as desired.

7. To make a Purim *tze-dakah* box, empty a paper Band-Aid box and cut out a slot on top for the money. Cover the box with contact paper or wrapping paper and decorate. Fill with all kinds of nosh.

8. Fill an empty toilet paper roll with an assortment of small candies and treats. Wrap the roll in colored cellophane, twisting each end closed, as shown. Secure the ends with tape or twist ties.

Cakes:

1. Numbers — Bake your favorite cake in a square or rectangular pan. Cut out the shape of the number you desire, joining several pieces when necessary. Ice the entire cake and decorate.

2. *Tzitzis* — Bake a large rectangular cake and cut it in the shape of *tzitzis,* as shown. Cover with white icing. With black icing, make stripes near the bottom of the cake. Attach white strings at each bottom corner.

3. *Upshirin* or Birthday — Bake one round cake and two square or oblong cakes. Using the round cake for the head, cover it with white frosting to which a tinge of yellow and red food coloring have been added. Use different colors for the hair, *yarmulke*, eyes, etc., as shown.
Use the second cake for the body, carefully cutting out a neck and an arm, and covering them with icing. Use different colors for the shirt. The third cake becomes the *siddur*.

To serve, assemble the cake on a large, sturdy piece of cardboard covered with aluminum foil.

4. Torah Scroll — Bake two jelly rolls and an oblong cake. Place one jelly roll alongside each end of the oblong cake, and frost the entire cake to resemble a *sefer Torah*.

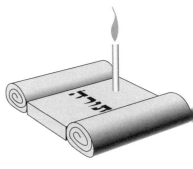

5. To make a drum cake, bake two or three round cakes. Put one on top of another, holding the layers together with icing or jelly. Frost the entire cake and arrange lollipops diagonally around the sides to look like a drum, as shown.

Cupcakes:

1. Write "Mazel Tov" or any other saying on a paper flag that has a toothpick attached. Stick the toothpick into a cupcake.

2. Cut out the shape of a Torah scroll from paper, glue it to a toothpick, and put it into a cupcake, as shown. Alternatively, attach the Torah scroll to

a lollipop and stick that into the cupcake. These are good ideas for a *Chumash* or *siddur* party, or a *siyum*.

3. Make chocolate letters using an *alef-beis* chocolate mold and place letters onto cupcakes, as shown at right.

4. Top a cupcake with a store-bought clown head. See illustration at left.

Cookies:

1. Cookie Pizza — Roll out a large piece of cookie dough into a round, flat "pizza" shape. Sprinkle with shredded coconut, marshmallows, chocolate lentils. etc. Bake until done and cut into wedges like a pizza.

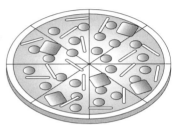

2. Roll out cookie dough into strips and shape them into letters. Make names or words, as shown.

3. Cookie Man — Roll out oatmeal or chocolate chip cookie dough into a circle. Stick a popsicle stick into the bottom. Decorate the dough to resemble a face, using shredded coconut for the hair, chocolate chips for the eyes, a piece of dried apricot for the nose, and "red hots" for the mouth. Bake as usual.

Sandwiches:

1. Use cookie cutters to cut out various shapes from hard cheese. Arrange the shapes on slices of bread when making grilled cheese.

2. Cut prepared sandwiches into interesting shapes, such as hearts, stars, etc.

3. Spread cream cheese on a slice of bread. Decorate it like a face, using shredded carrots for hair, pickle slices for eyes, cucumber for the nose, and a slice of red pepper for the mouth.

Ants on a Log:

Cut celery stalks into pieces, each about three inches long. Fill each piece with peanut butter and top with a row of black raisins, to resemble ants on a log.

To Make a Racing Car:

Fill a three-inch piece of celery with tuna and pat down. Insert a toothpick through each end of the celery and attach carrot rounds to each toothpick tip, to resemble wheels.

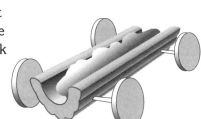

Make a Pizza Party:

Prepare the pizza dough before the children arrive. Distribute some dough to each child, along with a small, round baking pan. Provide ingredients for pizza toppings, such as cheese, tomato sauce, and oregano, and let each child prepare his or her own pizza.

Teddy Bear Challah:

Using round pieces of challah dough, form a teddy bear, as shown. Moisten the pieces of dough with egg or water to hold them together. Bake the challah as usual.

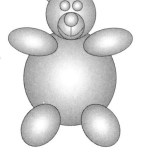

CHILDREN'S SIMCHA SECTION

Hamburger:

Place a peppermint patty between two round vanilla cookies to resemble a hamburger on a bun, as shown. Using green food coloring, tint shredded coconut to look like lettuce, and stick it onto the peppermint patty with honey. Spread more honey over the top cookie and sprinkle with sesame seeds, to look like an authentic sesame bun.

Ice Cream Soda:

Fill a cup with popcorn and stick in a piece of licorice as a straw.

Carousel:

Bake and ice a round cake to serve as the base of the carousel. Alternatively, use a round, flat piece of styrofoam covered with aluminum foil. Decorate the sides of the base with jelly beans or gumdrops, using toothpicks to hold them on. Carefully insert toothpicks into the bottoms of animal cookies and arrange them around the top surface of the base. Insert striped candy canes or straws for the poles. Then form a wide cone from a round paper plate and staple it together to the top of the carousel.

Jack-in-the-Box:

Fill a small box with goodies. Inflate a balloon and tape it inside the box to resemble a jack-in-the-box.

Chanukah Ideas:

1. Jello Menorah — Fill shnapps cups with lemon jello. Insert pieces of thin licorice for wicks, and line up the cups like a menorah.

2. Crispy Rice Cereal Shapes —

½ cup peanut butter	1 cup sugar
	5 cups crispy rice cereal
½ cup corn syrup	6 oz. chocolate chips

Melt the first 3 ingredients in a pot over a low flame. Mix in the cereal. Melt the chocolate chips and pour over the mixture in the pot. Mix well. Spread out mixture on a cookie sheet. Cut into dreidel shape as shown.

Lag b'Omer Box Lunch:

Decorate an empty egg carton by gluing on paper flowers. Fill each compartment of the carton with finger foods such as hard-boiled egg, cheese cubes, carrot or celery sticks, strawberries, grapes, and cookies. Close the carton and tie with a ribbon.

Clay:

2 cups flour
1 cup salt
1 Tbs. cream of tartar

2 Tbs. oil
2 cups water
food coloring

Combine dry ingredients. Then add all remaining ingredients. Heat over medium-low flame, until clay does not stick to the pot. Turn out onto a clean board and knead. Cool and store in an airtight container.

For Your Information...

VEGETABLE INSPECTION
Adapted from *The Koshergram,* published by *the Merkaz*

Inspection methods referred to are found on pp. 287-288

Artichoke:
Each leaf down to the heart of the plant must be inspected.[1]

Asparagus:
• Canned: Pour the liquid from the can into a lightly colored bowl and inspect the liquid. If any insects are found, the asparagus may not be used.[2,3]
• Frozen: Method A.
• Fresh: Treat as florets and follow Method E. After this treatment, peel the scales and discard.

Boston lettuce: Method B.

Belgian endive: Method C.

Broccoli:
• Florets: Method E.
• Frozen: Method A.
• Stalks: Method D.

Brussels Sprouts:
(Fresh and Frozen): Not

recommended, since the inspection methods are not reliable.[2,3]

Cabbage:
Shopping tip: Choose clean heads without soft spots and cracked bases.
Method C.

Cauliflower:
Cook, preserve, or refrigerate immediately after inspecting.
• Florets: Method E.
• Frozen: Method A.
• Stalks: Method D.

Celery:
• Leaves: Follow procedure for Parsley (for cooking).
• Stalks: Method D.

Dill:
• Dried: Permitted without inspection.
• Fresh, for cooking: Follow procedure for Parsley (for cooking).

Escarole:
Shopping tip: Choose fresh, firm heads.

---

1. Rabbi Pinchas Bodner.
2. Rabbi Shimon Schwab.
3. Rabbi Moshe Heinneman.

The views of the Poskim cited here are found in their recent articles on this subject. When a Posek is not cited, this does not necessarily mean that he disagrees with a given approach, but merely that he has not issued a written opinion on this specific issue.

Method B.

Iceberg Lettuce:
Shopping tip: Choose clean heads without soft spots and cracked bases.
•Method C.
•After the inspection, it is not advisable to reuse the store's wrapping.

Kale: Method B.

Onions:
Shopping tip: Choose firm onions without shoots.
•Peel until the second onion layer. The remainder of the onion may be used without further inspection.

Parsley:
•Flakes: Permitted without inspection.
•Raw: Not recommended.[2]
•For cooking: Treat the parsley sprigs as florets and follow Method E.
Cooking tip: To use as a seasoning when cooking, place parsley in a closed gourmet bag. Discard parsley after cooking.

Romaine lettuce:
•Leaves: Method B.
•Stalks: Method D.

Spinach:
•Fresh: Treat as florets and follow Method E.
•Frozen: Method A.

•It has been determined that the following vegetables, when grown in the United States, **do not** require inspection:

Alfalfa sprouts, bean sprouts, beets, carrots, corn, cucumbers, eggplant, green beans, knob celery, kohlrabi, mushrooms, parsnips, peas (canned or frozen), peppers, potatoes, pumpkins, radishes, squash, sweet potatoes, tomatoes, turnips, zucchini.

Shopping hint: To avoid as many problems of infestation as possible, always buy U.S. FANCY or U.S. GRADE A vegetables that are clean and crisp.

Shabbos Caution: Because of the Shabbos prohibition of selecting (בּוֹרֵר), whenever an insect is found on a vegetable, the insect alone may not be removed. Rather, the part of the vegetable containing the insect and an additional portion should be cut away, thereby effectively removing the insect from the vegetable. Any procedures requiring soaking the vegetable in salt water should not be done on Shabbos.

A Note on Inspecting Vegetables:

The surfaces of the vegetable should be inspected in proper lighting. If the leaf is translucent (e.g., lettuce), backlighting may also be used.

Methods of Inspection

The following is a summary of the methods suggested recently by some *Poskim* to inspect vegetables properly. Because there are different opinions regarding the appropriate cleaning and inspection methods, each individual should consult his Rav for a definitive ruling.

Method A

Some *Poskim* hold that frozen vegetables may be used without special inspection. Others hold that some appropriate form of inspection is required.[1,2]

Method B

Since infestation is so prevalent, only the most rigorous treatment will permit the use of the leaves.

In the **spring and summer**, *each* leaf must be washed well and carefully inspected on both sides.

In the **fall and winter**, when infestation is not as prevalent, the leaves should be soaked for a few minutes in a vinegar solution and flushed in water. Three leaves should be randomly selected and then inspected to determine if the soaking procedure did in fact remove all insects. If these three leaves prove to be insect-free, the remaining leaves do not need to be inspected.[3] If, however, even one of these three leaves is contaminated, then all the leaves of the vegetable must be inspected.[3] Others hold that under all circumstances, all the leaves must be visually inspected.[1]

Method C

Some hold that merely removing the loose, outer leaves allows one to use the entire vegetable without further inspection, if the vegetable

---

1. Rabbi Shimon Schwab.
2. Rabbi Moshe Heinneman.
3. Rabbi Shimon Eider.

is U.S.-grown. Nevertheless, it is still preferable to inspect three additional inner leaves and flush the remaining leaves in running water.[3]

There is another view that holds that all leaves must be soaked in a vinegar solution and then individually inspected.[1]

Method D

Remove all soil by flushing in running water, since insects may appear as specks of dirt. A vegetable brush is helpful for cleaning. Inspect stalks.

Method E

To clean florets, soak for a few minutes in lukewarm water (preferably a vinegar or salt water solution) in a light-colored bowl. Run finger through the florets and agitate them in the water by holding onto the stem. Inspect the water. If insects are present, empty the water and repeat this procedure until the water is insect-free.[1,2] Rinse the vegetable before using.

HELPFUL HINTS

Baking

For greatest volume when beating egg whites, let them stand before beating until they reach room temperature.

Never grease a tube pan when making sponge or chiffon cakes.

Your cake is done when a toothpick or knife inserted in the center of the cake comes out dry. Also, the top of the cake will spring back when lightly touched.

If the top of your cake is cracked, you may have overmixed, or used too much flour, too little liquid, or too high a temperature.

If there is a soggy layer at the bottom of your cake, you may have used too much liquid, or underbaked, undermixed, or underbeaten the eggs.

Baking powder loses effectiveness over time. To test if yours is still fresh enough to use, put ½ teaspoon of the baking powder into ¼ cup of hot tap water. If the water bubbles, the baking powder is still good.

If you have trouble getting your cake out of the pan, try placing the pan on a wet towel when it comes out of the oven. When the pan is cool, shake it gently and the cake will slip right out.

To frost a cake soon after baking, place the cake in the freezer while the frosting is being prepared. When the frosting is ready, the cake will be cool and will slip out of the pan.

Frosting

One cup of frosting is enough for one 8- or 9-inch round or square cake, or one 9x13-inch cake.

Two cups will frost one 8- or 9-inch layer cake or 30 cupcakes.

Challah

Knead dough by folding it, pressing it down, and turning it. Keep repeating these steps until dough is elastic and smooth.

If challah dough gets sticky, add a little oil, not flour.

To punch down dough, make a fist and punch the center. Pull the edges to the center and turn dough over. Let dough rest a few minutes after being punched.

If dough does not rise, it might not have been kneaded enough. Dough should be kneaded for at least 10 minutes. It should feel resilient when adequately kneaded.

If the top of the loaf cracks, too much flour was used for kneading.

Eggs

Store eggs in the refrigerator, preferably in the carton they come in. The closed container helps preserve freshness.

Eggs can be stored in the refrigerator for up to 4 or 5 weeks.

Hard-cooked eggs should be stored in the refrigerator as soon as they are cool, and should be used within one week.

Raw whites keep for 7 to 10 days if refrigerated in a tightly covered container.

Store eggs away from strong-smelling food, since they readily absorb odors.

Never wash eggs before you store them.

Vegetables

Onions won't cause tears if they are well chilled. Store them in the refrigerator in covered containers.

To keep dill fresh, store in the refrigerator in a tightly closed jar. It will keep about a month.

Don't store unwrapped carrots in the same place as fresh apples. The apples give off ethylene gas that causes a ripening process in fruits and in some vegetables. This can result in carrots acquiring a bitter taste.

Cauliflower will stay white if you cook it with a strip of lemon peel.

When baking potatoes, prick skin with a fork to let steam escape.

A little vinegar or lemon juice added to potatoes before draining will make them extra-white when mashed.

Freeze cabbage, then defrost for easy separation of leaves.

You can revive wilted lettuce by submerging it in a bowl of water to which a couple of tablespoons of lemon juice have been added, and refrigerating it for one hour.

Place potatoes in a cool, dark pantry and they will last for 2 weeks. Light causes them to turn greenish and taste bitter.

Do not keep potatoes near onions. They each emit a gas that will shorten the other's shelf life.

In order to prevent a potato kugel from turning brown:
1. Preheat oven
2. Mix all other ingredients together before blending or grating potatoes
3. Mix a few vitamin C drops into eggs before adding grated or blended potatoes.

Soup

Refrigerate soup after cooking. The fat will rise to the top and congeal for easy removal.

Long, slow cooking makes a good soup.

When freezing soup, always remember to leave room at the top of the container for expansion.

For children who won't eat vegetables, you can force vegetables through a sieve and mix into the soup, or blend the soup in a blender.

Meat and Poultry

To prevent turkey or chicken from becoming too brown when baking, cover with a tent of foil.

Always stuff turkey loosely if you don't want it to burst.

Use one cup of stuffing for every pound of turkey.

If your corned beef turns stringy or dry after cooking, it may be because it was removed from the cooking liquid too quickly. To keep the meat juicy, let it stay in the liquid until it's warm (not hot), then remove it and slice.

Rice and Pasta

Do not stir rice while cooking. This disrupts the starch on the surface of the rice and causes it to clump together.

For perfect rice, measure accurately and use a snug cover on the pot.

To reheat cooked rice, fill the pan with just enough water to cover bottom. Spoon in rice and steam for five minutes, until water is absorbed and rice is fluffy again.

If pasta sticks together, either not enough water was used to cook the pasta, or the water was not boiling when pasta was added.

A tablespoon of olive oil added to the already boiling water will keep pasta from sticking together and the water from foaming over.

Fish

Frozen fish does not have to be thawed before cooking.

Fish is a highly perishable food. It can be stored in the refrigerator for only a day or two.

After fish is purchased, rinse it quickly in cold water and dry it with a paper towel. Repackage it in an airtight plastic bag and store it in the coldest part of the refrigerator.

Fruit

Before peeling oranges or grapefruits, heat for a few minutes in a hot oven. The white membrane will come off easily when the heated skin is removed.

Ripe fruits should be refrigerated or stored in a cool place and used as soon as possible.

Wash all fruit (except for berries and cherries) before refrigerating.

Sort out berries, discard any moldy or spoiled ones before they infect the others, and refrigerate in a dry container.

To ripen fruits, keep them at room temperature away from the sun.

To speed up the ripening process, place fruit in a closed bag. Check daily and refrigerate as soon as they ripen.

To keep apple slices from browning, put them in a bowl of lightly salted water or lemon juice mixed with water.

To keep a cut apple from browning, pour some lemon juice over the cut surface and wrap tightly in plastic wrap.

Miscellaneous

To keep hot oil from spattering, sprinkle a little flour in the pan before frying.

If your recipe calls for bread crumbs and you have no dry bread available, use dry cereal. Make it into crumbs by using a blender, or put the flakes between waxed paper sheets and crush them with a rolling pin.

Ground herbs and spices last about a year. Whole spices and dried herb leaves last longer.

All whole-grain products, such as whole-wheat or rye flour or brown rice, should be kept in airtight containers in the refrigerator.

Seeds and nuts, both shelled and unshelled, keep best and longest when stored in the freezer. They can be used directly from the freezer.

Ideas for Leftovers

Leftover Chicken: Chicken Chow Mein, p. 105
Chicken Salad, p. 107
Chinese Rice and Chicken, p. 112
Chicken with Vegetables, p. 106

Leftover chicken or meat can be cut into small pieces and added to soups such as minestrone or vegetable.

Leftover Challah: Stuffing, p. 113
Bubby's Challah Kugel, p. 172
Apple Challah Kugel, p. 176
Pineapple Bread Kugel, p. 180

QUANTITY COOKING

Food	25 servings	50 servings	100 servings
Meat, poultry, and fish			
hamburger	9 lb.	18 lb.	35 lb.
frankfurters	6½ lb.	13 lb.	25 lb.
turkey or chicken	13 lb.	25-35 lb.	50-75 lb.
roast beef or veal	10 lb.	20 lb.	40 lb.
fish (large whole)	13 lb.	25 lb.	50 lb.
fish fillets or steaks	7½ lb.	15 lb.	30 lb.
Salads			
potato salad	4½ qt.	2¼ gal.	4½ gal.
coleslaw	4½ qt.	2¼ gal.	4½ gal.
baked beans	¾ gal.	1¼ gal.	2½ gal.
Vegetables			
cabbage (shredded)	5 lb.	10 lb.	15 lb.
carrots (cooked)	5 lb.	10 lb.	15 lb.
corn (frozen pkg.)	120 oz.	200 oz.	360 oz.
peas (frozen pkg.)	120 oz.	200 oz.	360 oz.
sweet potatoes (fresh)	7 lb.	12 lb.	18 lb.
Sandwiches			
bread	50 slices	100 slices	200 slices
butter	½ lb.	1 lb.	2 lb.
filling (meat, eggs, fish)	1½ qt.	3 qt.	6 qt.
Desserts			
sheet cake	1 10x12-inch	1 12x20-inch	2 12x20-inch
jello	¾ gal.	1¼ gal.	2½ gal.
ice cream (brick)	3¼ qt.	6½ qt.	12½ qt.
ice cream (bulk)	2¼ qt.	4½ qt. or 1¼ gal.	9 qt. or 2½ gal.
Beverages			
coffee	½ lb. coffee + 1½ gal. water	1 lb. + 3 gal. water	2 lb. + 6 gal. water
tea	1/12 lb. tea + 1½ gal. water	1/6 lb. + 3 gal. water	⅓ lb. + 6 gal. water
lemonade	10-15 lemons + 1½ gal. water	20-30 lemons + 3 gal. water	40-60 lemons + 6 gal. water

FOOD STORAGE CHART

FOOD	IN REFRIGERATOR	IN FREEZER
Uncooked Meats		
roasts	3 to 5 days	6 to 12 months
steaks	3 to 5 days	6 to 12 months
lamb chops	3 to 5 days	6 to 9 months
ground and stew meats	1 to 2 days	3 to 4 months
Cooked Meats		
cooked meat and meat dishes	3 to 4 days	2 to 3 months
Processed Meats		
frankfurters	7 days	1 to 2 months
luncheon meats	3 to 5 days	1 to 2 months
Uncooked Poultry		
whole chicken or turkey	1 to 2 days	12 months
chicken parts	1 to 2 days	9 months
turkey parts	1 to 2 days	6 months
duck (whole)	1 to 2 days	6 months
Cooked Poultry		
in broth or gravy	1 to 2 days	6 months
not in broth or gravy	3 to 4 days	4 to 6 months
Fish		
fat fish	1 to 2 days	4 months
lean fish	1 to 2 days	8 months
Eggs		
whites	2 to 4 days	9 to 12 months
whole eggs	4 weeks	9 to 12 months
yolks	2 to 3 days	9 to 12 months
Cheese		
cottage cheese	5 days	Not recommended
hard cheese	3 to 4 months	6 months
soft cheese	2 weeks	4 months
Ice cream		1 to 3 months

About Flour

The flour most commonly used is wheat flour, made from the wheat berry. Every wheat berry has three layers:

BRAN — the outer layer, which is rich in vitamins, minerals, and plant proteins.

GERM — the embryo of the wheat berry; a great source of vitamin E as well as the B vitamins, oils, proteins, and lecithin.

ENDOSPERM — the inner layer of the wheat berry; mostly starch, with very little protein, vitamins, or minerals.

WHITE FLOUR   Made from the ground endosperm of the wheat berry. By removing the bran and germ, many vitamins and minerals are removed.

WHITE ENRICHED FLOUR   White flour with approximately four vitamins returned to it.

BLEACHED WHITE FLOUR   White flour is bleached to ensure that the white color will last during the baking process. This bleaching removes any vitamins or minerals left in the flour.

UNBLEACHED WHITE FLOUR   White flour without the bleaching process. Baked product will be light brown or tan.

WHOLE-WHEAT FLOUR   Flour made from the whole-wheat berry. This has all the vitamins and minerals of the wheat berry. Sometimes, commercial whole-wheat flour can get rancid and stale, so it's best to buy it from a health food store where they can assure its freshness, or substitute whole-wheat pastry flour.

WHOLE-WHEAT PASTRY FLOUR   This has less gluten and protein in it than whole-wheat flour and has a more delicate and flaky texture. It is good for cakes and pastries—not for yeast breads.

GLUTEN FLOUR   Gluten is the protein portion of the wheat berry. Gluten makes the dough more elastic (good for kneading) and helps it to rise well.

RYE FLOUR   Made from whole rye berries. It contains very little gluten and it produces a heavy, yet chewy and tasty, bread.

CORNMEAL AND CORN FLOUR   Both of these are made from ground corn kernels. Cornmeal is coarser, while corn flour is finely ground.

SOY FLOUR   Made from ground soy beans. It is very high in protein and is usually added to other flours (1 or 2 tablespoons) to enrich the baked product.

STONE-GROUND FLOUR   This is flour ground by slow-moving stone mills, which give off less heat than high-speed mills. This flour is richer in nutritional value, since heat destroys some of the vitamins and minerals found in flour.

What to Serve...

A. When you plan to cook

A week of sample dinner menus
(All recipes except those marked with an asterisk can be found in this cookbook.)

Sunday
Grapefruit
Franks on Buns*
Baked Beans*
Tossed Salad
(substitute Homemade Pizza for
    Franks and Beans)

Monday
Vegetable Soup
Sweet and Sour Meatballs
Orzo
Health Salad
Fresh Fruit in Season

Tuesday
Melon
Baked Gefilte Fish Loaf

Cheese Kugel
Purple Cabbage Salad
Chocolate Chip Cookies with
    Milk

Wednesday
Lentil Soup
Baked Crispy Chicken
Potato Salad
Broccoli Salad
Applesauce with Cinnamon

Thursday
Onion Soup
Baked Ziti
Fish Cakes
Corn on the Cob
Chocolate Pudding

Sample Shabbos Menus
(All recipes except those marked with an asterisk can be found in this cookbook.)

Friday Night I
Easy Gefilte Fish
Chicken Soup with Kneidels
Pot Roast
Garlic Potato Kugel
Sweet Noodle Kugel
Marinated Vegetable Salad
Hot Apple Pie

Friday Night II
Gefilte Fish Loaf
Chicken Soup with Croutons
Sweet Chicken
Apple Kugel
Yerushalmi Kugel
Marinated Mushrooms
Lemon Meringue Pie

Shabbos Day I
Fancy Fruit Cup
Baked Salmon
Cholent (with potato kugel
    inside pot)
Cold Roast or Poultry
Bean Salad
Coleslaw
Amaretto Cake

Shabbos Day II
Chopped Liver or Egg Salad on
    lettuce, with cucumbers
    and tomatoes*
Fruit Soup
Cholent
Corned Beef or Schnitzel
Cucumber Salad
Potato Salad
Coffee Cake

Seudah Shelishis I
Fruit Salad
Sweet and Sour Salmon
Tossed Salad with Dressings*
Festive Pasta Salad
Techina
Parve Cheesecake

Seudah Shelishis II
Sliced Melon
Stuffed Baked Whitefish
Vegetable Trifle
Deviled Eggs
Tabouli Salad
Pineapple Tofu Cake

Melaveh Malka I
Ambrosia Drink
Salmon Wellington
Vegetable Casserole
Stuffed Shells
Cheesecake

Melaveh Malka II
Super Fruit Salad
Herring or Smoked Fish*
Easy Lasagna
Dairy Mushroom Quiche
Chocolate Mousse Pie

Special Foods for Jewish Holidays

Rosh Hashanah
Round challah, honey (to dip challah and apple in), fish head, apple, blackeyed peas, carrots, dates, pomegranates, leeks, beets

Erev Yom Kippur
Kreplach

Sukkos
Stuffed cabbage, kreplach

Chanukah
Dairy dishes, latkes, doughnuts

Tu B'shevat
Olives, dates, grapes, figs, pomegranates

Purim
Hamantashen, kreplach, vegetables

Pesach
Charoses, romaine lettuce, roasted shankbone, a green vegetable (celery, for example), eggs

Shavuos
Dairy foods (cheesecake, cheese blintzes)

Rosh Chodesh
A larger meal than usual is served, including a special dish in honor of the day.

Sample Sheva Berachos Menus

Sheva Berachos I
Mama's Fruit Salad
Stuffed Cabbage
Chicken Capon
Spanish Rice
Sweet Potato à la Pineapple
Almond Green Beans
Parve Ice Cream Cake

Place cucumber salad and corn
salad on table in serving bowls
for guests to help themselves.

Sheva Berachos II
Ambrosia Drink
Meatballs over Chinese Noodles
    or Rice
French Roast Meat
Marinated Mushrooms
Spicy Roasted Potatoes
Tricolor Vegetable Kugel
Easy Fruit Pie

Place cabbage salad and
marinated vegetable salad on
table in serving bowls for
guests to help themselves.

B. When you plan to have it catered

The menu suggestions in this section have been provided with the compliments of Sabel's Catering, Monsey, NY

Shalom Zachar

Chickpeas
Lima Beans
Assorted fruits: cut melons, strawberries, grapes, kiwis, pineapple,
    whole apples, pears, oranges
Assorted cakes: sliced sponge, chocolate, kokosh, marble, 7-layer,
    rainbow.
Brownies, lemon pudding
Nosh: potato chips, pretzels, popcorn, corn chips, assorted nuts,
    candy
Drinks: soda, beer

Suggestions:
- Use some exotic fruits as part of your platter, such as star fruit, mango, etc., if available.
- In winter, hot kugels are good.
- In summer, parve ice cream is nice.

Vach Nacht

Platters of assorted cakes: sponge, sprinkle, marble, chocolate, 7-layer, rainbow, mocha torte, fruit pie
Platters of assorted fruit: melon, pineapple, grapes, apples, oranges, pears
Nosh: chips, popcorn, candies, pretzels, assorted nuts
Gefilte fish
Hot kugels: potato, noodle, Yerushalmi, broccoli

Suggestions:
- It is customary for some groups to have a minimum of one minyan (10 men) wash and sit down for a full meal. This might include challah, gefilte fish, chicken, potato kugel, orzo, relish, and fruit compote.
- Please be aware that the custom is to have the young children of the local yeshiva come to the home of the newborn the evening before to say the *Shema* in the baby's room. The children are given *pekelach* (bags) of goodies — nuts, raisins, candies, or other nosh.

Bris

"L'chaim"
Liqueurs, schnapps, cordials, brandy
Platters of assorted cakes: sponge, marble, brownie, kokosh, bobka, individual tarts, fancy cookies

DAIRY MEAL
Assorted bagels
Platter of assorted smoked fish: whitefish, lox, sable, baked salmon
Platter of assorted pâtés: tuna, egg, mock chopped liver, eggplant, babaganoush, avocado

Assorted cream cheese: plain, strawberry, chives
Butter, margarine
Milk, orange and apple juice, coffee, tea
Assorted miniature danishes

Suggestions:
- Make sure to have aluminum foil and plastic bags handy for "guests on the go."
- Press butter into molds to form flowers or other nice shapes.

FLEISHIG MEAL
Large *seudah* challah
Individual challah rolls (at each place setting)
Sliced gefilte fish with *chrein*
Salads: relishes, cucumber salad, coleslaw, purple cabbage salad
¼ roast chicken per person
Side dishes: farfel, tzimmes, kugel, kasha varnishkes
Fruit compote or individual servings of parve ice cream

Suggestion:
- You might want to substitute a deli platter for the chicken.

Kiddush

Wine, schnapps, cordials, brandy
Trays of cake: Plain — sponge, marble, brownie; Fancy — 7-layer, rainbow, *petit fours*
Sliced gefilte fish with *chrein*
Hot potato kugel, Yerushalmi kugel, hot sweet noodle kugel, salt and pepper noodle kugel
Cholent with kishka
Soda

Suggestions:
- On ladies' tables, serve cordials and brandies.
- Place each slice of gefilte fish on a piece of purple kale, with a cherry tomato.

Engagement Party — Vort — L'chayim — Tena'im

It is customary on these happy occasions to open one's home for guests to come, in order to make a "*l'chaim*" and wish mazel tov.

Serving Suggestions:

Platters of assorted plain and fancy cakes, liqueurs, schnapps, and wines, and platters of fruits, platters of cut vegetables, and lots of nosh!

For a more formal party, might we suggest a sit-down dinner? (Please see *Sheva Berachos* for sample menu.)

To be different, why not a smorgasbord?

Sample Smorgasbord:

Displays of whole cakes, as many varieties as you like, on various raised platters.

Large fruit and vegetable displays, decorated with kale. Put dip into whole peppers that have been hollowed out.

A Chinese buffet set in chafing dishes, with foods such as:
sesame chicken, pepper steak, vegetable lo mein, egg rolls, lemon chicken, veal with garlic sauce, orange beef.

Bar with soda, liqueurs, schnapps, and mixed drinks (cocktails).

Pidyon ha-Ben — Sheva Berachos — Upshirin — Chanukas ha-Bayis (Sit-down meal)

Opener	*Seudah* Challah Individual challah rolls at each place setting Choice of: fresh fruit cup, ¼ pineapple, flute of fresh strawberries with whipped cream and lemon leaf, fruit sorbet
Appetizer	Choice of: vegetable crepe with mushroom sauce, Hawaiian meatballs over rice, baked salmon on kale with cherry tomato, cucumber with tartar sauce and slice of lemon

Soup	Choice of: vegetable medley, mushroom and barley, cream of asparagus, chicken with wontons
Main Dishes	Choice of: ¼ stuffed chicken, schnitzel, prime rib of beef, Chicken Wellington, baby lamb chops
Side Dishes (Starch)	Choice of: roasted small red potatoes, Spanish rice, cabbage noodles, shlishkes, kasha varnishkes, sweet potato souffle, orzo
Side Dishes (Vegetable)	Choice of: string beans with almonds, glazed baby carrots, Chinese vegetable medley
Salads/Relishes	Choice of: coleslaw, potato salad, carrot salad, pickles with olives, hot red/green peppers
Dessert	Choice of: pastries, parve ice cream or ices, poached pears, coffee (plain and flavored), tea

INDEX

Y

Z